David W. ty University, San Anton books on the Middle East and has traveled widely there on scholarly and diplomatic endeavors. He is a frequent consultant to US and European government

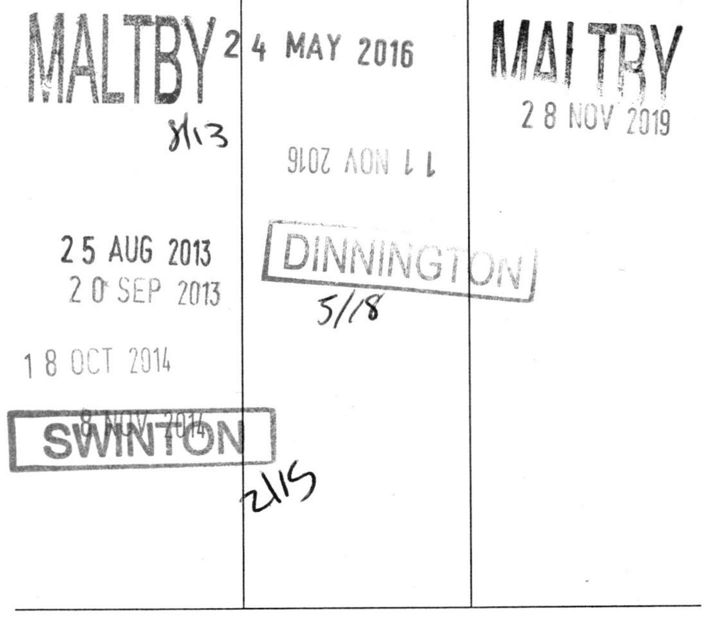

SYRIA
THE FALL OF THE HOUSE OF ASSAD

David W. Lesch

YALE UNIVERSITY PRESS
NEW HAVEN AND LONDON

First published in paperback in 2013

For information about this and other Yale University Press publications, please contact:
U.S. Office: sales.press@yale.edu www.yalebooks.com
Europe Office: sales@yaleup.co.uk www.yalebooks.co.uk

Set in Minion Pro by IDSUK (DataConnection) Ltd
Printed in Great Britain by TJ International Ltd, Padstow, Cornwall

Library of Congress Cataloging-in-Publication Data

Lesch, David W.
Syria : the fall of the house of Assad / David W. Lesch.
p. cm.
Includes bibliographical references and index.
ISBN 978-0-300-18651-2 (alk. paper)
1. Syria—Politics and government—2000– 2. Assad, Bashar, 1965– 3. Assad, Bashar, 1965—Political and social views. 4. Political leadership—Syria. 5. Syria—History—Demonstrations, 2010– 6. Protest movements—Syria—History—21st century. 7. Political violence—Syria—History—21st century. I. Title.
DS98.6.L475 2012
956.9104'2—dc23

2012021934

A catalogue record for this book is available from the British Library.

ISBN 978-0-300-19722-8 (pbk)

10 9 8 7 6 5 4 3 2 1

Contents

Preface

Choosing the title of a book can be a somewhat hazardous venture. This is especially the case when the subject matter of the book deals primarily with recent and current events. A number of things can occur in the time between the final submission of a manuscript to the publisher and the actual appearance of the book on the shelves. There may, then, be a few (hopefully a very few) parts of the book, including the title, that may become a bit outdated or seem rather out of place. When the title of a book is *Syria: The fall of the House of Assad*, I might be expected to be pretty darn sure that President Bashar al-Assad will fall. But what happens if Assad does *not* actually fall from power by the time the book is published? In fact, at the time of writing (perforce a phrase I use often in the book), it seems more likely than not that Assad will, in fact, survive the domestic uprising (which has already been going on for over a year) against his rule well past the publication date.

But I have gone with this title for another reason: whether or not he remains in power, Bashar al-Assad, in my mind, has already fallen. And thus the (more than) forty-year rule of the House of Assad – Hafiz al-Assad, who ruled from 1970 to 2000, and his son, who succeeded upon his father's death in 2000 – is over. This is the judgment of someone who got to know Bashar al-Assad fairly well and, at one point, had high hopes of him. Despite his shortcomings, I thought he could lead Syria to achieve its full potential as a country, and the Syrians to reach theirs as a people. Even if the event is more metaphorical than real, however, he has fallen in my estimation. Or maybe it would be more accurate to say that the authoritarian Syrian system has proved too difficult to overcome. Assad morphed into a real-life tyrant; this became most dramatically manifest in his sanctioning of the government crackdown of what were, at first, largely peaceful protests, inspired by the Arab Spring. He acted against his own people even though he may have deluded himself into thinking he was doing the right thing. I examine his journey to the 'dark side' (so to speak) throughout this book. In doing so, I analyze and trace the causes of the uprising in Syria, the nature of the government response, the development of the opposition movement, the varied – and often contradictory – reactions and policies of the international community, and the different outcomes the Syrian crisis may produce in the near future.

I have been traveling regularly to, and writing about, Syria for twenty-three years. The accumulation of experience and contacts in Syria created the opportunity for me, in 2004 and 2005, to extensively interview Bashar al-Assad, his wife Asma al-Assad, and other leading Syrian officials for a book published by Yale University Press in 2005 entitled *The New Lion of Damascus: Bashar al-Asad and modern Syria*. This unique access meant that I got to know Assad probably better than anyone in the West. At his urging, we continued to meet on a regular basis until late 2008, and I had meetings with high-level Syrian officials well into 2013. In the beginning, I was generally impressed with Bashar and the promise of his leadership. As an American interested primarily in improving the position of my country in the Middle East, I also tended to believe that the pressure on Syria that was applied by the US administration of George W. Bush was, for the most part, counterproductive, and that opportunities for a better and mutually beneficial US-Syrian relationship were being missed; even in retrospect, I still believe this. However, I clearly detected changes in Assad as he became more ensconced in power and survived threats to his rule. I saw these changes at close quarters and describe them in this book.

For now, let me just say that when Bashar unleashed Syria's military and security forces on the protestors, I was not the least bit shocked; if anything, my initial reaction was that of disappointment, sadness and ultimately even anger – anger that someone who was in a position to propel his country forward had failed so miserably to do so. On the contrary, Assad had degraded Syria.

Instead of creatively and courageously embracing the future, Assad chose a bloody path that is well beaten by an impressive list of brutal dictators from Middle East history. The shape of the future is still very much in doubt, but one thing is clear: the popular protests and rebellions of the Arab Spring have wrought a tangle of change in the Middle East that may take a generation to unravel. Bashar al-Assad, the person I came to know (and like), showed that he – and the hope he sparked when he came to power – is long gone. The Assads have lost whatever legitimacy they had. Their claim to fame was that they kept Syria together in the face of regional strife and maintained domestic stability. This is no longer the case. They have lost their mandate to rule. A return to the status quo ante, even if tweaked with some political reform, will not suffice. The office of the president of Syria, as it existed, is vacant – whether or not an Assad occupies it.

There are several people to acknowledge for their efforts in helping to make this book possible. I would like, first, to thank Heather McCallum, publisher at Yale University Press. This is the second book on which we have collaborated, and it was no less an enjoyable experience this time around. Heather is the type of editor who, at one and the same time, adeptly encourages and challenges the author, all of which leads to a better final product. The rest of the staff at and those working with Yale University Press have been marvelous, including Rachael Lonsdale and Clive Liddiard, who is an outstanding copy editor. I also want to thank my colleague-in-arms and fellow Syria expert, James (Jim) Gelvin, for reading an earlier draft of the book and to Mark Haas for his helpful comments on my work. Trinity University has continued to support my research and writing, and I am very thankful for its faith in my projects. In addition, I want to thank a research assistant, Krystal Rountree, one of my students at

Trinity University, in particular for helping me better understand various aspects of the social media with regard to the Syrian uprising – a topic she has researched and written on for one of my classes. My son, Michael Lesch, a student at Rollins College in Florida, also conducted some research for me, for which I am grateful. He has been to Syria three times already in his young life. My wish is that he can make another visit to a peaceful and prosperous Syria in the near future. Indeed, I firmly hope for all my dear friends in Syria, who are on both sides of the divide, that they can soon see and experience stability, freedom and prosperity. Often these things are born of conflict and despair, as we know all too well in my own country; but may the unrest and violence in Syria end soon, with the prospects of a brighter future alive and well and within their grasp.

Finally, I want to thank my wonderful wife, Judy Dunlap, for her unending support and encouragement, as well as for acting as the first line of defense in reading the rough drafts. I hope she takes the time to read the final version, so that she sees just how much help she really was. More to the point, she makes me insanely happy and serene, which more than compensates for the frequent moments of drudgery in writing a book. Thank you for making this very concentrated period of writing tolerable.

TURKEY
Tigris
Qamishli
Jarablus
Aleppo
Idlib
Raqqa
Euphrates
Orontes
Latakia
Jableh
Banias
Hama
Masyaf
Tartous
Homs
Dayr al-Zor
Mediterranean Sea
Tadmur
(Palmyra)
Abu Kamal
Al-Qusayr
LEBANON
An-Nabk
Beirut
IRAQ
Douma
Damascus
Qatana
Golan
Heights
Ezraa
Deraa
ISRAEL
JORDAN
0 20 40 60 80 100 Miles
0 100 km
36°
38°
40°
42°
34°

CHAPTER 1

The Hope

It wasn't supposed to be this way. Or perhaps it was inevitable . . .

For three decades, from the time an intra-Baath party coup brought him to power in 1970 until his death in June 2000, President Hafiz al-Assad was the ruler of Syria. By the early 1990s, though, his health was failing, and it was widely accepted that his eldest son, Basil, was being groomed for the top job – even though Syria is officially a republic, not a monarchy. Basil was viewed in Syria as a charismatic military figure who would seamlessly assume the presidency when the day came. But Basil was killed one foggy morning in 1994, in a car accident at a roundabout just outside Damascus International Airport.

Bashar al-Assad, the second-eldest son of Hafiz, was in his London apartment that January morning when he received the news that his older brother had died. Bashar, a licensed ophthalmologist who had graduated from Damascus University, was in London, studying for a postgraduate qualification in ophthalmology at the Western Eye Hospital. Of course, he returned to Syria to support a grieving family and to assist with the funeral arrangements, in a show of familial solidarity. He may or may not at that moment have entertained the idea that he might someday become president. But – whether by choice or compulsion – that is what he became, six years later, on his father's death. He could not have guessed that, eleven years on, he would face a popular uprising against his rule. Nor could he have suspected that – as a result of the regime's brutal response, which has already left thousands dead – he would one day be almost universally reviled as a bloodthirsty killer who has lost his legitimacy to rule.

This was a far cry from people's high expectations of Bashar when he came to power. Indeed, even before he assumed the presidency, in Syria he was being called 'The Hope' – as in the hope for the future.[1] After Basil's death, Bashar had been systematically elevated within the ruling apparatus and given more and more responsibility. He was appointed chairman of the Syrian Computer Society, a position that had been held by his older brother. He moved quickly through the ranks of the military, reaching the equivalent of brigadier general by the time of his father's death. In 1998, the all-important Lebanon portfolio was taken from Vice President Abd al-Halim Khaddam (who was not happy about it) and given to Bashar. It seemed to be a race against time to build Bashar's legitimacy and power base within the Baath party, the government and, especially, the military, to the point where he could succeed without serious opposition. If only his father could hang on long enough.

And his father did hold on just long enough: there was no serious opposition to Bashar al-Assad becoming president. Essentially, the generals in the state military-security apparatus gathered around Mustafa Tlas, Hafiz al-Assad's longtime – and loyal – minister of defense, to discuss the succession. No doubt most of the generals were Alawite, the minority Muslim sect in Syria that comprises 12–13 per cent of the population, which had dominated the ruling apparatus since the mid-1960s when the Baath party had consolidated its hold on power. The Alawites, a secular off-shoot of Shiite Islam that is considered by most Muslims to be heretical, had, for centuries, been an oppressed minority in the area that came to comprise Syria. Indeed, the great thirteenth- and fourteenth-century Sunni Islamic scholar Ibn Taymiyya, who leaned to the more rigorous – some would say puritanical – interpretation of Sunni Islam, issued a *fatwa*, or legal religious ruling, calling the Alawites greater infidels than the Christians, Jews or idolaters, and authorizing a *jihad* or holy war against them.

It was not until the French mandate over Syria in the period between World War One and World War Two that the fortunes of the Alawites (and certain other minorities in Syria, such as the Christians and the Druze) began to improve in a country that is 75 per cent Sunni Muslim. At the time of Syrian independence from the French, in 1946, the Alawites found themselves well positioned in the military: they had volunteered for and been recruited into the Syrian armed forces during the French mandate period, when Sunnis either looked down on military service or frowned upon it as collusion with the French in ruling over the country. When the socialist and pan-Arab neutralist Baath party started to win more and more parliamentary seats in the 1950s, and after it allied itself with important elements in the military to improve its political power in the divided and unstable Syrian political landscape, Alawite officers worked their way into the political mix and up the ladder, eventually becoming the dominant element in government as the primary arbiters of power. The February 1966 intra-Baath coup brought Hafiz al-Assad to a senior position in the new regime, as defense minister and commander of the air force. The Alawites were well represented from 1966 to 1970, but their position, especially in the military-security apparatus, improved immeasurably under Hafiz. This trend gained further momentum under Bashar, and Alawites are dominant in important sinecures in the regime (though over the years both Hafiz and Bashar also appointed Sunni Muslims to important posts in government).

The point is that the Alawites worked long and hard to obtain their positions of power and influence in the country, and they were not going to give those up easily. The Alawite-dominated military-security apparatus, as well as leading (mostly Sunni) businessmen tied into the regime, saw in Bashar al-Assad the best chance (or perhaps the least worst) of maintaining their political, economic and social positions and status. This, above all other reasons, is why Bashar became president. He was young, he had gained a certain amount of popularity, he was an Alawite – and, most importantly, he was an Assad.

On 11 June 2000, one day after his father died, Bashar was unanimously nominated by the ruling Baath party as president. There were no other nominees. The national assembly (or parliament) hastily amended article 83 of the Syrian constitution, which stated that the president of the republic must be forty years old – the minimum age was changed to thirty-four, the exact age of Bashar, who was born on 11 September 1965. On 24 June he was elected secretary-general of the Baath party at the Ninth Regional Congress meeting, the first such gathering of the Baath party for fifteen years. Three days later, the Syrian parliament voted 'yes' to the nomination, and in a nationwide referendum, Bashar received 97.29 per cent of the total vote (slightly less than the 99 per cent his father had regularly received to confirm his seven-year terms in office).

President Bashar al-Assad officially took the constitutional oath of office and delivered his inaugural speech in Damascus on 17 July 2000.

By Syrian standards, it was a remarkably enlightened speech, and it even went so far as to criticize certain policies of the past under Bashar's father. It served to confirm the suspicions among many inside and outside Syria – especially the pro-reform and pro-democracy elements – that Bashar was indeed a breath of fresh air who would lead the country in a new direction. In his speech, he made economic reform a clear priority; indeed, the frankness of his criticism of the previous system was unprecedented.

The new president declared that the state bureaucracy had become a 'major obstacle' to development, and he admitted that economic progress had been uneven, due, in large measure, to the state-dominated economy: 'Don't depend on the state. There is no magic wand. The process of change requires elements that are not the preserve of one person . . . Authority without responsibility is the cause of chaos.' He went on:

> We must rid ourselves of those old ideas that have become obstacles. In order to succeed we need modern thinking . . . some people may believe that creative minds are linked to age and that they can frequently be found with the old, but this is not quite accurate. Some young people have strong minds that are still lively and creative.[2]

And, in a subtle fashion, he seemed to lay the foundation for embarking on a different path from his father, proclaiming that 'the approach of the great leader, Hafez al-Assad, was a very special and unique approach and therefore it is not easy to emulate, especially as we remember that we are required not just to maintain it but to develop it as well'. Despite this reform-tinged rhetoric, Bashar did say that it would be impossible for Syria to become a Western-style democracy, calling instead for 'democracy specific to Syria that takes its roots from its history and respects its society'.

There was a genuine exuberance among many who had longed for change in Syria. Bashar brought into government a number of members of the Syrian Computer Society, people who could legitimately be called reformists. This added to the anticipatory environment, although the new so-called 'reformers' were more technocrats than pro-democracy elements. They were tasked with the job of modernizing Syria, implementing administrative reform in the various ministries to which they were assigned, and examining the economic weaknesses of the system and devising ways to correct it; they were not there to enact political reform. Besides, they had reached their privileged positions by being part of the system; they were not going to do anything substantial that would undermine it.

Bashar inherited from his father an authoritarian state. It was in a dilapidated condition, characterized by a stagnant economy, pervasive corruption and political repression. It was, as existed in a number of other authoritarian countries of the Middle East, a *mukhabarat* state – that is, one in which the security or intelligence services, in combination with certain trusted elements of the military, are dominant in controlling the population and in defending the regime against perceived threats, both internal and external. Hafiz al-Assad had largely established the *mukhabarat* state in Syria, having created a tangled matrix of overlapping security agencies during his time in power. With so much political instability in post-independence Syria, seething as it was with actual and attempted coups, many Syrians willingly accepted the Faustian bargain of less freedom for more stability that Hafiz al-Assad implicitly offered (or demanded). With chronic political instability and war on Syria's borders (in Lebanon and Iraq) an almost constant feature since the mid-1970s, it was not terribly difficult to convince most Syrians of the importance of stability above all else, even if this came at a considerable price. Under the Assads, therefore, it has been a constant mantra of the regime that it has performed its primary duty well – at times even achieving a modicum of socio-economic growth and opportunity – and that it is often the only thing standing between stability and chaos.

It has been an enormous challenge to provide that modicum of growth and opportunity, however. Syria is categorized as a lower-middle-income country, and is in the bottom third on most of the important international economic indices. It is a country that is dominated by the public sector, which was initially forged during the socialist-leaning and economic-nationalist post-independence period of the 1950s and 1960s, when countries were emerging from the shackles of British and French colonial rule. As Charles Issawi wrote at the time, three main shifts in power took place in the Middle East: 'from foreigners to nationals; from the landed interest to the industrial, financial, commercial and managerial interests; and from the private sector to the state'.[3]

This was, of course, well intentioned: it aimed at distributing wealth and political power more equitably, ending reliance on outside powers, eliminating corruption and restoring justice. A social contract with the people became common in such countries, with the regimes promising to establish adequate safety nets, and to provide employment, education and social services in return for compliance and obedience (if not obeisance). As typically happened in such economic systems, Syria instead developed a bloated and inefficient public sector that, for five decades, provided the support base for the ruling regime. In the process, it established a classic 'Bonapartist' state, where economic policy was primarily driven by regime survival, especially in a regional environment that was anything but benevolent. As time went on, the wealth was funneled to the state as the capital accumulator, and the government became the source of patronage, as a pervasive clientelist network was created in the military, bureaucracy, business community and other elements of society tied to the state apparatus.

Because of this dominant public sector that was tied into the political apparatus, when the Syrian economy faced a crisis situation – a fairly frequent occurrence, since Syria's agrarian and oil export-based economy was ultimately dependent on unpredictable rainfall (and drought) and on the volatile international oil market – the regime had sometimes to engage in what has been called 'selective liberalization'.[4] It had to be *selective* because of the following dilemma: if the Assads were to liberalize too much and/or too quickly, that could undermine the public sector patronage system that helped maintain the regime in power. Some contend that Syria's selective liberalization was directed as much by a desire to broaden the regime's support base during times of change as by the intrinsic need to improve its economic situation in general; therefore, significant elements of the bourgeoisie were brought – or dragged – de facto and de jure into a sort of coalition with the state.[5] This led to enhanced access to political power and to greater corruption in the private sector, with lucrative results for those willing to be co-opted. On the other hand, it may have, as Volker Perthes put it, 'amalgamated' these societal elements together behind the regime, and it did not lead to any acquisition of political power by the private sector.[6] Indeed, as Ghassan Salame wrote, this state of affairs could be described as 'bourgeoisies leaving politics to their masters who secure the stability these bourgeoisies need to enrich themselves'.[7] This is also what Patrick Seale called the 'military-mercantile complex',[8] which developed strong ties between the government and the large Sunni business class, whose support proved so crucial in 1982, when Hafiz al-Assad moved against the Sunni Muslim Brotherhood in Syria. The highlight – or in this case the lowlight – of the crackdown was the shelling of the city of Hama, the base of the Syrian Muslim Brotherhood: this killed some 10,000–20,000 people, many of them innocent civilians, though it did succeed in stamping out the violent Muslim Brotherhood uprising that had been going on since the late 1970s.

Both Hafiz and Bashar al-Assad opened up the economy at various times, and to varying degrees; but the primary beneficiaries were usually those already tied into the regime through familial, business and/or political connections. An already elite class enriched itself further, and especially under Bashar this resulted in a conspicuously unequal distribution of wealth. But it also meant that the elite were co-opted by the regime, in the sense that their socioeconomic status depended upon regime support; they could very rapidly lose that status if they displayed any sign of disloyalty or acted in any way that embarrassed the regime.

In addition to the burden of an overly dominant public sector, there were numerous problems that inhibited economic growth under Hafiz al-Assad, including:

- a very small and restricted banking system, and no stock market to organize capital;
- an inadequate regulatory regime and insufficient transparency, which is also related to a corrupt and politicized judiciary that is anything but independent (a major impediment to attracting foreign investment);
- a private sector that is too fragmented to lead the way in capital accumulation;
- rampant corruption and a vibrant black market; and
- the absence of any tradition of large-scale domestic capital investment (leading to a proliferation of small-scale enterprises and investment in non-productive areas, such as commerce, instead of manufacturing).

Moreover, as a noted 2002 United Nations study (the Arab Human Development Report) found, right across the Arab world there is a 'knowledge' deficit – a result of poorly performing and inadequately supported educational systems, combined with the brain-drain of those who receive an education in the West and choose to stay there, rather than return to their native countries.

One can see why Bashar al-Assad focused on economic reform in his inaugural speech. Nonetheless, there was a noticeably more open political environment in the months after Bashar took office, leading many to call this period the 'Damascus Spring'. The seven or eight months of the Damascus Spring were marked by general amnesties for political prisoners of all persuasions, the licensing of private newspapers, a shake-up in the state-controlled media apparatus, the provision of political forums and salons at which open criticism and dissent was tolerated, and the abandonment of the personality cult that had surrounded the regime of Bashar's father.

The regime appeared to be caught off guard by the precipitate growth in the number of civil society organizations and pro-democracy groups, and by the level of criticism directed at the government. It is generally believed that some of the stalwart elements in the regime (referred to at the time as the 'old guard' – those who had reached positions of power, especially in the military-security apparatus, under Hafiz al-Assad and had been loyal to him) basically approached Bashar and warned him of the deleterious effects on the regime's power base of his move to open up society. As one diplomat who served in Syria at the time told me: 'Probably some of the tough guys in the regime came to Bashar and essentially said, "Hey kid, this is not how we do things here." '[9]

As a result, most of the political and social reforms announced during the Damascus Spring were reversed directly or indirectly. This backtracking saw the re-imprisonment of a number of prominent pro-democracy activists. A winter of retrenchment set in; this was followed by a decade of some economic, monetary and administrative reform. There was, however, scarcely any trace of real political reform away from the single-party system that dominated this neo-patriarchal authoritarian structure, in which the state apparatus – and therefore the country as a whole – was dependent upon and subservient to the ruling regime, and particularly the Assad family.

Regional and international isolation

In March 2006, I gave a talk on President Bashar al-Assad and Syria at the Center for Strategic and International Studies in Washington, DC. I happened at the time to be in the camp that was advocating the establishment of dialogue with Syria and its president. After my talk, a foreign policy advisor on Vice President Dick Cheney's staff came up to me and said he understood what I had meant. He then grew more animated, waved his finger in my face and bellowed: 'But those sons of bitches are killing our boys in Iraq!' He was obviously referring to the regime in Syria.

It was at that moment that I realized what a visceral issue this had become among at least some important members of the George W. Bush administration. Administration officials were quite simply inordinately upset that Syria was not, in their opinion, doing all it could to prevent foreign fighters from entering and traversing Syria, crossing the border into Iraq, and fueling an insurgency that, at the time, had bogged down American efforts there following the 2003 US-led invasion and had sullied the reputation of the Bush team. There was genuine anger at Syria, and there continues to be residual anger in Washington over this. Sometimes emotional responses are not factored into the equation that deals with policy objectives or rationale, because they are difficult (if not impossible) to measure. On that March day in 2006, however, I learned that they did play – and may well continue to play – a role in the US–Syria dynamic.

My response to Vice President Cheney's staffer was twofold. First, I mentioned that I had volunteered on occasion at the burns unit at Brook Army Medical Center (BAMC) in San Antonio, Texas. BAMC's burns center was (and is) the primary treatment facility for burned soldiers flown in from Iraq and Afghanistan. In other words, it is quite possible that some of the severely burned soldiers I met at BAMC, many of whom will since have died from their injuries, were maimed by improvised explosive devices or suicide bombings that were, in a way, facilitated by the very man I had been meeting regularly in Damascus. So, yes, I was angry about this state of affairs as well, because I saw 'up close and personal' the end result.

Secondly, I told him that he (and, by inference, other like-minded administration officials) needed to role-play and view the world as though from Damascus, so that he could better understand Syria's motivations and policy objectives in supporting the Iraqi insurgency, by at least turning a blind eye to foreign fighters using Syrian territory to cross over into Iraq. If he performed this mental exercise, he would find that, when President Bashar al-Assad looked out from Damascus, he found himself virtually surrounded by actual or potential hostile forces. Much as his father had done when he was up against the wall in 1982 and 1983, faced with a domestic Islamist uprising and an Israeli invasion of Lebanon, Bashar realized that he had to fight back in an asymmetrical fashion that foiled perceived US threats, yet did not incur the wrath of the United States in the form of a full-fledged military response. It was a fine line to tread.

Bashar al-Assad came to power in 2000 in a threatening regional environment. The al-Aqsa *intifada* (uprising) had erupted a few months after he became president, when frustrated Palestinians in the Occupied Territories, following almost a decade of failed Israeli-Palestinian negotiations, rose up against Israel to demand more rights, autonomy and independence. Long the self-proclaimed champion of Palestinian rights in the Arab world, the Syrian government was compelled vocally to support the Palestinians and condemn Israel, thus spoiling at the outset any chances of developing a positive relationship with Washington and of restarting negotiations with Israel. Then, in rapid succession, came 9/11, the US invasion of Afghanistan and the 2003 US invasion of neighboring Iraq. The rules of the game were changing, and they were being dictated by the Bush administration in a way that placed Syria on the outside looking in.

Since the early 1970s, Syria had been able to straddle the regional and international fence. Hafiz al-Assad had relished this position, and it had allowed him to select whichever side of the fence to sit on, depending on the circumstances of the day. He was, after all, a foreign policy pragmatist. Alone of the major Arab actors in the Middle East, Syria could play this role. On the one hand, Syria is the cradle of Arab nationalism, in the forefront of the Arab world's confrontation states arrayed against Israel, and supportive of groups such as Hizbullah and Hamas. It also did not give in to what, in the region during the Bush years, was often called the 'American project'. On the other hand, Syria sent troops to support the US-led UN coalition forces that evicted Iraq from Kuwait in the 1991 Gulf War. Damascus has also entered into indirect and direct negotiations with Israel over three decades, often with US brokerage, coming tantalizingly close to an Israeli-Syrian peace deal in 1999–2000.

The Bush administration basically told Damascus that it could no longer play both sides of the fence: it had to choose one side or the other. After post-9/11 intelligence cooperation on al-Qaida (prompting one US official to say that Syria had 'saved American lives') the two countries' relations began to sour when the US invaded Iraq, a move that Syria opposed.[10] Essentially, Bashar al-Assad did not adequately adjust to the important underlying changes in American foreign policy after 9/11. This heightened Syria's exposure to US regime-change rhetoric, especially as the Bush doctrine defined US policy. Damascus thought the old rules of the game still applied, and US administration officials periodically led it to believe this was so. The Syrians may have been guilty of only hearing what they wanted to hear; but at the same time, the new rules of the game were being written in Washington – in the corridors of Congress, the Pentagon, the vice president's office and influential conservative think tanks, by those who saw Bashar and his regime as part of the problem, rather than as the solution. As the wars in Afghanistan and Iraq commenced and progressed, the focus of foreign policy power in the Bush administration shifted away from the State Department, leading to a more bellicose posture vis-à-vis Syria. State Department officials, including Secretary of State Colin Powell, made comments from time to time praising Syria's cooperation against jihadists crossing over into Iraq, which reassured Damascus that perhaps the old rules still applied; but in hindsight, these statements carried little weight in the US foreign policy-making apparatus, as Powell and the State Department in general were marginalized.

Thus Bashar's continued verbal assaults on Israel and his support for Hizbullah and Hamas well into 2003 played straight into the hands of the ascendant group of US foreign policy ideologues. Bashar was quite unaware that he and his regime were becoming more of a target. As President Bush stated on 24 June 2003, 'Syria must choose the right side in the war on terror by closing terrorist camps and expelling terrorist organizations.'[11] Syria assumed that the clear differences between al-Qaida on the one hand and Hamas/Hizbullah on the other were self-evident, as they were understood by most in the region. But these distinctions were apparently lost on the Bush administration.

No longer could the differences between Washington and Damascus be resolved as part of a Syrian-Israeli peace process; Syria now had to meet all of Washington's concerns before negotiations with Israel could even begin. From the point of view of Damascus, this was a non-starter, for it would entail relinquishing its few remaining assets (such as its ties with Hizbullah, Hamas and Iran) before the initiation of peace talks. As a result, Syria was regarded by the Bush administration as a rogue state, and, with the US invasion of Iraq, a series of accusations was hurled at the regime in Damascus – from harboring Saddam Hussein regime members and hiding Iraq's weapons of mass destruction (WMD) to supplying Iraqi fighters with military equipment. The most pointed accusation of all, however, would only gain momentum as the Iraq insurgency took shape: that the Syrian regime was actively assisting the insurgency financially and logistically. Now, according to US officials, Syria was *costing* US lives. It had crossed the line. Typical of US comments was one by a US Central Command (CENTCOM) official: 'If Americans are dying in Iraq because of Syrian policies, then this is something we are not going to tolerate.'[12] Although the language was rhetorical, as the Bush administration shifted its emphasis toward promoting democracy in the region, and especially in Lebanon, Syria's authoritarian regime became a natural target. Given the international revulsion over the assassination of former Lebanese Prime Minister Rafiq Hariri in February 2005 (by order of Damascus, in Washington's view), the subsequent Cedar Revolution in Lebanon, the evacuation of the remaining Syrian troops from the country by April, and the launch of a UN investigation into the Hariri murder, Bashar was clearly on the defensive, and regime change in Damascus seemed to be just a matter of time.

Responding to the US accusations, Bashar told me in 2004:

> Some see me as bad, some see me as good – we don't actually care what terms they use. It is not right to apply this term to Syria – I mean, look at the relationship that Syria has with the rest of the world; if you have good relations with most of the rest of the world, you are not a rogue state just because the United States says you are.[13]

Weathering these multiple storms took a great deal of ability – with a little bit of luck thrown in. Bashar al-Assad was no longer the untested, inexperienced leader. No one remains as president of Syria very long without being capable and cunning. In Middle East circles, Bashar was often compared unfavorably to his father; but one must remember that Hafiz al-Assad did not become 'Hafiz al-Assad the clever, tough leader and shrewd negotiator' overnight. He, too, had had a learning curve, particular points on which included being taken to the diplomatic cleaners (on separate occasions) by Egyptian President Anwar Sadat and US Secretary of State Henry Kissinger, during and after the 1973 Arab-Israeli war.

Bashar had to tread very carefully. As seen from Damascus, the invasion of Iraq implanted 150,000 US troops in a country on Syria's eastern border, armed with the Bush doctrine and fresh from a swift and – to Syrian eyes – shockingly easy military removal of the only other Baathist regime on earth. To the north was Turkey; while Syria had markedly improved its relationship with Ankara, Turkey was still a member of NATO. To the south, of course, was Israel, as well as Jordan, with which it had a long-standing mercurial relationship (and which, in any event, was a US ally). The only friendly neighbor was Lebanon, and even there various domestic factions were agitating more assertively for a Syrian troop withdrawal and for less Syrian interference.

In the fresh glow of the Bush administration's 'mission accomplished' in 2003, several implicit threats were directed at Damascus – threats that Syrian officials took *very* seriously: Syria could be next on the Bush doctrine's hit list. As such, it is no surprise that the Syrian regime (at the very least) turned a blind eye to insurgents crossing into Iraq. Damascus wanted the Bush doctrine to fail, and it hoped that Iraq would be the first and last time the doctrine was applied. Anything it could do to ensure this outcome, short of incurring the direct military wrath of the United States, was considered fair game. These are the actions of a rational actor, and most regimes would have done the same.

While certainly under pressure from the United States to do more on the border, Bashar also had to face a domestic constituency that identified strongly with the Iraqi insurgency. The minority Alawite Syrian regime was caught rather off guard by the popular reaction in the country against the US-led invasion of Iraq, particularly as manifested in *salafist* groups among the Sunni Muslim majority. Because Bashar still had not consolidated his hold on power, he could not afford to appear to be doing Bush's bidding – and nor did he want to. In fact, the more the United States pressured Syria, the more it compelled Bashar to appeal to a combination of Arab, Syrian and Islamic nationalism to strengthen his support base. As US pressure was stepped up following the Hariri assassination, Bashar orchestrated a nationalistic response that reinforced the portrayal of internal regime critics as accomplices of the West. In addition, the threatening external environment gave the regime something of a green light to crack down on civil society and democracy activists, some of whom, both inside and outside the country, were in contact with and were being supported by the Bush administration. With chaos reigning in Iraq and instability growing in Lebanon, it was not hard to remind the Syrian populace that US-promoted democracy could likewise rip the fabric of its own society apart. Trying to walk a fine line, Bashar did take some measures along the Iraqi border. At this time, there was little harm in meeting some of the US concerns; after all, it emerged soon enough that Damascus and Washington had a shared interest in stability in Iraq.

From the point of view of Damascus, it was fortunate that the Americans had got bogged down in a quagmire in Iraq. The United States was, therefore, in no position to turn its guns on Syria. Bashar could heave a sigh of relief. The more the United States was involved in Iraq, the less enthusiasm and ability it would have to widen what had become the neo-conservative agenda in Syria's direction. As one US military source said in April 2004, a full year after the invasion had begun, 'The Syrians know America can bark a lot, but what else can we do?'[14]

There is little doubt that the Syrians were trying to complicate things for the United States in Iraq. It must be said, nonetheless, that even if Syria had been the most compliant and helpful country on the planet toward the United States, the situation in Iraq would not have been dramatically different.[15] In other words, Syrian influence on the situation in Iraq was marginal; but from the point of view of Damascus, complicating the US position in Iraq even a little might have meant the difference between regime survival and joining Saddam and his cohorts on the 'ash heap of history'. But it was in Syria's interest to have a stable Iraq next door, once the US threat receded. It was also in Syria's interests to position itself as a friendly neighbor, the better to establish (or re-establish) the economic and business links it had begun to forge in the late 1990s, as well as to form a working relationship at the political level.[16]

Damascus certainly wanted the US presence in Iraq to be minimized, but it did not want Iraq to split up into its constituent parts. Syria has its own ethnic and religious cleavages, and having one state – Lebanon – violently implode for almost a generation was more than enough; it did not want the same thing to happen on its eastern border. In addition, the break-up of Iraq could potentially cause minorities in Syria to agitate for outright independence – a possibility that was brought home by the Kurdish nationalist riots in eastern Syria in March 2004, which were certainly motivated by the enhanced autonomy of the Kurds in Iraq.

So by 2005, the perception of Bashar al-Assad in the United States and much of the international community, including key regional actors, was quite negative; indeed, there was a steady clamor of disappointment in the Syrian president. Utterances from Washington and beyond regularly derided, even mocked, Bashar as incompetent, naïve and weak; indeed, when Bashar came to power in 2000, following his father's death, I pointed out in writing some of the similarities with the fictional character Michael Corleone from *The Godfather* movies, noting how Michael, like Bashar, was not originally selected to engage in (much less take over) the family business. A number of people suggested to me that the correct analogy was not with Michael, but with the weak, confused brother, Fredo. This was usually followed by some derogatory remarks that the 'real' leader of Syria should be Bashar's tough-minded older sister, Bushra, or even the president's cosmopolitan wife, Asma al-Assad. Particularly in Arab society, such a suggestion would be regarded as an attack on Bashar's manhood, i.e. his ability to lead.

Emblematic of the negative view of Bashar al-Assad in Washington in the early days of the Bush administration was the congressional testimony in 2002, when the Syrian Accountability Act was being discussed (the SAA, which established a series of economic sanctions against Syria, was signed into law by President Bush in 2004). This view helped establish an image of Bashar as inept. The diatribes against him emerged from the post-9/11 environment, at a time when Congress was on anti-terrorist steroids, each member trying to outdo the next in building up his or her anti-terrorist credentials. This group-think also contributed to congressional support for the US invasion of Iraq in 2003. Syria was an easy target, as was its president – 'low-hanging fruit', in the jargon of the time. It could easily be attacked verbally – and even militarily, in targeted strikes – with no serious repercussions. Giving testimony on the SAA before the House Committee on International Relations in September 2002, Dick Armey (Republican, Texas) claimed:

> Our inaction on holding Syria accountable for its dangerous activities could seriously diminish our efforts on the war on terrorism and brokering a viable peace in the Middle East . . . Syria should be held accountable for its record of harboring and supporting terrorist groups; stockpiling illegal weapons in an effort to develop weapons of mass destruction; and transferring weapons and oil back and forth through Iraq.[17]

The co-sponsor of the SAA, Eliot Engel (Democrat, New York) asserted: 'We will not tolerate Syrian support for terrorism. We will not tolerate Syrian occupation of Lebanon . . . I do not want to witness horrors worse than 9/11. I urge the Administration to get tough on Syria.' His colleague from New York, Gary Ackerman, chipped in: 'This is not too big a nut to crack. Syria is a small, decrepit, little terror state that has been yanking our diplomatic chain for years.' Alluding to the fact that President Bashar was a licensed ophthalmologist, Shelley Berkley (Democrat, Nevada) stated:

> I don't care if he's a doctor, a lawyer, a plumber, a carpenter – this is not a kinder and gentler leader. This is a kinder and gentler terrorist, and we don't need another one of those. He is no different from his father;

> perhaps, even worse because he should know better. This is a disgrace that this country isn't standing up to this terrorist and making sure that this type of behavior is not only condemned, but eliminated.

Bashar had been in power for a little over two years when these comments were made. They were based on a lack of knowledge in Congress of how Syria works – or, in many instances, does not work. For instance, Bashar had announced in the early days of his regime that he intended to authorize the opening of private banks in Syria, a novelty for a public sector-dominated country where most of the fluid capital found its way to Lebanese banks. When private banks had failed to materialize by 2003, Bashar was taken to task by some members of Congress and officials in the Bush administration for not following through on what he had promised – further indication of his ineptitude and prevarication. He could not be trusted.

The fact of the matter is that Syria is practically immune to innovation and short-term change because of an almost institutionalized convulsive reaction against it, all the way from the low-level bureaucrat to the head of a ministry. Change in Syria just does not happen quickly. It is incremental at best. As Syria's First Lady, Asma al-Assad, herself steeped in a financial background as a broker on Wall Street with J.P. Morgan before she married Bashar, commented to me:

> We have not had private banks in Syria for fifty years. Our public banks are not functioning . . . We have staff who do not speak English, who do not have computers. So we are on a very, very basic level . . . We had no idea how to do this. We don't have the experience.

Both of the Assads told me that the biggest mistake they made in this case was announcing the intention of establishing private banks to such fanfare. It created expectations that could not possibly be met in a year or two. A handful of private banks were, indeed, established in 2004 – a number that has since grown as other monetary reforms have been carried through; and in early 2009, the long-promised Syrian stock exchange commenced operations. This is the Syrian way, but in the sound-bite-oriented, four-year-term American sociopolitical system it did not happen fast enough.

Heightened expectations were Bashar's main problem from the very beginning. The first time we met, in May 2004, I half-jokingly mentioned to him that he had made a mistake in telling the media that he liked the music of Phil Collins. When the unknown second son of Hafiz al-Assad came to power in 2000, this widely reported snippet of information fed into an emerging profile of him as a pro-West, modernizing reformer who was not cut from the same cloth as his taciturn father. Bashar was an ophthalmologist, not the heir to the throne, as his more flamboyant and charismatic older brother, Basil, had been. He was the forward-looking head of the Syrian Computer Society, something of a computer nerd himself, and an avid amateur photographer. He liked the technological toys of the West.

Maybe Bashar is partially to blame for these raised expectations; after all, he did launch the Damascus Spring, which was quickly followed by a wave of political repression. But the main thing is that officials and commentators in the West failed to grasp that he had spent all of eighteen months in London, and they were not during the formative years of his life. He is the son of Hafiz al-Assad. He is a child of the Arab-Israeli conflict. He grew up amid the superpower Cold War. He lived the tumult in Lebanon. These are the relationships and historical events that shaped his *Weltanschauung*, not his sojourn in England. Israel is Syria's primary competitor. He is suspicious of the United States. Lebanon should be non-threatening at all costs, and preferably within Syria's sphere of influence. And he is the keeper of the Alawite flame. His hobbies might well include playing with Sony camcorders and listening to the Electric Light Orchestra; but maintaining Syria's traditional interests has always been his obligation.

CHAPTER 2

Surviving

By early 2005, it seemed that Bashar al-Assad had made it through the worst that the US invasion of neighboring Iraq had to offer. But regional and international pressure would increase exponentially over the next few months. It is important to go over in some detail what happened to Syria (and to Bashar) at this time, because it sheds light on the regime's actions, its determination to hold on to power, and the leadership's belief that it would emerge victorious when confronted by an even more lethal threat in 2011.

On 14 February 2005, Rafiq Hariri, the billionaire businessman and former Lebanese prime minister, was assassinated by a massive car bomb in Beirut. Syria was immediately held at least indirectly responsible for the killing, with many in the region and in the international community – certainly in Washington – suspecting that it had been carried out by order of Damascus. The US ambassador to Syria was recalled the day after the assassination. The United States, Europe (particularly France, whose then president, Jacques Chirac, had been close to Hariri) and most of the Arab world (especially Saudi Arabia, whose royal family had also had close ties to him) were united in calling on Syria to withdraw its 14,000–16,000 remaining troops from Lebanon. Those who held Syria responsible for the murder believed Damascus thought the Lebanese leader had been working to force the Syrian troops out of Lebanon.

This was Bashar al-Assad's severest test to date, and it gave additional ammunition to those who wanted to contain Syria (if not to generate regime change). Although Bashar had reduced Syria's troop presence in Lebanon by over 50 per cent since he came to power, he now had to cave in to regional and international pressure and implement a complete withdrawal in April 2005.

Syria cooperated to a minimal extent with the UN investigation into the murder. However, some UN Security Council members (such as Russia, China and Algeria) were opposed both to any expansion in the breadth of the investigation and to the imposition of tougher sanctions against Syria. By early 2006, the focus of the Bush administration's attention seemed to have shifted more toward Iran's alleged attempts to develop a nuclear weapons capability. From the perspective of Damascus, the threat receded somewhat as the United States sank deeper into the quagmire of Iraq. Even the UN investigation process slowed considerably, thus easing the angst in Damascus, where naturally the whole affair was viewed as a political instrument wielded by the Bush administration to put pressure on the Syrian regime.

The Bush administration and anti-regime Syrian exile groups overplayed their hand vis-à-vis Damascus in late 2005. This followed the seemingly damning preliminary UN report, which implicated figures close to the Syrian president in the Hariri murder, including Bashar's brother, Maher al-Assad (commander of the Republican Guard and the army's elite Fourth Armored Division), and his brother-in-law, Asef Shawkat (head of Syrian intelligence). But Bush and the exiles underestimated the staying power and resilience of the regime: quite unexpectedly, Bashar used the crisis atmosphere to consolidate his power. As Syrian expert Joshua Landis put it at the time, Bashar may have lost Beirut, but he gained Damascus. In other words, he used the internal fallout from 'losing' Lebanon to push aside domestic foes and albatrosses. This was manifest in the forced resignation of Vice President Abd al-Halim Khaddam at a Baath party congress meeting in June 2005. Even though Khaddam gave some damning interviews once in exile, the fact that he was doing so *from outside Syria* was evidence that Bashar had consolidated his position. In addition, with the intense anti-American feeling in the region, the more the Syrian exiled opposition appeared to attach itself to the United States, the more it became discredited in Syria; and the more Bashar appeared to stand up to Washington, the more popular he would become – and not only inside Syria, but throughout the Arab world generally. Bashar continued his maneuvering by reshuffling his cabinet in early 2006 and implanting loyalists in the military-security apparatus. A senior Syrian official was asked in December 2005 if his country would make concessions, muddle through or lash out in order to escape from the burden of international pressure: he responded that Syria would do all three. That is the Syrian way.

US-Syrian confrontation

Bashar adeptly survived 2005. It was not easy, though. One of the ways in which Damascus could get Washington off its back was by offering more cooperation on Iraq. At the end of February 2005, Syria captured and handed over to the Iraqi authorities Saddam Hussein's half-brother, Sabawi Ibrahim al-Hassan al-Tikriti, as well as twenty-nine other fugitive members of Saddam's regime. Sabawi reportedly was one of the leading organizers and financiers in Syria of the insurgency in Iraq, and he was number thirty-six on the list of the fifty-five most wanted Iraqis compiled by the US authorities.[1] Since the Syrians took more time to apprehend Sabawi than Washington thought was warranted (Damascus believed US intelligence was faulty), the gesture did not ingratiate the regime with the Bush administration.

With international pressure building on Syria over the Hariri murder, any concessions on Iraq were ignored. Indeed, it was reported that there were several clashes during 2005 between US and Syrian soldiers along the Iraqi-Syrian border, including a prolonged firefight during the summer that ended in the death of several Syrians.[2] There were also reports that US Special Forces units had been carrying out missions into Syria. In the aftermath of the Hariri assassination, the United States turned up the heat on Damascus. In addition, political flashpoints in Iraq led to heightened American pressure on Syria along the border, in an effort to lessen the chances that insurgent activities could disrupt political developments – a theme that would be repeated in coming years. In October 2005, President Bush called Syria one of the Islamic extremists' 'allies of convenience'.[3] Ironically, even though important elements in the Bush administration favored the overthrow of the Assad regime (or at least sufficient pressure being brought to bear to induce a change of behavior), others feared that too much pressure might lead to Assad's fall from power, which could result in something much worse: greater instability in the region and/or the possibility of an Islamist regime coming to power in Syria. This policy divide regarding the Assad regime would reappear in 2011.

The way Damascus viewed matters, then, perhaps it made sense to hold the Iraq card close to its chest, just in case things took a turn for the worse . . . As things turned out, they did not; but it was clear to Damascus that its ability to control the flow (at least to *some* extent) of insurgents into Iraq was of considerable value to the Americans. But how far was this politicized by the Bush administration in an attempt to explain away the deteriorating situation in Iraq? A number of studies in late 2005 and early 2006 concluded that foreign fighters represented well below 10 per cent of all insurgents in Iraq. Military officials were regularly quoted as saying that 95 per cent of the insurgents in Iraq were homegrown. One former intelligence official said that he thought the senior commanders were 'obsessed with the foreign fighters because that's an easier issue to deal with . . . It's easier to blame foreign fighters instead of developing new counterinsurgency strategies.'[4] General John P. Abizaid, the head of CENTCOM, said on 2 October 2005, in a television interview on *Meet the Press*, that he recognized the need to avoid 'hyping the foreign fighter problem'. On the other hand, Abizaid and others quickly pointed out that even though the foreign fighter contingent was relatively small, they provided most of the suicide bombers, since they were more likely to be affiliated to, or to sympathize with, al-Qaida, and therefore the damage they inflicted was disproportionately high compared to their numbers. It is clear that there was confusion and disagreement in Western circles on the extent of the foreign fighter influence in Iraq at the time and on what role Syria was playing in this; there was even more disagreement on how to deal with Syria over this issue. With its own ambiguous position on the subject, Damascus did little to clarify matters – which is probably how Syria wanted it. It was hedging its bets.

Things were looking up for Bashar at the start of 2006, as the situation in Iraq appeared to be rapidly deteriorating. This was highlighted by the bombing in February of the al-Askariyya mosque in Samarra, a venerated Shiite shrine. The sectarian warfare between Sunni and Shia, which had been simmering and episodic prior to this point, seemed to erupt after the bombing, which was suspected to have been perpetrated by al-Qaida in Iraq. All of a sudden, the prospect of unbridled chaos in Iraq allowed the United States and Syria to develop converging interests: neither of them wanted disintegration. For the Syrians, sectarian warfare and the break-up of Iraq could spill over into their country, with equally devastating consequences, and could even spark an unwanted regional conflagration. On the prospects of this, and reflecting on recent events, President Bashar commented in a Saudi newspaper in 2007:

> We say that the biggest threat in the region right now is the sectarian one. This is why we in Syria have started to act independently with our Iraqi brethren. We hosted many delegations from tribes and different religions. We had them conduct direct dialogues and meet with each other. We didn't witness at the popular level what we are witnessing at the political level, which means that until now the sectarian dispute is limited to the political arena . . . Arab states must deal with Iraq not on a sectarian basis but as a whole. Without its Arab identity . . . Iraq will be divided . . . and this will have direct repercussions on us, on you and on other states.[5]

Syria began both to reject and to accept the US occupation of Iraq, and to work more earnestly with the recognized Iraqi government. As such, Syrian-Iraqi diplomatic relations were finally restored in November 2006, following a visit to Baghdad by Syrian Foreign Minister Walid al-Mouallem, and the two countries signed a security cooperation agreement in December 2006, as well as some trade accords.

Riding coattails to opportunity

The Israel–Hizbullah war of summer 2006 also improved Bashar's regional position: Israel was unable to 'defeat' Hizbullah, and a 'victory' for Hizbullah was a victory for Syria. Bashar had very few strategic assets left as of early 2006, and Syrian foreign policy under the Assads is all about having leverage for quid pro quos, particularly regarding Israel's return of the Golan Heights. The Bush administration had basically said to Bashar: 'There is nothing you can do to hurt us, and you have nothing to offer us.' The actions by Hamas and Hizbullah in summer 2006, however, showed that these quasi-state and sub-state actors could make a significant difference in the Middle East political and strategic landscape, thus providing Syria with more regional diplomatic leverage. Bashar rode Hizbullah leader Hassan Nasrallah's popularity to boost his own on the home front, as well as his regime's popular legitimacy in the region. Maybe now Syria could regain a seat at the diplomatic table and utilize its new-found leverage to restart Syrian-Israeli negotiations and engage the United States in a dialogue on more equal terms.

There was no shortage of signals emanating from Damascus after the 2006 war that Syria was prepared to resume negotiations with Israel. A debate ensued inside and outside the Israeli government on whether to explore Syrian intentions. But Israeli Prime Minister Ehud Olmert remained steadfast in rejecting Bashar's peace overtures for the time being – partly because he did not want to negotiate from a position of perceived weakness, following the debacle in Lebanon. It was also widely believed that the Bush administration was pressuring Israel not to re-engage with Syria, in order to maintain the US-led isolation of Damascus.

Then came the Democratic victory in both houses of Congress in the November 2006 midterm elections, widely seen as a repudiation of Bush's foreign policy. This was followed by the publication in early December of the bipartisan Iraq Study Group report. The Group was charged with producing recommendations on Iraq, but commissioners soon saw that Iraq's problems were so tightly interwoven with those of its neighbors that they concluded that the question of improving the US position in the Middle East overall would have to be addressed. Accordingly, they advocated a broader regional diplomatic offensive, including a call for the United States to re-engage with Syria.

Syrian officials, however, were both disappointed and angry over the refusal of the Bush administration to change course. They met Iraq Study Group representatives, and several US senators visited Damascus and met Bashar in December 2006. Syria hoped a corner had been turned with the United States, but it would be disappointed for the time being. Discouraged, Bashar concluded that he must wait until another administration came to power in Washington, which, regardless of political party, could only be better than Bush.

By early 2007, it was time to concentrate on other matters. It was certainly in Syria's interests to do what it could, even if its influence was marginal, to help stabilize the situation in Iraq. From the point of view of Damascus, the ideal outcome would be a strong authoritarian government in Baghdad that maintained the country's Arab character and that was favorably disposed to Syria, coupled with a near-term US troop withdrawal. This might also minimize Iranian influence, which had been (and would continue to be) considerable on account of the Shiite control of the Iraqi government: despite their close strategic relationship, Syria and Iran do not see eye to eye on several issues, one of them being the makeup of the Iraqi government. Accordingly, Damascus played host to a variety of Iraqi factions – Sunni, Shiite and Kurdish alike – seeking to maximize the limited political influence it had in Iraq, as well as the potential lucrative business and economic benefits as Iraq recovered from the war.

In addition, stability in Iraq would help Syria with its Iraqi refugee problem. Depending on the source, estimates of the number of Iraqi refugees entering Syria ranged from 500,000 to 1.4 million. Whatever the actual figure, clearly Syria's largely altruistic move to open its doors to Iraqis escaping the tumult of sectarian warfare placed a tremendous strain on an already brittle Syrian economy. Most of the Iraqi refugees settled in and around Damascus, forcing up rents, reducing the availability of housing for ordinary Syrians, overcrowding the schools and generally contributing to inflationary trends in the country. Crime also spiked upward as the disposable income of the refugees evaporated and job opportunities remained scarce. Support from international organizations for refugees in Syria was slow and inadequate, so the Syrian government was stuck with the lion's share of the bill.

In the course of 2007 and 2008, the United States and Syria seemed to dance around the issue of foreign fighters in Iraq: sometimes Damascus received praise for its efforts; at other times it was urged by US officials to do more. On the one hand, a National Intelligence Estimate on Iraq released in February 2007 concluded that external actors (including Syria) would not likely be a 'major driver of violence', and that most of the violence appeared to be driven by internal factors.[6] On the other hand, at a 26 April 2007 briefing, General David Petraeus, who had become commander of the multinational forces in Iraq in January 2007, stated that '80 to 90 percent of the suicide attacks are carried out by foreigners' channeled into Iraq by a 'network that typically brings them in through Syria'. He said the Syrians had to do more to 'crack down' on the trafficking of insurgents into Iraq, although he stopped short of saying that Damascus was supporting the militants.[7] Within the Bush administration, Petraeus had actually been advocating a policy of engagement with Syria, as a way of sealing the border, and he offered to travel to Damascus to facilitate military and intelligence cooperation; but apparently his plan was vetoed by the White House.

In April 2007, the new speaker of the House of Representatives, Nancy Pelosi, led a bipartisan delegation of congresspersons for a high-profile visit to Syria and a meeting with Bashar al-Assad. This was certainly a far cry from the antagonistic attitude Congress had had toward Syria at the time of the Syrian Accountability Act. The seesaw effect in the US approach to Damascus was more a reflection of domestic politics in Washington (between the Republican administration and the Democrat-controlled Congress) than any sort of intended foreign policy ambiguity.

Regardless of this, it was quite confusing to the Syrian regime, and it would continue to be so, because schizophrenic US actions vis-à-vis Syria would continue throughout the remainder of the Bush administration.

According to American military intelligence officers, there appeared to be some low-level US-Syrian military and/or intelligence cooperation in 2008, with Syrian sources passing information to US forces so that they could target insurgents inside Iraq. In addition, Syria stepped up its arrests of foreign fighters inside the country. As one US military official stationed in northern Iraq, along the Syrian border, said: 'We don't really deal directly with the Syrians, but I will tell you that they have been relatively good in the near recent past, arresting people on their side of the border.'[8] Several US officials in Iraq stated at the time that the number of foreign fighters crossing into the country from Syria had gone down from about ninety per month to about twenty per month (and down from an estimated high of 120 per month at the peak of the violence in 2007). This reduction in the flow of foreign fighters also had to do with the relative success of the 'surge' of US military forces in Iraq, initiated by Petraeus in early 2007, and – maybe even more importantly – with US efforts to win over Sunni tribal confederations to the US cause (the Sunni 'Awakening'), after they had become alienated over the years by the extremist tactics and beliefs of al-Qaida elements in Iraq.

It seemed as if US-Syrian interests and cooperative efforts were finally aligned with regard to Iraq. This paralleled Bashar al-Assad's rapid emergence from US-led isolation, highlighted by his attendance at a Euro-Mediterranean summit meeting hosted by French President Nicolas Sarkozy in July 2008. This was a major breakthrough for the Syrian president, coming as it did on the heels of French gratitude for Syria's positive role in constructing the Doha agreement in May 2008, which put to rest (for the time being) a crisis in Lebanon that threatened to spiral out of control. Bashar was playing the role he had repeatedly said he wanted to play – that of facilitator. He preferred not to sever relations with Iran, Hizbullah or Hamas; instead, he wanted to utilize Syria's unique capacity to play both sides of the fence in order to facilitate Iranian, Hizbullah and Hamas engagement with the West, in the process elevating Syria's status.

Bashar was confident that he had placed the country on the right side of the strategic equation in the inter-Arab arena, especially after Israel's heavy-handed military action in Gaza against Hamas at the end of 2008 and early 2009. He consistently refused to give in to what, in the region, was called the 'American project'. It is almost as if the Arab world moved closer to his consistently held position, rather than the other way around.

The burgeoning cooperative attitude between Syria and the United States appeared to come to a halt on 26 October 2008, when American forces carried out a daring cross-border raid into Syria, near the frontier town of Abu Kamal, and killed a senior al-Qaida operative by the name of Abu Ghadiya, who apparently had been in charge of a Syrian facilitation network since 2005. Officially, the Syrian government denied the claim and expressed outrage over what it viewed as an unwarranted attack. Syria announced the closure of the American School and the American Cultural Center in Damascus – hardly an earth-shattering response.

Bashar knew, however, that he could do little in any tangible way to respond in kind. He was also smart enough to pay attention to the polls, which showed that Barack Obama, who was much more favorably disposed to diplomatic engagement with Syria, was likely to win the US presidential election. The fact that Bashar was able to hold off those in the Syrian leadership who wanted a more aggressive response was a sign that his vision of Syrian foreign policy had imposed itself on the Syrian foreign policy-making apparatus. He did not want to jeopardize the momentum toward a US-Syrian rapprochement when Obama came to power in January 2009. More importantly in the immediate term, though, following the Abu Kamal raid Syria decided to scale back cooperation with the United States over foreign fighters.[9]

In addition, the Bush administration's influence in the Middle East had been considerably circumscribed over its Iraqi policy and the lack of any tangible movement on the Israeli-Palestinian issue. To make up for the diminished US role in Middle East diplomacy, regional players began to enter the Middle East negotiations as arbiters and brokers, especially Qatar and Turkey; indeed, many were surprised by the announcement in May 2008 that Turkey had been brokering indirect Syrian-Israeli peace negotiations. This not only revealed the diplomatic vacuum in the region that the United States should have filled, but it also indicated that Syria was indeed serious about peace with Israel (contrary to the lamentations of the Bush administration that Damascus only wanted the benefits of being involved in a peace process and was not prepared to make the necessary sacrifices). Unfortunately, the Israeli offensive in Gaza in December 2008 and January 2009 forced all sides to cancel the negotiations.

The walls of isolation surrounding Syria were crumbling fast. High-level diplomats from a host of European countries beat a path to Damascus in late 2007 and 2008. Even the Israelis deemed Bashar's peace overtures worth exploring, as he continued to maintain the strategic choice for peace with Israel (despite a September 2007 Israeli attack on a suspected Syrian nuclear facility, which sparked an investigation by the International Atomic Energy Agency (IAEA)).[10] As with the US cross-border raid into Syria from Iraq in October 2008, this did not alter Bashar's overall course. He responded in a relatively measured fashion. He knew he could not do much more anyway, but he did not want to sour the relationship with the United States just when an anticipated Obama presidential victory might herald a new diplomatic environment.

Barack Obama's victory in the 2008 presidential election seemed to create another opportunity to improve the US-Syrian relationship; indeed, in 2009 and 2010 high-level US and Syrian officials met on a regular basis. In June 2009, the Obama administration announced that it would return the US ambassador to Damascus, and in early 2010 an ambassador-designate was chosen. But ideology and anti-Syrian institutional inertia often trump logic, and moral absolutism buries compromise. Obama was not able to wave a magic wand and immediately build a productive relationship with Syria. The legacy of the Bush administration resulted in tremendous distrust on both sides of the equation. The situation was not helped by a raft of UN resolutions, a UN tribunal continuing to investigate the Hariri assassination, an IAEA investigation into Syria's alleged nuclear site, and the Syrian Accountability Act. All of these things found their way into the US-Syrian dynamic, and they could not be easily disentangled, especially as the Obama administration was compelled to deal with other important domestic and foreign policy issues soon after it came to office in 2009. What, during the Bush years, could have been a sagacious foreign policy of dialogue and cooperation with Syria to combat Islamic terrorism, foster peace with Israel and promote political space in Lebanon instead ended up in a neo-conservative ideological straitjacket.

Gaining confidence

Over the years, I saw Bashar al-Assad grow more comfortable as president – perhaps too comfortable. When I first met him, in 2004, he was still a bit unsure about the world around him. Particularly befuddling to him was US policy. In 2005, he was defensive and angry, especially as he had ordered the withdrawal of Syrian troops from Lebanon (something for which he felt he should have received at least a little credit, even if it was primarily due to international pressure). In early 2006, having survived the worst that 2005 had to offer, he began to feel more secure in his position and more sure of his future. In the summer of 2006, when I met him during the Israel–Hizbullah war, it was apparent to me that Bashar's confidence had grown, perhaps in proportion to the regional perception that Hizbullah had inflicted a defeat on – or had at least survived – the Israeli onslaught. His anger at the United States turned into cockiness, as if the Bush administration had taken its best shot and he was still standing.

In May 2007, amid Bashar's re-election in a referendum to another seven-year term, I noticed something in him that I had not detected before: self-satisfaction, even smugness. Ever since first meeting Bashar I had found him to be unpretentious, even self-deprecating. Despite the very serious circumstances surrounding him, he never seemed to take himself too seriously: to my invitation to talk about what he felt had been his biggest achievements, he responded that perhaps we should spend more time on his biggest failures. He is not a commanding figure at first glance: soft-spoken, gregarious and with a childlike laugh – not the typical profile of a dictator. However, for this very reason he commands attention. Beneath him lies the pyramidal Syrian political and military structure. He has got where he is and has stayed there despite – or perhaps because of – his unassuming appearance.

The election of 2007 generated tremendous mass support for the re-elected president. Mingling with the throngs of supporters around Umayyad Square in Damascus over two days, I sensed that a good portion of this outpouring of affection was genuine. Though, of course, much was prearranged: in Syria, when one group – be it a ministry or a private corporation – starts to organize celebratory events, others rapidly clamber on board to generate a tidal wave of support. (Equally, in a *mukhabarat* state, where one never knows who might be a government informant, no one wants to be seen *not* to support the president's re-election.) Bashar had finally been able to tap into that aquifer of support that he had apparently built up, and for the first time he was able to experience it in grand style. It seemed a cathartic experience for him, after all that had happened in the previous two years. In a personal meeting with him on 'election day', I found him genuinely touched by the celebrations and parades in his honor; more importantly, he seemed to drink it in. It all reminded me rather of actress Sally Field's emotional 1985 Oscar acceptance speech – *you like me, you really like me!*

And yet he ran unopposed, in a yes–no referendum vote. Visiting a polling station, I observed that each 'voter' had to tick the 'yes' or the 'no' box – in public – with a band playing and people singing pro-Bashar tunes. It would be an intrepid voter who ticked 'no', especially with security personnel no doubt watching closely. The Bashar posters draped over virtually every upright structure and hanging from virtually every window, and the 'I love Bashar' (in English and Arabic) pins, pendants and billboards were at odds with the way he had up to then eschewed such 'cult' behavior. Bashar understood that the over 97 per cent vote to re-elect him was not an accurate barometer of his real standing in the country. He said it was more important to look at turnout rates, since those who did not vote could probably be added to those who voted 'no'. According to Syrian estimates, the voter turnout rate was 75 per cent, so still a very favorable response for Bashar.

This was the first time I felt that Bashar had begun to believe the sycophants – that to lead the country was his destiny. His view of his position had certainly evolved since the early years of his rule. In the 1950s, the US authorities had frequently referred to friendly dictatorships as 'transitional authoritarian regimes' (i.e. with US guidance and support, those countries would 'transition' to democracy). More often than not, of course, the transitional authoritarian leaders did not want to transition: they liked the power and, in many cases, were convinced that the well-being of the country was synonymous with their retention of power. I wondered at the time whether Bashar had passed the tipping point in this regard.

By late 2007, Bashar felt vindicated, which contributed mightily to his renewed sense of confidence. Syria was even invited to attend the Annapolis conference that the Bush administration sponsored in November to jump-start the Middle East peace process. European and Middle Eastern diplomats were beginning to travel to Damascus to meet Bashar and other Syrian officials, and Bashar's schedule was filling up.[11] While not claiming outright victory, Bashar certainly believed that the noose had been removed from around his neck; indeed, time was on *his* side now. Syrian officials scoffed at the popular notion that their country could be brought in from the cold à la Libya, i.e. that a warm US-Syrian relationship awaited Damascus if only it would give up Hizbullah, Hamas and Iran, in the same way as Libyan leader Muammar al-Gadafi had renounced weapons of mass destruction and made amends for the 1988 Lockerbie bombing. On the contrary, the Syrians believed they had stayed the course and that it had proved to be the correct one: it was the United States that needed to be brought back in from the cold. The 2008 presidential election and the victory of Barack Obama (in a resounding renunciation of the Bush presidency) allowed the *United States* – not Syria – an opportunity to make amends.

A seat at the table

Bashar – and Syria – wanted to be taken seriously by the international community. In a telling exchange in July 2006, during the Israel–Hizbullah war, I asked the Syrian president what he thought of President Bush's expletive that had inadvertently been caught on tape at the G8 summit meeting earlier in the month: in a conversation with British Prime Minister Tony Blair about the conflict in Lebanon, Bush had said, 'Yo Blair, you see, the ... thing is what they need to do is get Syria to get Hizbullah to stop doing this shit and it's over.' Despite the US president's misreading of Syria's (lack of) influence over Hizbullah, Bashar's reaction was unexpected and interesting: 'I love it. I love that he [Bush] said that. It makes me feel great, because at least he is thinking about Syria. He is thinking about us.' Syria was not behind Hizbullah's actions, and Damascus was lucky the Israelis knew that and decided not to take out their wrath on Syria as well. But the very *perception* that Syria could do some damage gave it some utility, some leverage, some more arrows in what had been a near empty quiver.

But, as many Syrians have pointed out over the years, Damascus wants to be seen as a problem *solver*, not a problem *seeker*. One might say that Syria sees its ability to create problems – which it believes it has every incentive to do when threatened – as translating into an ability to solve problems. Certainly Bashar was consistent with me in trying to advocate the utility of Syria in the region. If Syria is denied this role, its leverage in the region is drastically reduced. In other words, Damascus was loath to completely sever its ties with Hamas, Hizbullah and Iran, as they provided Syria with diplomatic leverage. On the contrary, Bashar saw his country as a conduit for the West to develop a dialogue with these very entities.

In late 2008, Bashar certainly believed he could now sit back and see how things unfolded – for example, the policy direction of the new Obama administration when it took power a few months later. He felt empowered politically: 2008 had been a pretty good year for him. There had been the Doha agreement, which had temporarily enhanced the Syrian position in Lebanon; French President Sarkozy had welcomed Bashar in Paris on Bastille Day, along with other heads of state, including Israeli Prime Minister Ehud Olmert (this had signaled a significant breach in the West's attempts to isolate Syria and was a major victory for Bashar). And perhaps most important of all, the Bush administration was all but gone, swept away in a presidential election that brought to power someone whose foreign policy philosophy was a direct repudiation of Bush's. With Barack Obama in power, perhaps traditional diplomacy would make a return. From the point of view of Damascus, perhaps the old rules of the game would return as well.

I always thought that, if Syria wanted to be taken seriously, it had to make a much better job of public diplomacy. Bashar – and Asma al-Assad – were more adept at it than his father had been, but that is not saying very much: Hafiz al-Assad barely engaged in it at all, and indeed seems to have had a healthy disdain for it. As Bashar gained confidence in his international standing, he became more comfortable with public diplomacy. To him, it was a matter of trust, and he was very suspicious (as is Syria as a whole) of the outside world. His public diplomacy at the domestic level improved by leaps and bounds. For example, I was with him (and his wife) at a reception following a special concert at the new opera house in Damascus in May 2007. Bashar did a superb job of 'working' the room, listening intently to every person he engaged with; and by the end of the evening he had spoken personally to everyone present. I saw him 'work' the balcony, so to speak, when he was viewing the parade to celebrate his re-election in front of his very modest presidential office in the Rowda area of Damascus. He made sure to make eye contact with and to point toward as many of the people marching in front of him as he could, and even invited whole families from the street to spend some time with him on the balcony; there he spoke to each member of each family and listened to what each of them had to say. It was very impressive – and it was very effective.

But Bashar is definitely not all-powerful. He fights against systemic corruption and an institutional, bureaucratic and cultural inertia in the country. On many issues he has had to negotiate, bargain and manipulate the system to get things done, and I have witnessed this at first hand. The array of bargains struck by his father at the elite level – i.e. unswerving loyalty in return for personal enrichment – sometimes had the regime sincerely saying and wanting to do one thing, while the actions of important groups that were connected to (or actually inside) the regime forced it to do something quite different. There is really nothing Bashar could have done about it without undermining his support base, especially given the threatening regional environment, when he needed all the friends he could muster, inside and outside the regime.

He told me something in October 2008 that offered some insight into his thinking. We were talking about the potential for elevating the indirect Syrian-Israeli peace negotiations brokered by Turkey that had begun earlier in the year to direct talks with Israel. He said he really did not want to move to the next level without greater assurance of success; he was 'new to this game' and, since it was his 'first time doing this', he 'could not afford to fail'. He had made his decision on negotiations with Israel, and he had placed people around him that agreed with this decision. But there were elements who did not agree with him, and so Bashar believed he had one shot at it, and he had better get it right. He therefore moved cautiously.

That is one very important reason why, from his perspective, it is absolutely essential that the entire Golan Heights, up to the 4 June 1967 line, should be returned to Syria. This is vital to his domestic legitimacy, to his legacy-in-the-making (especially compared to that of his father, who 'lost' the Golan as minister of defense during the 1967 Arab-Israeli war). In essence, maybe he could get rid of the 'security' in 'security state'. This has always been the lure for Bashar: the Golan Heights in exchange for concessions on foreign policy and domestic issues.

At a meeting with him in late 2007, I got a sense that this trade-off might have been more real than most people think. In my discussions with Bashar, 80 per cent of what he told me was the standard Syrian line, or else something that would appear in newspapers in the coming days. But about 20 per cent was more off the cuff, especially as he felt increasingly comfortable with me over the years. Those were the gems I was looking for, which really gave me some valuable insight into the man. On this occasion, we were talking about trade-offs regarding a peace agreement with Israel and severing ties with Hizbullah, Hamas and Iran, as well as about remaking the Syrian system. He rocked back on his chair, gazed up at the ceiling and said with emotion: 'If I get the Golan back, I will be a hero.' In a sense, the systematic embedding of the return of the Golan in the minds of two generations of Syrians, while previously an obstacle to the conclusion of an Israeli-Syrian agreement, could actually have worked in favor of peace: it would have empowered the Syrian regime – it would have empowered Bashar – to deliver on heightened levels of expectations and responsibilities domestically and regionally as the price of peace. But this would only be viable so long as Bashar was in control and maintained his seat at the diplomatic table.

Before the 2011 uprising, there was still a good bit of leftover anti-Syrian inertia in the Obama administration, in the Pentagon and intelligence community, and in Congress. This is to say nothing of the negative image of Syria in the minds of the American public. Then the raft of UN resolutions, the UN tribunal investigation into the Hariri assassination and a sanctions regime put in place by the Bush administration all complicated any improvement in US-Syrian relations. The United States has a way of painting a picture of foreign leaders that is based on whether they are for or against US interests. At different times in the 1950s and 1960s, Gamal Abd al-Nasser was viewed as a possible ally and as an implacable foe, depending on where he positioned Egypt in the superpower Cold War. Saddam Hussein was our friend in the 1980s and our enemy in the 1990s. I do not know if they changed as much as our perception of them did. The fact that Assad was not traditionally groomed to be president and that, in the eyes of many Syrians, he gave up his vocation to serve his country won him some breathing space in Syria. The regime exploited this to buy him a long learning curve, and he delivered enough amid constant pressure for a time to warrant it. But then came the Arab Spring, and all bets were off.

CHAPTER 3

Syria is Different

In late 2010 and early 2011, Syria seemed a fairly stable place, especially compared to Tunisia, Egypt and Yemen, where events were beginning to bubble. Bashar al-Assad had improved his own and his country's image; earlier in the decade, and particularly in the aftermath of the Hariri assassination, that image had been tarnished. In Paris in December 2010, the Syrian president and his wife were described as cosmopolitan visitors and were widely photographed in their haute couture clothes, visiting trendy museums and being hosted (if not feted) by the French elite.

Even the Special Tribunal for Lebanon (STL), established under UN Security Council Resolution 1757 on 30 May 2007 to indict and try suspects in the Rafiq Hariri assassination, shifted its focus away from Syria. By late 2010, it was being widely reported that the STL was planning to issue indictments for four members of Hizbullah in connection with the assassination.[1] Even though Hizbullah is the crucial ally of Damascus in Lebanon and facilitates Syrian influence, and even though many in the Syrian leadership still believed their country to be the ultimate target of the STL, diplomatic pressure on Syria eased substantially on an issue that had been a looming nightmare for the regime ever since the UN investigation commenced in 2005.

Within a two-day span in December 2010, there were separate stories in two leading US newspapers praising various aspects of Syrian society, history, culture and the new direction of its government. The headline and sub-headline of a story in the tourism section of the 26 December issue of the *Los Angeles Times* read: 'Syria a Bright Star in the Middle East: Tourism is on the upswing in Syria, with a more modern government, lavish hotels sprouting up and cuisine and culture evolving in striking ways.'[2] Next day the *New York Times* ran a feature entitled 'Preserving Heritage, and the Fabric of Life, in Syria'. In the story, the creative and socially sensitive efforts to preserve the old city district of Aleppo were lauded, and the endeavor was dubbed 'one of the most far-thinking preservation projects in the Middle East, one that places as much importance on people as it does on the buildings they live in'. The national and local governments were praised for spearheading the project and outsourcing the effort to a German non-profit group and the Aga Khan Trust for Culture.[3]

All seemed to be well.

And yet, a year later, the Center for the Study of Islam and Democracy sent an email to its readership with the following headline: 'ACT NOW to stop Bashar Assad's killing machine in Syria.'[4] This – and the many other negative references to the Syrian president and his cohorts which consistently appeared as the Syrian uprising gained momentum throughout 2011 – shows how far Bashar had fallen in just twelve months.

In February 2011, a leading Israeli newspaper detailed the months of effort put in by then-Senator John Kerry (chairman of the Senate Committee on Foreign Relations and one of President Barack Obama's confidants on foreign policy) to restart the Syrian-Israeli peace negotiations. Kerry had reportedly met Bashar al-Assad five times in Damascus in the previous two years and had frequently spoken to him on the telephone. The same article stated that, on one occasion, Kerry and his wife had dined with Bashar and Asma al-Assad.[5] Hollywood icons Brad Pitt and Angelina Jolie visited and dined with Syria's First Family. The First Lady also had what quickly became a controversial *Vogue* magazine feature on her in March, at the same time as the uprising was brewing in Syria and only a short while before it erupted. The title of the article was 'Asma al-Assad: A Rose in the Desert'. The opening lines of the article were as follows:

> Asma al-Assad, Syria's dynamic first lady, is on a mission to create a beacon of culture and secularism in a powder-keg region – and to put a modern face on her husband's regime. Asma al-Assad is glamorous, young, and very chic – the freshest and most magnetic of first ladies. Her style is not the couture-and-bling dazzle of Middle Eastern power but a deliberate lack of adornment. She's a rare combination: a thin, long-limbed beauty with a trained analytical mind who dresses with cunning understatement. *Paris Match* calls her 'the element of light in a country full of shadow zones'. She is the first lady of Syria.[6]

Yet, paralleling the increasingly disreputable image of her husband, on 26 December 2011, CNN.com ran a feature on the First Lady entitled 'Will Asma al-Assad take a stand or stand by her man?'[7] Amid the rising level of violence and death in Syria, the writer of the article asked: 'What must Syria's first lady be thinking now? Could she do anything to stop the bloodshed?' In essence, it concluded that she had decided to stand by her man, perhaps ignorant of, or even complicit in, the violence.

In retrospect, Bashar al-Assad's apparent complacency or denial of the facts amid the turmoil of the Arab Spring in Tunisia, Egypt and Yemen was vividly on display in an interview he gave to journalists from the *Wall Street Journal* in late January 2011.[8] Assad stated in the interview that the protests in those countries signaled a 'new era' in the Middle East, where the rulers would need to meet the rising political and economic demands of the people: 'If you didn't see the need of reform before what happened in Egypt and Tunisia, it's too late to do any reform.' He went on:

> Syria is stable. Why? Because you have to be very closely linked to the beliefs of the people. This is the core issue. When there is divergence . . . you will have this vacuum that creates disturbances.

This was a reference to Syria's position on Palestinian and Israeli issues, as well as to Bashar's perceived triumphal resistance to the 'American project' in the region. The Syrian president also seemed confident in the level of reform he had implemented in Syria over the years. He admitted that he wished there had been more, but commented that his country needed more time to build up institutions and improve education, in order to absorb such levels of reform. Reform could, he said, be counterproductive if society is not yet ready for it. In this vein, he asked: 'Is it going to be a new era toward more chaos or more institutionalization? That is the question.'

In its February 2011 issue, *Forward Magazine*, a pro-government (it has to be or else it would not be published in Syria!) English-language monthly produced in Damascus, dovetailed Bashar's *Wall Street Journal* interview with two essays, one by a leading Syrian commentator and the other by one of the president's closest and most influential advisors. This generally interesting periodical focuses primarily on economic, business and cultural issues in Syria, but it usually includes one or two political commentaries. Everything, and especially the political commentaries, is vetted by the Ministry of Information before it goes to press. Both articles in the February issue reflected the president's and the regime's sense of immunity from the virus of protest spreading elsewhere in the Arab world. The editor-in-chief of the magazine, Dr Sami Moubayed (whom I know quite well and of whom I think highly), is a professor of international relations in the country and one of its foremost commentators. He has access to high places in Syria, and therefore his essays often reflect regime sentiments. For this issue he wrote a piece entitled 'Lesson from Egypt: West is not Best'. In it, Moubayed repeatedly hammers home the point that the dictators in the Arab world who had either fallen by then (President Ben Ali in Tunisia) or were on their way out (President Husni Mubarak in Egypt and President Abdullah Saleh in Yemen) were being run out of office by widespread popular protest primarily because over the years they had been the lackeys of the West, and particularly of the United States:

> There are two kinds of leaders in this region: those who rely on their people for support, and those who rely on the West. Ben Ali, Farouk

> [King Farouk of Egypt, overthrown in a coup in 1952], the Shah [Shah Muhammad Reza Pahlavi, the US-backed ruler of Iran, overthrown in 1979 by Islamist revolutionaries led by Ayatollah Khomeini], and Mubarak all relied on the West, but the West abandoned them without blinking when it was clear that their regimes were no longer useful. The other kinds of leaders are those like President Gamal Abdul Nasser of Egypt and Bashar al-Assad of Syria. When Nasser faced the Suez war of 1956, the people of Egypt came out in his defense. When he stepped down in 1967 [following Egypt's defeat in the June 1967 Arab-Israeli war] the people of Egypt came out in the millions, asking him to stay in power. The same applied to Syria's Assad, whose people rallied around him during the difficult years of George W. Bush's presidency. The overnight generation of Egypt fans [*sic*] reflects the dreams and ambitions of young Arabs who desperately want similar street revolts against their own aged and ailing despots. These Arab leaders, many being friends of both Ben Ali and Mubarak, have terrorized their own people with a stick – given to them by the West – for over 20 years.[9]

In what is now almost self-prophetic irony, Moubayed ends his editorial:

> What is so beautiful about the Tunisian and Egyptian stories is that this time, it wasn't flamboyant and inexperienced young officers toppling . . . [the] young king. Nor was it turbaned clerics toppling an autocratic and aging royal, like Iran 1979. It was also not US tanks rumbling into Tunisia, as was the case with Baghdad 2003. It was the people of Tunisia – the young and old, the intellectual, and the unemployed. It was the glorious people of Egypt, who said, 'enough is enough'.[10]

In this same issue of *Forward Magazine*, Dr Bouthaina Shaaban wrote a piece entitled 'The Real Evils Plaguing the Region'.[11] Shaaban has been close to the Assad family for over twenty years. She was a translator and advisor to Hafiz al-Assad, and she is very close friends with Bushra al-Assad, Bashar's older sister (who also happens to be married to Asef

Shawkat, the head of Syrian intelligence). Shaaban was placed in the Foreign Ministry when Bashar came to power; after falling out with the longtime minister of foreign affairs, Farouk al-Sharaa, she was appointed minister of expatriates. A few years ago, Shaaban re-entered the inner sanctum of the regime by being named Political and Media Advisor to the Office of the President. Her office is located in the Rowda building in Damascus, where Bashar spends most of his official time as president. I have interviewed her on a number of occasions, and again she is someone for whom I have high regard. In addition, she is known among diplomats and analysts as one of the more pro-Western of Bashar's advisors over the years. What she writes and states publicly no doubt directly reflects Bashar's thinking and is culled from meeting and talking with him at length on these issues.

Like Moubayed, in her essay she castigates the West for being at the root of the unrest that had hit Tunisia, Egypt, Yemen and elsewhere. Interestingly, she seems to recognize the pervasive socioeconomic problems in the Arab world, and by implication also in Syria:

> Is this the time for Arab masses to go to the streets to force their will on governments which have, for decades, imposed their will, slogans, gods, failures, alliances and differences on their peoples without achieving any of their aspirations? Grievances, frustration, betrayal and political, economic and social failure accumulated, while the Arab ruling elites did not feel the simmering anger of the masses? There is no doubt that the needs of millions of young people throughout the Arab world need to be addressed in a manner different to what governments have used so far. This is a generation living in the 21st century; it needs to get seriously involved in building their country and their future. The reasons for this rage are complicated. They cannot be explained away by unemployment or poor living conditions. Mohammad Bouazizi, who provided the spark to the Tunisian revolution, was a university graduate working on his fruit and vegetable cart until he felt insulted and humiliated by the forces of oppression. His desperation pushed him to set fire to his body which stood for the body of the whole generation. His suicide was the last straw

> which removed the barrier of fear built between his generation and the might of governments. This is what sparked the call for change throughout the Arab world. So, it is a cry for the dignity humiliated by seeing their people besieged in Gaza and seeing six million Palestinians placed in large prisons inside their occupied country, occupied since 1948 and in refugee camps and being killed on a daily basis amidst Arab impotence.

She identified what, to her mind, were the real reasons for unrest: not only socioeconomic problems, but also neglect of – and Arab complicity in – the Palestinian problem, Israeli brutality and related US policies. In other words, if an Arab leader, such as Bashar al-Assad, has been on the correct side by opposing such policies and by supporting the Palestinians and other Arabs suffering under stagnant, obsequious autocracies and foreign imperialism, he should be safe, because he is on the side of the people. She went on:

> it is easy to trace the critical moments which accumulated rage in the Arab conscience, particularly as a result of their government impotence and silence regarding the tragedies which befell Iraq and Palestine. This feeling is ignored by American and western decision makers because they actually aim at humiliating the Arabs assisted by the ability of oppressive government forces to quell the voice of Arab masses calling for solidarity.

She ended: 'If anger is directed today against governments and aims are to change rulers and their methods, there is no doubt that the position of these rulers over the question of the liberation of Palestine from Israeli occupation will be a major factor in what happens over the coming weeks and months.'

Correct identification of symptoms; wrong diagnosis.

Why did Bashar al-Assad – and the Syrian regime – think Syria was different?

As Bouthaina Shaaban wrote, it was the self-immolation of a young man that began the so-called Arab Spring in late 2010. Twenty-six-year-old

Muhammad Bouazizi humbly worked a fruit and vegetable cart in the town of Sidi Bouzid, in Tunisia. But police confiscated his produce because he supposedly lacked the proper permit – probably one that required a bribe to acquire. So, on 17 December, he set himself on fire in what he hoped was a final act of despair and anger. Little did he know that he would light a fire under the entire Arab world.

The clue as to why what happened in Tunisia, Egypt and elsewhere in the Arab world did happen lies in the profile of Muhammad Bouazizi. For he is far from alone, as the events he unleashed have shown. The Arab world is full of (predominantly) male, urban twenty-somethings who are either unemployed or underemployed. They cannot make ends meet. Those who are married and have children often cannot provide adequately for their families, while those that do manage to scrape by usually need to hold down two or three jobs. Young single men do not earn enough to provide a dowry – or even to offer the merest glimmer of hope of a financially secure future, which might win them consent to their marriage. They expected more than this. They were promised more than this – especially the throngs who acquired a college education.

As MIT scholar Philip Khoury wrote in a seminal article in the 1980s, the disaffected youth had been mobilized but not assimilated.[12] Back then, Khoury was talking about the rising appeal of Islamic fundamentalism in Egypt; but the profile applies equally to the populist protest movements that erupted in 2011, because the vehicle by which anger and frustration are expressed matters less than the cause. Youths all over the Arab world are being mobilized every day – by being educated. They are led to believe that this education will lead to a decent job, allowing them to make enough money to eke out a living, have a family and even have a future. But they are not getting these things: they are not being assimilated.

In many Arab countries in the 1950s and 1960s there was a social contract between the government and the people. One of the clauses was free education all the way through college. As a result, hundreds of thousands graduated from college every year. The problem in the non-oil-rich

Arab countries such as Tunisia and Egypt, where the Arab Spring began and became a tidal wave (and also in a country such as Syria), was that their moribund economies, stunted by socialist-inspired state-capitalist policies, corruption and rising birth rates, could not provide enough jobs for all these college graduates. For that reason, the public sector often became the employer of last resort; it often turned into a bloated vessel of civil servant purgatory.

The vestiges of these long-standing regimes in the Arab world today have been haltingly trying for decades to shift to more market-oriented economic systems. It is a wrenching process that must be carefully calibrated by the ruling regimes if they want to stay in power: engaging in too much reform and too quickly can lead to immediate economic instability and subsequent political unrest. Since staying in power is paramount for these regimes, the reform process has been a zigzagging one that has proved uneven and inadequate.

Though they led to some GDP growth, some easing of the flow of capital and some infrastructural improvement, these incomplete market reforms also exacerbated the unequal distribution of wealth, widespread corruption and relative poverty. The economies did not expand fast enough, especially as the populations were largely made up of under-thirty-year-olds, so jobs were scarce and good jobs went to the privileged. Thus the gap between mobilization and assimilation widened. This gap is what has produced the level of societal anger and frustration that has been witnessed throughout much of the Arab world – it is not a question of absolute poverty. That is why the middle- and lower-middle-class educated strata are often the ones to initiate and lead protest movements in the Arab world, whether Islamist or secularist. Combine all of this with a lack of any real political space, pervasive corruption and decades of political repression and one ends up with a highly combustible mixture. The events of the Arab Spring were not the first manifestations of anger and frustration by the masses against entrenched, corrupt regimes.[13] There had been episodes of this in the past in a number of Arab states, such as the bread riots in Egypt in the 1970s and 1980s, when subsidies for basic foodstuffs were reduced; however, a combination of state repression and strategic backtracking usually kept the regimes in power. But not this time. The demonstrations seemed larger and angrier, and they were fueled by new instruments of protest.

Muhammad Bouazizi was humiliated; and then he was in unimaginable pain for over two weeks, before he died on 4 January 2011. He did not deserve his fate. But his fate may well determine the destiny of the Arab world.

The day after Bouazizi's self-immolation, the protests began in Tunisia, first of all in his home town. Then, via Facebook and mobile phone feeds, the images gained greater currency, appearing on the Arab satellite news agency Al-Jazeera, based in Qatar. The protests gained momentum, and the government's response also grew, inevitably leading to more violence and deaths. Pretty soon, protestors were vigorously demanding the departure of the septuagenarian President Ben Ali, who had ruled in an increasingly authoritarian fashion for decades. The uprising reached the capital, Tunis, on 13 January 2011, and the following day Ben Ali fled to Saudi Arabia. Such a thing had never before happened in the modern history of the Middle East: a popular uprising had overthrown an entrenched regime. All of a sudden it was a new Middle East. Popular will matched with popular assertiveness could bring down decrepit, corrupt old regimes, despite the apparent asymmetry in power between the repressive apparatus of the government and the masses. But the mobilized youth in Tunisia and Egypt – and soon elsewhere in the Arab world – had the great equalizer: technologically savvy use of social media. The barrier of fear seemed to be broken with the events in Tunisia; and, with the liberating use of social media to mobilize, inform, plan and spread the news, the decades-old monopoly control of information by repressive regimes was a thing of the past.

Taking notice in neighboring Egypt were many who had at least as many grievances against the authoritarian regime of the octogenarian leader, Husni Mubarak, who had been president of Egypt ever since the assassination of his predecessor, Anwar Sadat, in 1981. Deliberately and with supreme irony choosing 25 January – National Police Day – to launch the popular protests in Cairo, people of all stripes began to march toward

Tahrir Square, long the political epicenter of popular politics in Cairo (the name itself meaning 'liberation'). Although there were protests elsewhere in the country, the local, regional and international focus fell squarely on Tahrir.

The government responded at first with police repression, although the relatively well-respected military first stood by on the sidelines. Later on, after it took control of the streets in order to prevent total chaos, the military showed itself unwilling to fire on demonstrators. Once the military essentially decided not to launch a bloody crackdown, it was all over for Mubarak. Though himself a military officer, the president was not powerful enough to overcome the self-interest of his generals, who wanted to maintain their hard-won lofty political and economic status, which had been built up over the decades and would be lost if they chose the wrong side of history. As a result, on 11 February, it was announced that Mubarak had stepped down as president and had turned over authority to the Supreme Council of the Armed Forces.

While the events of early 2011 were at their most spectacular in Tunisia and Egypt, there was also serious popular protest in Yemen, Bahrain and Libya. While all these movements targeted long-entrenched authoritarian regimes, and while the circumstances in the various countries resembled those in Tunisia and Egypt in some ways, in other ways the conditions in each individual country were unique. Less dramatic but still significant protests also rumbled in Jordan and Morocco, while oil-rich Arab states such as Saudi Arabia tried desperately to forestall any potential discontent spreading to their countries by injecting billions of dollars of oil money into social services and wage increases, at the same time promising ambiguous political reforms. It seemed that no country was immune to the contagion of protest born of pent-up anger and frustration.

It is almost certain that Bashar al-Assad was absolutely shocked when the uprisings in the Arab world started to seep into his country in March 2011. I believe he truly thought he was safe and secure and popular in the country, and was beyond condemnation. But this was not the case in the Middle East of 2011, where the stream of information via the Internet, Facebook, Twitter, YouTube and mobile phones could not be controlled as it once had been. The 'perfect storm' in the Arab world of higher commodity prices (which made basic items more expensive), a youth bulge (which created a gap between mobilization and assimilation) and even Wikileaks (which revealed the profligate lifestyles of the ruling elite) threw into sharp relief the widespread socioeconomic problems, corruption and restricted political space. In this, Syria was no different. And after the popular uprisings in Tunisia and Egypt led to the removal of the *ancien régime* in each country, the barrier of fear of the repressive apparatus of the state was broken.

Assad's thought Syria was different; he was obviously wrong. As mentioned above, Assad portrayed his country in interviews as almost immune from such domestic unrest. The mouthpieces of the Syrian regime consistently echoed this view, even to the point of expressing support for the protestors in other Arab states. Indeed, calls by anti-Assad elements inside and outside the country for similar protests to be held in Syrian cities in January and February failed to elicit much of a response, as only a few dozen showed up, rather than the hoped-for thousands. These protests usually fizzled out rapidly or were easily snuffed out by security.[14] There just did not seem to be the same energy for opposition in Syria as in other countries, and this only made the regime feel that much more secure.

Assad's supporters also emphasized that the septuagenarian and octogenarian leaders of those other Arab countries had been out of touch with their people and had been corrupt lackeys of the United States and Israel. The implication, of course, was that Assad – at forty-five years of age relatively young – was in synch with the Arab youth. He had also consistently confronted the United States and Israel in the region and had supported the resistance forces of Hamas and Hizbullah. He could thus brandish credentials that played well in the Arab street – not only in Syria, but throughout much of the Arab world. This may have bought him some time, but it was a misreading of the situation – or a denial of it. As it turns out – and as will be described in the next chapter – Syria was suffering from many of the same underlying socioeconomic woes that existed in the non-oil-producing Arab countries and that created a well of disenfranchisement and disempowerment, especially among an energized and increasingly frustrated youth.

However, there were indeed certain differences between Syria and such countries as Tunisia and Egypt that led many to believe that the Syrian regime could weather the storm of the Arab Spring – or at least be one of the last to be subjected to it. Because of Syria's turbulent political development following independence, Syrians have generally disdained to engage in activities that could produce instability and chaos. They only have to look across their borders, on either side, toward Lebanon and Iraq – two countries that, like Syria, are ethnically and religiously sectarian – to see how political disorder can violently rip apart the fabric of society. Of course, this trepidation was constantly stoked by the regime to reinforce the necessity of maintaining stability at all costs. It frequently portrayed itself as the only thing standing between stability and chaos. So long as Assad remained the only viable alternative in the minds of many Syrians, they were not going to participate in an opposition movement that could destabilize the country. For the many Syrians who were ambivalent, the lack of support for the opposition was not necessarily a vote of confidence in the regime. Thus, if a viable opposition could emerge in concert with the weakening of the regime, Syrians could jump *en masse* from a sinking ship, potentially making the end of the Assad era a rapid one.

Over the years, Bashar al-Assad had carefully maneuvered his most loyal allies into the military-security apparatus, government ministries and the Baath party. Following Syria's withdrawal from Lebanon in April 2005, there was a reconfiguration of the Syrian hierarchy. Then, a few months later came the Baath Party Regional Congress, at which Bashar asserted his authority, got rid of potential enemies and brought in more loyalists. In February 2006, a Cabinet reshuffle resulted in Bashar's most hand-picked and loyal Cabinet to date. This was a clear indication that *his* people were beginning to monopolize all the important positions in the state. Any sense that Bashar's authority might be inhibited by a remnant of the 'old guard' from his father's days was gone.

The fate of the Syrian military and security services is also closely tied to that of the regime. In contrast to Egypt, these institutions have not been separate from the political leadership. In 2011 they aggressively led the violent action against the protestors. Moreover, the regime has been careful to use the most loyal divisions in the military – particularly those made up largely or entirely of Alawites – to spearhead the crackdowns in the cities and towns that have generated the most unrest.

Memory of the Syrian military action ordered by Hafiz al-Assad in 1982 in Hama against Islamic militants – action which, according to many reports, killed up to 20,000 people – certainly weighed heavily on the minds of many Syrians as they contemplated active opposition. With the brutality of the 2011 crackdown, it appeared that the regime wanted to remind Syrians that it was willing to go to similar lengths to eliminate any resistance, and that it had the necessary loyalty of the military, the party and the government. The repressive apparatus of the state – military, *mukhabarat*, paramilitary groups – was daunting to anyone contemplating taking it on.

On a related issue, the Syrian regime, infused as it is with Alawites in important positions, had always portrayed itself as the protector of all minorities in a country that is 75 per cent Sunni Muslim. As well as the Alawites, there are various Christian sects in the country (comprising about 10 per cent of the population), plus Druze (3 per cent) and a smattering of Jews and various obscure Islamic sects. In addition, there are Sunni Kurds in Syria, most of them in the northeast sector of the country; they account for approximately 10 per cent of the population. Although the Kurds have often been a restless minority in Syria under the Assads, with two uprisings against the regime that were forcibly put down (in 1982 and 2004), the Syrian government has, from time to time, made concessions to them (as in spring 2011, in the early stages of the protests) in order to pre-empt any large-scale rebellion.

The Assads have skillfully played the minority card over the years, practically guaranteeing for themselves at least a 20–30 per cent loyal support base in the country by playing on fears of the potential for repressive Sunni Muslim rule and/or instability, in which minorities typically pay a high price. Then there are loyal Sunnis from the business class (part of the military-mercantile complex discussed in Chapter 1), and Sufi Muslims (mostly Sunni), who tend to have a broader and more tolerant view of other Muslim sects and non-Muslim religions, and who have been actively cultivated and supported by the Syrian government under the Assads (especially Bashar). When all these elements are added together, they probably account for close to half of the Syrian population. For an authoritarian ruler, this is not such a bad thing: employing coercion, a pervasive spy apparatus, carefully constructed tribal and family alliances, bribery and the tactics of divide and rule, maintaining control over the remaining half of the population is not as difficult for a minority-ruled regime as it would, on the surface, seem.

Bashar al-Assad himself used to be generally well liked in the country – or was not generally reviled. There were no Wikileaks reports detailing the extravagant lifestyle of Assad – as there were with Tunisian President Ben Ali – because he does not have one. Stories of Bashar and Asma al-Assad going out shopping or for dinner in Damascus and elsewhere without bodyguards, and of the president driving his own car, became the stuff of urban legend. This did, in fact, occur on occasion, especially early on in Bashar's tenure; but soon enough the stories multiplied to the point where almost every Syrian claimed to have seen the couple out. The image, of course, was that he and his family were normal people – not distanced from the masses, but rather aware of and concerned about their problems, because they engaged with the public. Bashar's supporters would talk about him almost as a prophet, delivered to Syria to bring the country forward and claim its rightful place of importance in the region.

By becoming president, Bashar gained a good bit of credit in the eyes of the Syrian public, for giving up his passion, ophthalmology, to serve the country when it needed him most. Of course, as pointed out in the previous chapter, this was also promoted as regime propaganda, and it may have bought Bashar a long learning curve and more public patience with his incremental reform efforts, simply because he had not been groomed from the beginning to be president. His is the image of a good family man with a beautiful, cosmopolitan and civically active wife. Despite the fissiparous pressures both within and outside his country, he kept it together for a decade despite all the odds, and in doing so earned no small debt of gratitude from the Syrian people. Through it all, there was some economic growth (albeit uneven), as well as fiscal, administrative and education reform that is perhaps too easily dismissed today.

Finally, Syria's internal and external opposition was, for most of 2011, uncoordinated and often divided, with no generally recognized leadership. The Syrian regime has done a good job over the years of ensuring this. As we shall see, since the beginning of the uprising there have been various attempts by Syrian opposition groups in exile to come together and present a unified, inclusive front. At first, this was more important in terms of attracting international support; but it was also vital in order to offer a real choice to those Syrians who supported the regime simply because there was no legitimate alternative. To date, the results of these efforts have been decidedly mixed.

In Syria (as in Iraq following the US invasion of 2003), there has always been a general feeling that the opposition in exile was (and still is) illegitimate. There is a divide between those who have had to deal with the repressive regime while living under it and those who were forced out of Syria or who left the country, and who lost touch with Syrian reality as they lived in relative comfort. The opposition elements and organizations outside Syria have also been tainted (whether or not legitimately) by their often close relationship with Western officials and by the funding they have received from the United States and some European countries. A similar scenario fatally hampered attempts by US-supported Iraqi exile groups to establish a power base in Iraq after the invasion, because they were seen to be riding in on the back of American tanks. With antipathy toward US policy at an all-time high throughout the first decade of the twenty-first century and into the second, any opposition group that is too closely associated with the United States (or with any other country that is regarded as acting out of self-interest) would have a very difficult time gaining traction with most Syrians. It was easy for the regime to paint the opposition inside and outside the country as tools of the imperialists, because actual imperialist interference (as well as associated regime propaganda) was commonplace in Syria during the first couple of decades after independence.

In any event, the numerous attempts from late January through early March 2011 by anti-Assad activists and organizations to ride the momentum of change witnessed in Tunisia and Egypt and to foment similar large-scale demonstrations in Damascus failed spectacularly. As mentioned above, instead of hundreds of thousands of protestors gathering on announced dates and at appointed locations, only a handful turned up. This seemed to confirm the almost universal predictions of analysts, commentators, diplomats and scholars (including this one) that the Arab Spring would not come to Syria any time soon or in any significant way; and if it did, the Syrian regime would be the hardest nut to crack and most probably the last in the Arab world to collapse. So, come mid-March, Bashar al-Assad had to feel pretty good about his chances.

But none of this was enough to eliminate the protests entirely or to reverse the increasing boldness of many Syrians, particularly the youth, in continuing to confront the military and security forces. A storm was quickly brewing.

CHAPTER 4

No, It's Not

Deraa is a city of some 70,000–100,000 people near the border with Jordan, in southwestern Syria. It is the capital of the Deraa Governorate, located about sixty miles due south of Damascus, on the road that leads to Amman, the Jordanian capital. This part of Syria, as with most of its rural areas, is agrarian based. As such, its economy has suffered disproportionately, due to a long drought in what is already an arid region.

It is here that the Syrian uprising effectively began.

During the first week of March, at a school in Deraa, reportedly ten children aged between nine and fifteen decided to do what children at this age do the world over: be mischievous. Inspired by a slogan from the Egyptian uprising, they decided to write 'Down with the Regime' on the wall of their school. The schoolchildren (and subsequent protestors) used the word *nizam* (system or regime) rather than *hukuma* (government), revealing the specific target of frustration to be the system rather than the government. This may indicate that they are more interested in issues of social justice and corruption than in democracy as such.[1] It is also an example of protestors expressing their anger in wall graffiti or in street demonstrations because there was no other avenue, such as through elections, to kick out the existing rulers. The *mukhabarat* is generally sensitive to anti-regime sentiments, and this sensitivity was probably heightened by what had transpired in Tunisia and Egypt. So they would be under orders to be especially vigilant in detecting signs of discontent. The upshot was that local security officials arrested the schoolchildren and, according to many reports, sent them to Damascus, where they were interrogated – and apparently even tortured – despite attempts by their families over two weeks to negotiate their release.

In a governorate or province such as Deraa, the three most important people are the governor, the *mukhabarat* chief and the Baath party head. Indeed, this is the case in all provinces. Which of these three is the most influential depends on the province and on the particular circumstances in that province. One may be sure, however, that in the regional atmosphere in the Middle East in March 2011, when the antennae of security services across the region were particularly pricked, the most important of the three in Deraa was the security chief. The decision to arrest the children was not untypical in Syria, but the social – and maybe even the psychological – environment had changed, thanks to the widespread coverage of (and fascination with) the events in Tunisia, Egypt and elsewhere.

On 15 March, a few hundred protestors, many of them family members and relatives of the imprisoned children, marched in front of the Omari mosque in downtown Deraa. They called for the release of the children, as well as for reform of the corrupt and repressive system of government that allowed such arbitrary – almost ridiculous – acts of excessive force. The protests grew to several thousand. Syrian security forces, attempting to disperse the crowd, opened fire and killed four people. The next day, the crowd ballooned to about 20,000. They attended the funerals of those slain the previous day, chanted anti-government slogans and inflicted damage on government offices that were symbolic of the Syrian *mukhabarat* state in Deraa: the Baath party headquarters, the governor's office and the headquarters of the security forces (which in Deraa were led by one of Bashar al-Assad's cousins).

Daily protests continued. Matters escalated when Syrian forces carried out a more vigorous crackdown on the protests on 23 March, when security agents raided the Omari mosque, which had been turned into a makeshift field hospital, treating wounded protestors and offering refuge to those in fear of their lives. At least fifteen civilians were reportedly killed, and hundreds wounded. In addition, basic services to Deraa were cut off – electricity, water and mobile phone networks – and funerals were banned, as they had become focal points for protest. By the evening, government forces had surrounded Deraa and were not allowing anyone in or out: it was being quarantined and, as with any quarantine, the Syrian government hoped to isolate the contagion and exterminate it before it had a chance to spread. The clampdown had begun. As Joshua Landis prophetically wrote at the time:

> Deraa is very poor and Islamic – it epitomizes everything that troubles Syria – a failed economy, the population explosion, a bad governor and overbearing security forces. It is an explosive brew. Even if the government can contain violence to Deraa for the time being, protests will spread. The wall of fear has broken. Apathy of the young has turned to anger. YouTube, Aljazeera, and cellphones have changed the game and given the people a powerful weapon to fight authority. The country is under intense pressure and ready to explode. There is too much unemployment and too little freedom.[2]

The underlying factors

In 2005 I wrote the following:

> almost every Syrian . . . realizes that systemic economic reform is absolutely necessary, and the government cannot continue the zigzag approach of Bashar's father – there needs to be sustained change. Economic growth in Syria for 2003 was approximately 3 percent, which is too low to create enough jobs for the growing population, especially among 15- to 24-year-olds . . . where unemployment is estimated at about 30 percent. Countrywide, unemployment is estimated at between 20 percent and 25 percent, although it could be higher and rise even further. If this were to continue unabated, it would be a recipe for social

> unrest . . . [and] with the repressive apparatus of the state, if this unrest occurs, things could get very ugly, and Bashar would be faced with some incalculably tough decisions.[3]

In examining what might happen without real economic reform, I wrote that 'at worst, the country could implode, with regime instability leading to a potential civil war among Syrian's varied ethnicities and religious sects, with radical Islamist groups waiting in the wings to assert themselves as the political, social, and economic environment deteriorates'.[4] Basically, not enough was accomplished.

Bashar al-Assad's inauguration speech certainly indicated that the economy was the immediate priority – as it should have been. He mentioned that the 'other domains' in society 'did not keep up with the excellent political performance' of his father. Bashar understood that Syria's infrastructure was largely built up in the 1970s and 1980s, and with it were created many opportunities in the public sector, which accounted for approximately 20 per cent of the workforce. As Bashar told me, this was 'a temporary good, but you cannot build an economy in this way. In the 1990s we started thinking about supporting the private sector, but with the changes in the world [i.e. globalization], we are stumbling. We tried to develop but we had some bad ideas.'[5]

There was, indeed, some economic reform during the first decade of Bashar's rule. Private banks were established in 2004: although things started slowly, their number grew throughout the decade, reaching thirteen by 2010, including two Islamic banks. Some important monetary reforms were implemented: loan interest rates were cut and the various exchange rates were consolidated (although the effects of these reforms were limited, due to the need to cover the fiscal deficit, which had grown in recent years). The long-awaited stock exchange, the Damascus Securities Exchange, was established in 2009 (although its listings were few and were usually companies whose ownership was closely tied to the regime). Steps were taken to make Syria investor-friendly, allowing foreign investors in 2007 to receive loans and other credit instruments from foreign banks, using profits to repay the loans through local banks. During Bashar's rule,

Syria attracted an impressive amount of foreign investment, especially from Gulf Arab states and development funds, although most of it went into tourism and the real estate development sector, rather than into industry and manufacturing. That said, the tourism sector grew to make up 12 per cent of GDP by 2010, bringing in over $8 billion in hard currency.[6] With Syria truly standing at the crossroads of history, the country's tourist sites are some of the most spectacular, yet (over the past few decades) least visited in the world. The sector became a focus for Assad's government, and tourism has grown accordingly over the last decade, although much more planning is still needed in terms of systemic, coordinated touristic development. So promising appeared to be the steps the government was taking in terms of economic reform and integration into the international community that, in a report on Syria by the respected Oxford Business Group (OBG) (*The Report: Syria 2010*), the regional editor for Asia and the Levant wrote:

> The successful steps which Syria has taken in liberalizing its economy have been matched by its achievements on the international stage, where it is enjoying revived relations with the US and has forged key trade partnerships with the EU. I am confident OBG's new report accurately and comprehensively reflects Syria's growing regional prominence and steady economic progress.[7]

The government, trying to reduce public expenditure and (haltingly) make the economy more market oriented, incrementally raised prices – that is, reduced subsidies – on basic items such as petrol, heating oil and cement. And the socialist compact of free education and other services began to be redressed, as nominal charges were introduced even for education at public institutions. In addition, at a more macro level, the regime under Bashar tried, with some success, to improve the general education system in Syria, as well as the level of expertise in the various government ministries, by hiring more people on merit rather than on the basis of family connections. Syria (as indeed the Arab world generally) has suffered from a chronic deficit in skill sets applicable to the modern economy. The United Nations Arab Human Development Report of 2002 famously concluded that the Arab world's knowledge deficit was the highest of all the major economic zones in the world. Syria has been a prime example of an archaic, stagnant, overcrowded and underfunded educational system from primary school to university. Bashar has made some inroads in this regard, primarily by increasing pay for teachers, reworking curriculums and allowing for (and building) a number of private universities across the country, although these are of variable quality. As Bashar commented to me on several occasions, Syria, like India, had to find a niche in the global economy that would give it added value. He recognized that Syria is a relatively poor country, with few resources; therefore, as he told me, 'the raw material is the brain'. But he could not just make changes on the margins and truly expect to improve the economy and assuage the general temperament of the population for long. He needed finally to engage in systemic change; however, he could not (or would not), and so frustration with the government and disillusionment with him spread beneath the surface.

Bashar was fighting a steeply uphill battle. Not least among his problems were those Syrians with entrenched interests who would lose their socioeconomic status if market-oriented reforms proceeded apace. That is why the regime sometimes seemed to be 'speaking out of both sides of its mouth': it felt compelled to cater to different powerful constituencies. There were those who advocated wholesale reform to turn Syria into a market economy. And then there were those who, although they recognized the need for at least some reform, believed it should proceed very slowly, so as not to cause economic dislocation and potential political instability. These differences were generally associated with different orientations in terms of trade, commerce and investment. Usually those who promoted a more rapid transition to a market economy pushed for a more robust trade relationship with the West, such as the European Union Euro-Mediterranean Partnership initiative, to which Syria signed up in 2004 (although its membership was never activated, due to political concerns among members of the EU and certain thresholds established by the EU that Syria did not meet). On the other hand, there was a powerful bloc in government which believed that economic relations with the West were too vulnerable to politics, a notion that gained traction in Damascus after the US Congress passed the Syrian Accountability Act and the Bush administration signed it into law in 2004. These folks support more efforts to develop trade relations with the East rather than the West; they look more toward Russia, Iran, India and China, and would like to develop a strong economic relationship with neighboring countries, such as a rebuilding Iraq and especially Turkey, with which Bashar had dramatically improved relations. Syria in early 2005 agreed to a plan to reduce its $13 billion debt to Russia (going back to the days of the Soviet Union) by 80 per cent, and Damascus renegotiated debt terms with a number of its other creditors as well, so Assad made good progress on reducing its heavy foreign debt burden. Sure enough, in any visit to a luxury hotel in Damascus during the 2000s one would find a phalanx of Chinese, Indian and other businessmen looking for investment opportunities in the country.

The experience of a friend of mine speaks volumes for Bashar's delicate balancing act over economic reform. It was summer 2010, and my friend was chairman of one of the private banks in Syria. I saw him for coffee in what had been the Le Meridien Hotel in downtown Damascus, though it had just been taken over by the Turkish Dedeman chain (in itself an indication of the way the Syrian economy was moving). He had just come from seeing Abdullah Dardari, the deputy prime minister for economy and the leading advocate in government for more market-oriented reform. After our get-together, he had a meeting with Muhammad Hussein, the minister of finance and someone who was known to strongly support a slower pace of reform and a more aggressive search for trade partners in the East. I asked my friend why he was meeting both of them: 'Because I don't know which one is going to win, and I want to be on good terms with the one who does.'

Emblematic of the competing interests in Syria was the announcement by Bashar al-Assad at the 2005 Baath Regional Congress meeting that his country would pursue the social market economy approach, which had succeeded for the most part in Germany. The idea behind this was that there would be a gradual adoption of market reform without wholesale abandonment of the social safety net characteristic of socialist-style economies. Unfortunately, this led in Syria to the zigzag approach and the ad hoc liberalization mentioned above, which did not go far enough in terms of effective, broad-based market-oriented economic reform, but at the same time diminished the social safety net to which many Syrians had become accustomed.

As a result of economic problems and deficiencies indigenous to Syria, as well as the negative effects of the global economic downturn of late 2008, the Syrian economy by early 2011 was sputtering. The International Monetary Fund (IMF) estimated that Syria's GDP in 2010 grew by 3.9 per cent, down from 6 per cent in 2008. The Central Intelligence Agency (CIA) estimates that Syrian economic growth slowed overall to 1.8 per cent. Whatever the number, it is clear that the Syrian economy did not attain the 6–7 per cent growth rate necessary to arrest (still less to reduce) the high unemployment rate, which is estimated to be around 20 per cent on average. This rate is much higher still among those aged under twenty-five, reaching approximately 53 per cent of females and 67 per cent of males. And about 60 per cent of the 22 million people in Syria are aged below twenty-five – a figure consistent with other developing countries in the Middle East. The annual population growth rate in Syria is estimated at 2.5–3 per cent, one of the highest in the region. Quite simply, Syria's economy is not keeping up with population growth, especially the number of jobseekers entering the market each and every year.

Syria's economic well-being has been said to turn on seasonal rainfall and on the price of oil, because agriculture and oil production make up such large swaths of the economy. The agricultural sector traditionally accounted for about a quarter of Syria's GDP (and about a quarter of the workforce). But with drought dominating the 2000s, this figure dropped to 17 per cent of GDP, thus reducing food production, driving up food prices and adding to the unemployment problem. Furthermore, with more farm laborers unemployed, many of them headed to the cities in search of work, adding to the overcrowding, congestion and rising rents in Syria's largest cities. The entire Arab world is more dependent than any other region on food imports; and therefore, the rising prices of basic commodities in the wake of the 2008 global financial crisis hit countries such as Syria disproportionately hard. Foreign direct investment (FDI), after charting some impressive gains in the first seven years of Assad's rule, began to head in the other direction in 2009: it fell some 28 per cent from 2008, due primarily to the global economic downturn, which hit FDI in almost every country.[8]

Prior to the uprising, oil trade constituted about 28 per cent of Syria's annual revenue; about 95 per cent of oil exports went to European markets, particularly Italy and Germany.[9] In 2010, Syria produced approximately 385,000 barrels of crude oil per day, down considerably from the peak of 610,000 barrels in 1995. Overall reserves are dwindling, although during Bashar's presidency the government has contracted with numerous foreign oil exploration companies to locate more reserves, and before the 2011 uprising began there had been some promising results. Even with new oil finds, however, rising oil consumption – due to Syria's continued industrialization and its steadily growing population – suggests that Syria will be a net importer of oil within the next ten years.

Because of these multiple problems, in 2010 some 30 per cent of Syrians were living below the poverty line, and 11 per cent were living below the subsistence level – and both these figures have no doubt increased due to the uprising. So grave is the problem that fighting poverty became the mantra of the regime in the few years preceding the uprising, although it was not able to do much to combat it. Matters have not been helped by the million or so Iraqi refugees who settled in Syria following the US invasion of Iraq in 2003, placing extra strain on the Syrian economy.

Beyond all the facts and figures, one of the most serious problems facing the Syrian economy has been the growing inequality in the distribution of wealth in the country during Bashar al-Assad's time in power. Efforts at privatization and other market-oriented reforms have tended to add to unemployment, yet enrich the privileged few who are tied into the regime politically or by family connections. What began to develop in Syria in a much more noticeable fashion under Bashar was not a liberal capitalist system, but a 'cronyocracy'. Crony capitalists benefited from selective privatization that appeared to be funneled toward those who were already economically and politically in a position to take advantage of it. As such, Bashar's cousin Rami Makhlouf (principal owner of SyriaTel, the country's largest telecommunications corporation) and Firas Tlas (known as the 'king of sugar'), son of Mustafa Tlas, the long-serving defense minister under both Hafiz and Bashar al-Assad, have become economic oligarchs, monopolizing important sectors of the Syrian economy and becoming the gateway for many of the domestic and foreign investors who want to do business in Syria. This explains why the anger and frustration of the Syrian protestors in 2011 were directed almost as much against Rami Makhlouf as against his cousin, the president. They were both seen as part and parcel of the same problem, i.e. pervasive corruption and privileged access to wealth. A conspicuous *nouveau riche* came into being under Bashar al-Assad, especially in Damascus, where luxury boutique hotels, expensive restaurants and high-end shopping centers were built, largely with Gulf Arab money, to house, feed and clothe the upper class, separating them even more from the rest of the population not only in terms of wealth, but also in style of living and expectations. This was also the case in Syria's largest city, Aleppo. What went on there and in Damascus under Bashar was completely at odds with the origins of the Baath party in Syria in the 1950s and 1960s: in those years it allied itself with the rural population against the large landowning families and urban notables who monopolized power and wealth in a skewed capitalist environment.

So the socioeconomic problems that existed in Tunisia, Egypt and elsewhere in the Arab world also existed in Syria. The gap between mobilization and assimilation in Syria was growing, along with the feeling of frustration and anger, particularly among an increasingly disenfranchised and disillusioned youth.

A further significant factor that increased the level of frustration and anger in the general population was corruption. According to any of the indices that rate the world's countries on corruption, transparency, accountability and ease of doing business, Syria always ranks in the third quartile or lower. For example, the Corruption Perceptions Index for 2010 listed Syria at 127 out of 178 countries. In the Middle East and North Africa region, Syria was placed fourteenth-equal out of nineteen countries (with only Iran, Libya, Yemen and Iraq behind it).[10] At the individual level, corruption has become a way of life, and palms have to be greased for just about everything – from fixing a plumbing problem to repairing a pothole in the street; from getting a license to start a business to obtaining a favorable judgment at court. And this way of life in Syria was exploited by the rich and powerful: if you were well connected, you got better service. This certainly wore people down over the years, especially when they could see the elites in society get away with almost anything – for the most part connived at and sanctioned by the Syrian government.

Repression

The *mukhabarat* or security/intelligence services in Syria are expansive and omnipresent (or at least they seem to be and want to appear to be). It is a fairly obscure aspect of Syrian society, but there are estimated to be 50,000–70,000 full-time security officers in the various security branches, in addition to hundreds of thousands of part-time personnel; by 2011 there was one intelligence officer for roughly 240 people. Funding for the security services, estimated at over $3 billion per year, traditionally has made up over a third of Syria's military budget.[11]

There are fifteen security branches that make up the *mukhabarat*. Of these, Air Force Intelligence, Military Intelligence, General Intelligence (which also contains a Palestinian branch that deals with Palestinian and Israeli issues) and Political Security (which monitors dissidents and the media, and oversees censorship activities) are the most important. Not only is this system oppressive, but the repressive activities of the *mukhabarat* are often quite arbitrary. Pre-emptive fear and intimidation are useful tools that are frequently employed by security agents to deter potential unrest and disruptive activities by real or perceived opposition elements inside and outside the country. As a result, there is a certain level of countrywide paranoia, which the regime uses to maintain control over the population. As one Syrian man moaned: 'The garbage collectors are intelligence agents. Sometimes we think even our wives are working with the intelligence. All phones are monitored. We live in hell.'[12]

One of the results is that the *mukhabarat* have been given a tremendous amount of leeway to ensure domestic stability and to protect the regime. In what is almost always a threatening environment in the heart of the Middle East, this is not unexpected. But the *mukhabarat*'s accumulation of empowerment over the years, overseen – if not sanctioned – by the government, has led to systemic recklessness, which has obviously backfired against the regime. After all, it was their collective hubris in arresting and manhandling the Deraa schoolchildren that launched the uprising.

I have observed this phenomenon at close quarters a number of times in Syria. On one occasion in late 2007, *when I was traveling to Syria for a scheduled meeting with the president*, I was detained at the airport, my passport was confiscated and I was interrogated for three hours. The security officer, a colonel, tried to intimidate me – mainly by twirling what I assumed was a loaded pistol around the table in front of me, almost as if we were playing Russian roulette. I was released only after I convinced the colonel to call the president's office to confirm the meeting. The right hand did not know what the left hand was doing, and nor did it seem to care – a disconnect that is both dangerous and an abdication of authority.

When I met Assad, I expressed my consternation at being detained. I told him that, a few days after my return to the United States, I was due to give testimony in front of the Senate Foreign Relations Committee, promoting US-Syrian dialogue. I asked him what would have happened if I had not convinced the officer to make the call. What if I had been incarcerated or even tortured? It could have instantly turned someone considered a friend of Syria at the time into an enemy. I strongly suggested to him that he needed to rein in the security forces, because the freedom he allowed them could come back to haunt him.

Syrians faced this sort of arbitrary repression on a daily basis. Most Syrians know someone who has been arrested, tortured or interrogated by the *mukhabarat*. Most Syrians know where the 'red lines' are in terms of what not to say or do, but the *mukhabarat* appear to have no red lines; and Bashar al-Assad, who seems to view the security organs as a necessary evil, is reluctant to control them (or incapable of doing so).

Syrians grew tired of the *mukhabarat* state, especially when, in early 2011, they saw the popular revolts in Tunisia and Egypt seemingly throw off the yoke of repression and move against the police and security services. They saw regular people in other Arab states say 'no' to presidents having a lifetime mandate to rule. Gone are the days when presidents and prime ministers ruled for decades. Yet between them, Hafiz and Bashar al-Assad have ruled Syria for forty-two years.

People want to be able to choose their rulers, to hold them more accountable, and to have some sort of say in the future of their countries. Political space is so restricted in Syria. Having witnessed the Arab Spring in Tunisia, Egypt and elsewhere, many Syrians have begun to wonder 'why not here?' This is what is known as 'demonstration effects', when events in one country inspire similar events in neighboring countries; that is why revolutions or uprisings are often clustered in time.[13] Of course, not only did these effects cross borders into other countries during the Arab Spring – most dramatically from Tunisia into Egypt and Libya – but the knowledge of this phenomenon compelled certain countries to take steps to prevent such a transfer and/or to forestall regional and international foes from taking advantage of the opportunity to sow domestic unrest. As Mark Haas writes,

> Reinforcing the fears of subversion due to the power of demonstration effects is the proclivity for politicians to assume that international ideological rivals will provide aid to the latter's ideological allies throughout the system in an attempt to promote political change in targeted states. In these ways, international ideological competitions tend to be translated into domestic struggles for power and legitimacy.[14]

Seen in this light, the Syrian regime's paranoia regarding conspiracies against it hatched on the outside, with willing internal accomplices, is hardly unexpected.

In the early, halcyon days of the Arab Spring, however, the power of the street – buoyed by the instruments and technology of social media – was on full display, knocking out one authoritarian leader after another. Of course, there are numerous questions now about what exactly will emerge in the aftermath of the Arab Spring. Will it indeed be better – and better for whom? Is all of this but the opening act in a long drawn-out play that may take a generation to resolve? But back in the volcanic and hopeful period of the movement in early 2011, its galvanizing effects were incalculable. Anything was possible. Or so it seemed.

CHAPTER 5

The Regime Responds

Deraa was not the only Syrian city in which protests erupted in the latter half of March 2011. There were also protests about the same time in Banias, a fairly conservative, Sunni-dominated city on the Mediterranean coast. The demonstrators were protesting against the regime's anti-Islamic decrees of recent years, particularly a ban in the summer of 2010 on female schoolteachers wearing the *niqab*, the veil worn by the more observant and traditional women in Syria. Protests popped up in a number of others cities around the country as well, notably in Homs, Kurdish-dominated Qamishli, al-Hasaka, Hama and Latakia, as well as in some suburbs of Damascus. No doubt the channels of information-sharing offered by the new technology – satellite television, the Internet, Facebook, Twitter and mobile phones – spread word of the protests quickly all over the country, thus sparking more of them. As in Banias, however, the initial protests in these cities tended to focus more on issues that were important locally rather than nationally, as at this point there was little or no coordination among the protestors. The protest marches sprouted up quite organically in different cities in different parts of the country, highlighting the breadth of the systemic problems in Syria. The protestors tended to rail against corruption and repression wherever they were, but organizationally they were anything but coordinated at this time.

And there were as yet very few calls for the fall of the regime, although pictures and posters of Bashar al-Assad were being torn down or defaced. The protestors primarily wanted the regime to implement long-promised reforms and to chart a new direction, dictated by what had happened recently elsewhere in the Arab world. In some respects, it was a giddy, almost cathartic moment for many Syrians, before the harsh reality of the regime crackdown set in. Reflecting on those early days, one protestor commented on the first anniversary of the uprising, in March 2012, that 'it was better than joy, it was better than love. What was amazing was that suddenly everyone felt like family. Your feeling of disconnection from society is broken, and suddenly you are with people who agree on this one thing you have all been afraid to talk about.'[1]

In response to the growing protests, the Syrian government announced a series of reforms on 24 March 2011. This repeated the pattern of fallen regimes in Tunis and Cairo, and of other Arab governments that were experiencing problems at the time in Bahrain, Libya, Yemen, Jordan, Saudi Arabia and Morocco. Regime insiders told me that Bashar went back and forth in his mind between making concessions (and a concessionary speech) and cracking down. The 24 March announcement included the formation of a committee to investigate and bring to justice anyone who had committed unlawful acts, including government soldiers who had killed protestors. The government spokesperson, Bouthaina Shaaban, also stipulated that the wages of government workers would be raised by 20–30 per cent, and there would be cuts in income tax and pension increases. She spoke in general terms about new health reforms, judicial reform, the relaxation of media restrictions, the establishment of a new mechanism to fight corruption, and about allowing more political parties to compete in elections. She went on to say that she wanted to

> relay the condolences of President Bashar al-Assad to the families of the victims [in Deraa]. President Bashar al-Assad cannot accept that even a single drop of blood is spilled, and I am a witness when he gave orders not to shoot any live bullets, even if a member of the police, the security or any other government agency is killed. This does not refute the fact

> that there were some mistakes or some actions that were not satisfactory. The demands of the people of Deraa and the rest of the Syrian people across all the provinces are legitimate. All legitimate demands will be met, but in a calm way.[2]

The most important announcement made by Shaaban, however, at least on the surface, was that the government promised to form a committee to study the need to lift the state of emergency that had been in place in Syria since 1963. The committee would be composed of senior lawyers and would complete its investigation – and supposedly offer its recommendations – within a month. The emergency – or martial – law refers to Decree No. 51, implemented on 9 March 1963, one day after the Baath party assumed power in a coup. It declared a 'state of emergency' that was ostensibly designed to thwart the perceived military threat from Israel; but of course, it was then used to stifle and arbitrarily eliminate internal challenges to the regime. The law allowed the government to make pre-emptive arrests, override constitutional and penal code statutes, and suspend habeas corpus. It barred those arrested from filing court complaints or having a lawyer present during interrogation. In the wake of the emergency law, Supreme State Security Courts (SSSCs) were established; these could arbitrarily try and sentence those detained and arrested on the grounds of protecting the state.

Bashar al-Assad has acknowledged that one of the primary demands of civil society and democracy activists has long been the elimination of the emergency law and its associated institutions, such as the SSSCs. He has admitted that the law has been abused by the government on a number of occasions as a form of repression against political dissent. But he has never backed down from the necessity of having the emergency law, basically stating that Syria needed it, given the dangerous context, with the Muslim Brotherhood, Israel, instability in Lebanon and Iraq, and external interference by regional and international powers constantly threatening the country. He told me, however, that 'we cannot use it as an excuse for something depending on our mood. It cannot be employed in the wrong way.'[3] He added: 'The emergency law is not used to suppress freedoms but to suppress terrorism, and there is a huge difference. Frequently in the past this law was used in the wrong way.'[4]

'Where is Bashar?'

Amid the escalating protests, associated violence and rising death tolls, by the last week of March that was the question many people were asking. Other than through his putative spokesperson, Bouthaina Shaaban, the world had not heard a peep out of Bashar. Reflecting these sentiments at the time, I wrote the following in an essay:

> Where has Syria's President Bashar al-Assad been? He has been conspicuous by his absence in the face of growing protests and associated violence in his country. Such has been the silence emanating from Bashar that rumors were rampant that he had been overthrown in an internal coup. He is set to address the nation in a televised speech. Why did he wait for over a week to appear when Syrians were desperate for some direction – leadership – out of the wilderness of rising uncertainty? . . . Maybe Bashar was realizing that he could carve out a more lasting legacy by moving forward instead of reaching into the past . . . The possibilities are breathtaking, but Syria needs a hero. Has Bashar assembled a critical mass of support behind him against the expected backlash from status quo elements? Time will tell, but first things first: Bashar must LEAD. This is his moment . . . He can change the course of Syria ultimately by giving up power himself sooner rather than later. He cannot be president for life. A country cannot have political pluralism unless there are presidential term limits or else the ruling party simply becomes a vessel through which authoritarianism is expressed. This is what happened to Syria in the first place with the Baath party. Will he set term limits? Will he change Syrian history by giving up that with which he began to feel so comfortable?[5]

During the week following the outbreak of significant protests in Syria, I sent several notes direct to Bouthaina Shaaban, at her personal email address, asking her to pass them on to Bashar al-Assad. I have since learned from a high-level regime insider that my messages were in fact read by Bashar. Although I have been told by Syrian officials that my comments and suggestions are taken seriously, obviously on this occasion my advice was ignored. This is perhaps why the Syrian *mukhabarat* did not particularly like me: it considered my access to the president to be dangerous.[6] One of my messages was an essay I wrote, which a few days later was published as an opinion piece. In it – in effect my message to Bashar – I wrote the following:

> But there is still time, however much it is shrinking, for Bashar to move forward in a positive way that does not result in the dangerous collapse of another Middle Eastern country. Rather than trying to muddle his way through, he should consider measures of true political reform rather than bits and pieces of co-optation masquerading as reform. Actually implement reform, do not sanction studies to do something that may or may not lead to actual reform. Bashar needs to seriously think about setting presidential term limits, establishing real political parties, holding elections subject to independent judicial review and international observers, and a follow through with the long-promised end to almost 50 years of emergency rule. Bashar can establish a lasting legacy that is in tune with the changing political landscape in and the future of the Middle East ... Unfortunately, Syrian leaders – indeed, the Syrian system – tend to convulsively recoil from reform of this magnitude. These days in the Middle East, however, getting ahead of the curve rather than behind it is much more conducive to one's political health.[7]

There are some possible reasons why Bashar waited for over a week before personally responding to the growing crisis. As I said previously, it is my firm opinion that the Syrian president, indeed the Syrian leadership, was caught off guard by the rapidly increasing intensity of the protests. They were complacent. The regime was rocked back on its heels by the events at Deraa. I am sure there were pronounced differences in the inner circle surrounding the president over how to react. Should the protests be repressed ruthlessly, as had been the Syrian way in the past? Or should

Assad grasp the moment to make meaningful political reforms? The regime appeared to be talking out of both sides of its mouth, saying one thing while forces on the ground did another, giving the impression that no one was really in charge.

Bashar is also someone who does not typically act or decide important issues in an expeditious fashion. It is difficult to discern exactly what was going on in those first few days and weeks, as the Syrian decision-making process is fairly opaque. But my understanding is that it is quite compartmentalized: there are small groups of advisors close to the president who advise him on different important issues, such as Lebanon, Israel, domestic politics, the economy, relations with the United States, etc. Some people 'serve' on more than one of these ad hoc committees, and often competing viewpoints are deliberately placed in the same group, so that the president can hear different opinions. The Syrian president tends to be very deliberate in his decision-making, often mulling things over for quite some time before making a final decision. This is not a system that is built for quick, efficient responses and reactions. It is actually more of a system that, in areas of domestic unrest, reacts instinctively to smother it before it grows out of control.

One high-ranking Syrian official informed me in December 2011, at a meeting in Europe, that one of the driving forces behind the regime's response in the initial stages of the unrest had been *not* to do what the Tunisian and Egyptian presidents had done. The logic is inescapable: Ben Ali and Mubarak were removed from office in short order; therefore, Bashar should pretty much do the opposite of what they did (or so the thinking went, according to this official). These other leaders gave in too easily and appeared weak. This may have affected the nature of Bashar's initial responses. In my emails to Bouthaina Shaaban, I beseeched her to get Bashar in front of a camera, to talk eye to eye (so to speak) with the Syrian people and to explain a way forward with real reform. As Bashar had a not insignificant level of popularity in Syria before the protests, and as that popularity had not yet been frittered away, I believed at the time that he should utilize his biggest asset – his ability to connect with the people – to get ahead of the curve while there was still a chance. After all, if Ben Ali and Mubarak had announced their reforms, including their own exit from office, before Muhammad Bouazizi self-immolated and before Tahrir Square became the epicenter of change in Egypt, they would have been hailed as visionary reformers, rather than condemned as dictators so desperate to cling onto power that they belatedly announced hasty measures (which, in any case, no one believed they would actually implement). I asked the Syrian official I spoke to in December why Assad did not go in front of the cameras, instead of merely delivering live televised speeches to the People's Assembly, to the Cabinet, and at Damascus University. The official told me that a number of people had tried to get him to do this for the very same reason I have just mentioned; but there had been other, obviously more influential members of the inner circle, who strongly cautioned against this because it was what other – by now former – Arab leaders had done. Maybe they thought it would be a sign of weakness for the president to admit any mistakes. Maybe they thought Bashar might be able to dissociate himself from the crackdown by 'connecting' at a more personal level with the Syrian people, thus making their own positions more vulnerable. Or perhaps it was Bashar's unmistakable commitment to what is often the fiction of institutions that compelled him to speak first at the People's Assembly in late March, to be filmed speaking to his newly sworn-in Cabinet in April, and to address a cast of supporters in an auditorium at Damascus University in June. It could be that Bashar, who is not the greatest orator and does not have a commanding presence, felt (or his advisors did) that he needed to be surrounded by supporters as a kind of prop, to create the spectacle and theater of drama he was seeking. Maybe he just likes a crowd – and the almost scripted applause and adulation that are so familiar to anyone who has heard speeches by him or his father at such venues. Whatever the reason, in my mind it was a huge error.

Bashar (kind of) addresses the nation

In conversation with a top Syrian official in April 2011, I described Bashar al-Assad's speech to the People's Assembly on 30 March – his first direct public comment on the unrest engulfing his country – as 'pathetic'. I had also been saying as much on the airwaves. The Syrian official responded by saying: 'David, you know I have been reading and hearing your commentaries, and some people back in Damascus are upset with you on this; and I would be mad at you, too, except that I agree with you.'

There was a great deal of anticipation regarding Bashar's 30 March speech. Many were hoping – perhaps hope against hope – that the Syrian president would be magnanimous and humble, announcing serious political reforms. They were to be disappointed. Many Syrians in the opposition later identified Bashar's speech as a turning point, i.e. their disappointment in the speech really galvanized the protests in addition to the fact that the Syrian president did not punish his cousin, the governor of Deraa. A number of Syrians concede that if he had done one or both of these things, the uprising may never have occurred.

I should like to examine the speech very closely, because I think, especially with the benefit of hindsight, that it is quite illuminating. It casts a good deal of light on the disposition of Bashar al-Assad and the regime in general, including on the policies they would implement to deal with the uprising.

Soon after he began his speech, he made it clear what his primary objective was with regard to the protests: 'My responsibility remains that I should protect the security of this country and ensure its stability. This remains the ever-dominant feeling in my heart and mind.'[8] He was going to keep his end of the great Faustian bargain originally struck with the Syrian people by his father: less freedom in return for more stability. He went on to explain why he had waited for well over a week to address the nation; he also fired his opening salvos against the nebulous external forces that, in his view, were behind the unrest (something that would become a common theme with the regime) and alluded to the new social networking weapons utilized by these forces:

> I know that the Syrian people have been waiting for this speech since last week, and I intentionally postponed it until I had a fuller picture in my mind . . . our enemies work every day in an organized, systemic and scientific manner in order to undermine Syria's stability. We acknowledge that they had been smart in choosing very sophisticated tools in what they have done, but at the same time we realize that they have been

> stupid in choosing this country and this people, for such conspiracies do not work with our country or our people.

After recognizing what had happened elsewhere in the Arab world and its inevitable effects on Syria, he went on to focus on Syria's national unity and unique characteristics – characteristics that give it a special place in the Arab world and that almost destined it to be a target of regional and international conspiracies:

> Syria is not isolated from what is happening in the Arab world. We are part of this region. We influence and are influenced by it, but at the same time we are not a copy of other countries . . . We in Syria have certain characteristics which might be different internally and externally from others. Our foreign policy has been based on holding to our national rights, holding to pan-Arab rights, to independence, to supporting Arab resistance when there is occupation. The link between domestic and foreign policies has always been the Syrian citizen. When the Syrian citizen is not the heart of domestic and foreign policies, this is a deviation, and it is the job of the country's institutions to correct this deviation. The net outcome of these policies has been an unprecedented case of national unity which has been the real force which has protected Syria during the past years when pressures intensified against Syria . . . We have been able to maintain Syria's central role and position. But this has not deterred the enemies. Of course, I have just started to talk about this conspiracy, and then I will move to the internal situation so that satellite TV stations will not say that the Syrian president considered all that has happened a foreign conspiracy.

Bashar tried to hit on popular traditional themes in Syria regarding the nature of threat, particularly so-called external forces, harking back to the days of the 1950s and 1960s, when fighting off European and superpower imperialism and interference was practically a full-time occupation. This became the *raison d'être* of the Baath party itself and the womb from which it was born in Syria. The Baath party slogan of 'freedom, unity and socialism' betrayed the foreign-policy applications of Baathist ideology: 'freedom' meant freedom from external occupation and influence; 'unity' in this sense meant Arab unity, the need to fight off the pernicious advances of European imperialism – and, in the post-World War Two period, the Cold War interference of the superpowers; and even 'socialism', which would seem to have only domestic application, was also meant to free the country from the shackles of capitalism, by which the Western powers interfered through the vehicle of economic imperialism.

These themes persisted under the Assads, and while much of the energy behind Arab nationalism and pan-Arab unity died throughout most of the Arab world following the devastating loss to Israel in the 1967 Arab-Israeli war, it remained very much alive in Syria, framing the Syrian paradigm of foreign relations, which, in the Baath point of view, was – and continued to be – intimately tied to the domestic environment in Syria. Indeed, toward the end of his speech, the Syrian president commented that 'the secret of Syria's strength lies in the many crises it faced throughout its history, particularly after independence. We have to face the crises with great confidence and with a determination to win.' The fact that Assad asserted that conspiracy and terrorist activity were at the root of the protests also gave sanction to the government's harsh crackdown. After all, as he had pointed out earlier in his comments to me regarding the (mis)application of emergency law, it should be used to suppress terrorism, not freedom.

Therefore it came as no surprise that, once Bashar had introduced the idea of a foreign conspiracy, he would continue to harp on it. The following excerpts from the speech are examples of this:

> And I am sure you all know that Syria is facing a great conspiracy whose tentacles extend to some nearby countries and far-away countries [a less than subtle reference primarily, but not exclusively, to Israel and the United States], with some inside the country. This conspiracy depends, in its timing not in its form, on what is happening in other Arab countries . . . Some satellite TV stations actually spoke about

> attacking certain buildings an hour before they were actually attacked. How did they know that? Do they read the future? This happened more than once . . . They will say that we believe in the conspiracy theory. In fact there is no conspiracy theory. There is a conspiracy . . . What we are seeing today is a stage . . . the last stage for them is for Syria to get weaker and disintegrate because this will remove the last obstacle facing the Israeli plans.

In a reference to the attempted demonstrations in February that failed to materialize, and in another backhanded swipe at Qatar (home to Al-Jazeera TV), whose cordial relationship with Damascus soured over various issues (particularly Iran) even before the uprising, Bashar continued:[9]

> In the beginning they started with incitement, many weeks before trouble started in Syria. They used the satellite TV stations and the Internet but did not achieve anything. And then, using sedition, started to produce fake information, voices, images, etc., they forged everything. Then they started to use the sectarian element . . . We have not yet discovered the whole structure of this conspiracy. We have discovered part of it but it is highly organized. There are support groups in more than one governorate linked to some countries abroad . . . Deraa is on the frontline with the Israeli enemy, and it is the frontline of defense for the hinterland.

Bashar also made several references to the post-Hariri environment, in which Syria persevered and survived the tremendous regional and international pressure:

> [Part] of what has happened is similar to what happened in 2005. It is a virtual war. I said at the time that they want us to surrender . . . using the media and the Internet, although the Internet was not as widespread as it is today . . . The United States wanted to impose on us reform and democracy. We fought against this project in the Arab summit and it failed.[10]

Only several pages into the speech did he begin to sprinkle references to some of the real socioeconomic problems at the root of the protests. What is interesting is that, in many of these references, he stated that the reforms announced had been decided at the Baath Party Regional Congress meeting in 2005, and he dwelt more on why there had been a delay in implementing the reforms than on the socioeconomic reasons for them. In addition, he clearly wanted anyone who was listening to know that he was not announcing reforms in response to protests; he was merely reiterating what had been announced six years earlier. He did not want to be seen to be caving into protests, since he and his advisors probably thought that would set an unhealthy precedent and show weakness, à la Ben Ali and Mubarak:

> I am not adding new things, but when you know how we think we harmonize our visions. So, did we make these reforms because there is a problem or because there is sedition? If there was no sedition wouldn't we have done these reforms? If the answer is yes, it means that the state is opportunistic, and this is bad. If we say that these things were made under the pressure of certain conditions or popular pressure, this is weakness. And I believe that if the people get the government to bow under pressure, it will bow to foreign pressure . . . The things I announced Thursday [24 March] were not decisions because those were the decisions of the Baath Party Regional Conference in 2005 . . . When we proposed these ideas in 2005 there was no pressure on Syria [actually there was tremendous pressure, the most there had been prior to the 2011 unrest] . . . This does not justify lagging behind on other issues, but we did not focus much on political issues like the emergency law and the party law. The reason is that when there are human issues at stake, they cannot be postponed. We can postpone a party statement for months or even years, but we cannot postpone providing food for children for breakfast . . . The measures announced last Thursday did not start from square one . . . The former government started these studies and they will be a priority for the new government [see the next section].

In one of the few accurate references to what happened in Egypt and Tunisia and their applicability to Syria, he said in the latter part of the speech: 'When the revolution started [in Tunisia and Egypt], we realized that the causes lie in the way wealth was distributed, not only in terms of corruption but also in terms of geographical distribution. This is something that we have tried to avoid, and we are calling for a fair distribution of development in Syria.'

Despite these references to Syria's socioeconomic problems, the speech was clearly dominated by the attempt to place the blame on external forces and on the seditious activities of their domestic co-conspirators; indeed, the word 'sedition' was used repeatedly during the speech (as some of the excerpts above show). Toward the end of his speech, in a clear – and chilling – warning to opposition elements, Bashar said: 'The Holy Quran says, "sedition is worse than killing". So all those involved intentionally or unintentionally in it contribute to destroying their country. So there is no compromise or middle way in this. What is at stake is the homeland and there is a huge conspiracy.'

Bashar and the Syrian leadership concluded very early on in the uprising that the battle was on and that the protests had to be eliminated. The regime had to reassert control and stability through force and would play on the penchant of the Syrian population to believe conspiracy theories. He ended his speech thus: 'I shall remain the faithful brother and comrade who will walk with his people and lead them to build the Syria we love, the Syria we are proud of, the Syria which is invincible to its enemies.' That he ended his speech with the word 'enemies' revealed the direction the regime was taking in terms of its public evaluation of the main source of the crisis, as well as the nature of its response.

It was no surprise that in his speech Bashar blamed the protests largely on conspirators inside and (especially) outside the country. Anyone who has spent time in Syria can recognize this national paranoia. This conspiratorial mindset is commonplace even among the educated elite, many of whom attended university in the West. The problem is that there have been just enough foreign conspiracies in Syria over the decades to lend credence to such claims. And the regimes of both Hafiz and Bashar al-Assad have nurtured this paranoia through propaganda and censorship, in part to justify the necessity of the security state. So the Syrian president probably figured he was preaching to the converted, certainly within the parliamentary chamber in which he was speaking. And a good many Syrians outside the chamber probably believed it; but in the new information age, a growing number of people could no longer be cowed or brainwashed as they had been in the past. The Arab Spring had changed the perspectives and the level of demands of ordinary citizens. By blaming unseen forces of conspiracy, the government denied responsibility for (and recognition of) the very real socioeconomic and political problems, and for the growing clamor of Syrians expressing frustration with the government for lack of accountability, corruption, political repression and rising poverty. Bashar al-Assad did not adequately address these issues, which had become much more important to ordinary Syrians because they saw in other Arab countries a way finally to combat them.

More 'reforms'

Beyond his closest supporters, the reactions to Bashar's 30 March speech were almost universally dismal. It was variously described as farcical, disingenuous, disappointing, delusional and proof of his duplicitous character – or (as I described it) 'pathetic'. In the wake of the speech, protests broke out across the country (apart from Syria's two largest cities, Damascus and Aleppo) and were followed by violent crackdowns by government forces. The regime was probably taken aback that the speech was apparently not the panacea they perhaps thought it would be. Soon thereafter further efforts were made to ameliorate the situation.

In fact, the day before the speech it was announced that there would be a change of government, and the long-serving prime minister, Naji al-Otari, tendered his resignation, though he agreed to stay on until a new government was formed. This move was not unexpected, as other Arab governments experiencing the unrest of the Arab Spring did something similar, usually with similarly disappointing results. It seemed that people across the Arab world were out for much more than simply a change of nameplates in the various ministries of government.

On 31 March, Bashar established a committee to study the termination of the 1963 emergency law. Of course, there was much skepticism, as Bashar has tremendous executive power, especially in times of crisis, and so most believed this was simply another diversionary or delaying tactic. Rather than appointing a commission to study the possibility of lifting the emergency law, many wanted a clear announcement that it was in fact going to be lifted. Studies to investigate the possibility of this, that or the next reform had been common over the years, and had usually ended up with little or nothing actually being done. So while there is some sense in not just lifting an important and long-standing governing statute without replacing it with something well thought out, the people in Syria wanted a more definitive statement by the president. That same day, Bashar issued a decree raising the wages of state employees, as from 1 April. Again, this was widely seen and criticized as a cynical attempt to purchase the loyalty of the bloated Syrian public sector.

Amid continuing protests, Bashar appointed Adel Safar, the former minister of agriculture, as the next prime minister charged with forming a new government. On 4 April, the governor of Deraa was sacked, and Bashar appointed Muhammad Khalid al-Hannus in his place. No doubt the regime, by appearing to lay the blame for the violence and deaths in Deraa on the outgoing governor and some security officers, hoped that this would be seen as a positive response to the anger expressed by the residents of Deraa. It didn't work.

On 6 April, again in an attempt to secure the support of important constituencies in Syria, the government announced concessions to the Kurds, who make up about 10 per cent of the population and who mostly live in the northeastern portion of the country (see Chapter 3). There had been serious Kurdish protests against the government in the past over issues of citizenship and cultural identity. The most recent of these had occurred in 2004 and had been violently put down by the security forces, especially in the Kurdish city of Qamishli. Now it was announced that the 250,000 Kurds and their descendants who had been stateless in Syria since the early 1960s (after, according to the government, illegally crossing into Syria from Turkey) would be granted citizenship. The government also made the Kurdish New Year (*Nawrooz*) a national holiday.

Also on 6 April, the government, in an obvious attempt to appease conservative and traditional Sunni Muslim elements in the country, announced that the ban on female teachers wearing the *niqab* would be rescinded, and that those teachers who had been sacked would be rehired. In addition, it was announced that the only casino in Syria, just outside Damascus, would be closed: the casino had been an affront to the more conservative Muslims. Along the same lines, the regime also allowed the formation of a pro-government Islamist party (the Muslim Brotherhood had been banned ever since the late 1970s). On 14 April, the government announced the release of hundreds of political prisoners who had been arrested since the uprisings began – though only those deemed to have been 'not involved in criminal acts'.

All of these efforts culminated in Assad's speech to the newly sworn-in Cabinet on 16 April, a speech that was broadcast to the nation and that afforded the Syrian president another opportunity to outline his plan for reform. During this speech he announced the lifting of the emergency law. He told the ministers seated around the table that he had had extensive discussions with activists from a number of Syrian governorates in an attempt to understand the exact nature of their complaints. He said that 'there is a gap which started to appear between state institutions and the Syrian citizens' and this gap must be closed, with more links created with the people.[11] He mentioned that a 'broad dialogue' had to be established, in order to understand the full nature of the problems in the country. He spoke a great deal about the economy, saying outright that 'the economy is the biggest problem'. He spoke on a wide range of issues regarding the economic situation in Syria, and he correctly focused on the problem of unemployment, commenting that it was the most significant issue facing Syria: 'We have a large number of unemployed young people . . . When young people feel that they have no prospects, they will be frustrated and may reach despair.' Perhaps driven by despair, they may take actions to bring about change, which 'is a challenge, not only economic, but rather a national one strongly linked to Syria's stability'.

Assad talked of the need to improve agriculture, which made up approximately 60 per cent of the workforce; perhaps this reinforced his choice of Adel Safar as the new prime minister. He spoke of the necessity of confronting corruption and the common practice of bribes, and of the need to build strong state institutions, to make Syria more investor-friendly, and to enact administrative reform to make the state and the economy work more efficiently.

He spoke briefly on political reform, such as encouraging more 'participation in decision-making' and beginning to study efforts to reform the party law and to bring in a new media law. He also reiterated the citizenship law for the Kurds, and used this as an opportunity to promote the importance of national unity – a recurring theme in his speech.[12]

The speech, then, covered a great deal of ground. The problem is that it focused very little on what most people wanted to hear: specific political reform that would lead to an end to the violence and the dismantling of the security state. In addition, it sounded quite similar to his inaugural speech in 2000 (which also focused on economic issues and corruption), to the messages surrounding the 2005 Baath Party Regional Congress meeting, and to a number of other speeches Bashar had made over the years. It was not terribly new, and it was not what the opposition wanted to hear. This was critical, because at this point Bashar could still have come back from the brink. Most opposition elements, if convinced that Bashar was serious about reform, would have been willing to give him one more chance. If anything, the perceived prevarication and the repetition of past utterances only reinforced the notion that the regime was trying to give the impression of change without really changing at all. The tiger still had his stripes.

On 19 April, the government approved legislation lifting the 1963 emergency law, a key opposition demand. Two days later, Assad signed the decrees ending the state of emergency and abolishing the Supreme State Security Courts. The problem with this was that, while the emergency law was lifted, there were other existing and newly implemented presidential decrees that were equally restrictive, such as making members of the security forces immune to prosecution or making membership of the Muslim Brotherhood punishable by death. Another law was also passed 'to protect national security, uphold the dignity of the citizenry, and combat terror'. The Syrian population knew what this type of ambiguous, overarching law meant: it gave security forces wide latitude to interpret what was a threat to national security or the dignity of Syrian citizens. To many Syrians, the emergency law continued in all but name.

Syrian activists were losing patience, as was the international community, especially since the violent reaction of the regime continued to escalate – and so did the death toll. They had heard many of these promises before. What they really wanted to see was actual implementation, not prestidigitation.

CHAPTER 6

Opposition Mounts

The protests and demonstrations that began in Syria in spring 2011 were not the first manifestations of opposition to the regime of Bashar al-Assad. In hindsight, the 'Damascus Spring' of 2000 may have opened the door for civil society (or democracy) activists in Syria: during and after it, they established important personal and organizational connections. It also encouraged a boldness that hitherto had been virtually nonexistent, and – perhaps most important – led to heightened expectations. When these were subsequently dashed, a greater level of frustration built up over time.

In September 2000, in the midst of the Damascus Spring, civil society elements (intellectuals, professionals, etc.) drafted what became known as the 'Statement of 99' (or sometimes 'Manifesto of 99') – a statement signed by ninety-nine Syrian civil society activists that outlined many of the goals of the nascent movement, launched in the aftermath of Bashar's inaugural speech. It was carefully worded. As Alan George wrote:

> There was no demand for the wholesale democratization of Syrian institutions; no ideological flavor; no attack on the manner in which Bashar al-Asad had come to power. None of the signatories had significant histories of anti-regime activism and the authorities were thereby denied

> the chance to condemn them as 'well-known enemies of the state' or 'agents of Israel'.[1]

Bolder still was the so-called 'Manifesto of the 1,000' (also known as the 'Basic Document' by its supporters) that was published in a Lebanese newspaper in January 2001. While reinforcing many of the earlier civil society and pro-democracy objectives, it went even further by explicitly attacking the foundation of Baathist rule and advocating – indeed demanding – a multi-party political system; it decried the regime's mantra of economic reform before political reform, stating that the former would fail unless 'preceded and accompanied by a comprehensive package of political and constitutional reform'.[2] This seemed to be something of a turning point for those officials in the regime who had been hesitant about the political opening-up of the previous year, giving them more ammunition to pressure the Syrian president to turn back the clock. Sure enough, a series of decrees was soon issued by the government, restricting or terminating almost all of what made the Damascus Spring in the first place. Many point to an interview that Bashar al-Assad gave the London Arabic-language newspaper *Al-Sharq al-Awsat* (8 February 2001) as a clear indication of the onset of the Damascus 'winter'. In what became a common refrain for the rationale behind cracking down on democracy activists, and as something of a precursor to similar arguments made by the Syrian regime in 2011, Bashar said the following:

> When the consequences of an action affect the stability of the homeland, there are two possibilities ... either the perpetrator is a foreign agent acting on behalf of an outside power, or else he is a simple person acting unintentionally. But in both cases a service is being done to the country's enemies and consequently both are dealt with in a similar fashion, irrespective of their intentions or motives.[3]

Following upon this, high-level officials from the government toured the country, holding meetings in cities and at universities to condemn the civil society movement and to reiterate that to continue along the same path would be to court disaster and tear apart the delicate fabric of the country in a way that could be exploited by hostile outside forces, such as the United States and Israel. The democracy activists were compelled to back off; but they did not totally abandon their attempts to pressure the regime to engage in political reform and lift the hated emergency law. Many – including such prominent figures as Riyad Seif, Michel Kilo and Riyad Turk – were constantly harassed by security forces or even sent to prison.

The next big surge of opposition activity occurred in 2005 and 2006, in the aftermath of the Hariri assassination of February 2005, the resulting withdrawal of Syrian troops from Lebanon in April, and the tremendous international pressure on the Syrian regime that followed, led by the United States, France and Saudi Arabia. Indeed, many were convinced by autumn 2005 that Bashar al-Assad's days in power were numbered – especially when the preliminary report of the UN committee investigating the Hariri assassination essentially indicated that the Syrian regime was responsible and directly implicated the Syrian president's brother, Maher al-Assad, and his brother-in-law, intelligence chief Asef al-Shawkat.

Most notable was the issuing, in October 2005, of what was called the 'Damascus Declaration for National Democratic Change', often just known as the 'Damascus Declaration'. This was a statement signed by over 250 leading opposition figures inside and outside Syria that called for peaceful and gradual reform toward a democratic, non-sectarian state. The signatories included the panoply of mostly secular opposition elements that went back to the late 1970s.[4] The heterogeneous nature of this group, however, quickly led to a number of internal antagonisms, especially as the Syrian government intensified its crackdown on democracy activists, painting them as willing accomplices of those countries that were trying to secure the downfall of the regime in the aftermath of the Hariri assassination. It does seem as though the Syrian opposition, especially those members who were in exile at the time, severely overplayed their hand in late 2005, wrongly assuming that the regime was on its way out. The regime was not nearly as brittle as they thought, and they failed to account for such countries as Russia and China, which opposed the increased international pressure on Syria that the Bush administration pursued in the United Nations. By coming out so openly in favor of stepping up the pressure on Damascus and by calling for regime change, these opposition members became discredited in the eyes of most Syrians, who saw them as nothing more than dupes of the West, taking advantage of a situation of which they (having been outside the country for many years in most cases) had little knowledge or understanding. Like the Iraqi National Congress that rode in on US tanks during the 2003 invasion of Iraq, many of the exiled opposition groups were seen as being – and sometimes were – on Washington's payroll.

When Abd al-Halim Khaddam – unceremoniously removed as vice president by Bashar at the Baath Party Regional Congress meeting in summer 2005 – joined the Syrian opposition and became vocal in his criticism of Assad and the regime, many thought he would lend legitimacy and momentum to the opposition. In fact, quite the reverse happened. The very opposition he joined had, for years, targeted Khaddam: he was widely known to be corrupt and had been part and parcel of the repression they had been fighting. His interviews railing against Assad and the regime seemed self-serving and disingenuous. If anything, Khaddam's role only exacerbated existing fissures in the Syrian opposition.

As an indication of the fracturing of the opposition, in March 2006 Khaddam teamed up with the head of the Syrian branch of the Muslim Brotherhood, Ali Sadr al-Din Bayanouni (exiled in London), to form the National Salvation Front (NSF). The Syrian Muslim Brotherhood was, of course, outlawed in Syria, and in fact membership of it in Syria was punishable by death. Bayanouni had, however, meticulously cultivated a new, more moderate image of the Syrian Muslim Brotherhood, saying he was for democracy, the protection of minority rights and a non-violent, peaceful approach to change. But the Syrian Muslim Brotherhood was not (and is not) a monolithic bloc. Bayanouni hails from Aleppo and leads a faction of the Brotherhood that appears to be more moderate. There is another faction based in Hama, scene of the 1982 massacre, which tends to be more militant. These two main factions have sometimes worked with, and sometimes against each other, often having to orchestrate short-lived compromises – a state of affairs that continued right into the Syrian uprising of 2011–12.

Many signatories to the Damascus Declaration wanted nothing to do with the NSF, especially if it included such unsavory figures as Khaddam. They had also always been suspicious of the Sunni-dominated Muslim Brotherhood, fearing that, if ever it did come to power or play a significant role in any successful opposition movement, it would dilute (or even reverse) the secular nature of Syria and threaten the status of religious minorities such as the Christians, Druze and Alawites. After a couple of years of notoriety, the NSF had faded away by 2009, especially when the Muslim Brotherhood split from the group amid improving Saudi-Syrian relations over Lebanon. Saudi support, particularly of the financial kind, was critical to the NSF, and after the Hariri family was reconciled with Damascus, the NSF's hand became considerably weaker. Khaddam faded away even faster, shutting down his private anti-Syrian satellite channel and living a far quieter life in exile in Paris.

Syria's emergence by 2008 from the cold of international isolation, combined with the victory in the US presidential election of Barack Obama (who had espoused a return to diplomacy and dialogue with countries such as Syria), further diluted the message of any Syrian opposition group. The regime was in the ascendant, and it leveraged its newfound legitimacy to continue its crackdown on democracy activists. By 2009, Ammar Qurabi, head of the National Organization for Human Rights in Syria, could say:

> In reality the NSF was always weak and it has done nothing. The Muslim Brotherhood thought Khaddam would bring international contacts and regimists but that amounted to nothing . . . We can talk of the NSF split, but the Damascus Declaration is the same . . . Some groups have split from it, the other leaders are in prison. At the moment, none of the opposition has any real influence . . . both inside and outside of Syria. At the moment the strongest thing [is] the security [services], the strongest thing is the regime.[5]

Opposition and the Arab Spring

On 26 January 2011, in al-Hasaka in northeast Syria, a man by the name of Hasan Ali Akleh poured petrol over himself and set himself alight. Apparently, not unlike the Tunisian Muhammad Bouazizi's self-immolation, this was in protest at government policies. But this action did not garner as much attention as Bouazizi's, and nor did it immediately light the fuse to an uprising. It was, however, a portent of things to come.

In early February, social media sites inside and outside Syria, hoping to have the same impact as social media sites in Tunisia and Egypt, called for a 'Day of Rage' across Syria on 4–5 February to demand reform by the government. Groups from outside Syria sent in large quantities of satellite modems, mobile phones, computers and other social media gizmos, in preparation for what might come. But the turnout for the Day of Rage was very disappointing for the organizers (for more on low turnouts, see Chapter 3). A number of activists inside Syria were contacted by security forces ahead of the event, to warn them not to engage in protest activities. The fear factor seemed to be working for the regime. A leading activist in Damascus, Suheir al-Atassi, lamented at the time that 'Syria has for many years been a kingdom of silence'.[6] The calls also had too much of a Syrian expatriate character to them, which in Syria instantly creates suspicions. Ribal al-Assad, a cousin of Bashar al-Assad and director of the London-based Organisation for Democracy and Freedom in Syria, also added:

> The campaign was a bit outrageous. First, they've chosen a date that reminds people of the uprising of the Muslim Brotherhood [at Hama in 1982]. People don't want to be reminded of the past. They want change, but they want it peacefully. And the picture they used on Facebook, a clenched fist and red color like blood behind. It was like people calling for civil war and who in his right mind wants that?[7]

But the arrest and reported torture of the children of Deraa changed all this, and became perhaps the signature event of the uprising. They were Syria's Muhammad Bouazizi. It seems to have had a visceral effect on many people in Syria, especially because it happened to children. The reckless nature of this act became a potent symbol of the decades of arbitrary repression by the regime. Considering what had happened elsewhere in the Middle East, the security forces should have been more careful. Many people had simply had enough of the arrests without warrants, the government refusal to disclose the whereabouts of those detained, the unfair trials, the incarcerations for even the mildest expressions of dissent or dissatisfaction (with the government claiming this 'weakened the nation's morale') and, of course, the torture. In a situation that was much more combustible than the regime had ever thought, the arrest and torture of the children of Deraa moved the protest meter to a whole new level. Some might say it was serendipitous or accidental. Others might say it was inevitable, as the hubris of the security forces was bound to get the regime into trouble sooner or later. As Peter Harling, the Damascus-based regional project director for the International Crisis Group, eloquently commented at the time, 'Subdued societies simply will no longer tolerate the many forms of abuse, large and small, to which they had grown accustomed – including crude propaganda, rapacious corruption and unaccountable violence; as a result, any attempt to deal with brand-new expectations via age-old methods can only backfire.'[8] The disparate opposition had uniformly been tortured by the *mukhabarat*.

By 15 March protests and scuffles with security forces had broken out in Deraa, Dayr al-Zor, al-Hasaka and Hama. Small demonstrations sprang up in Damascus. That same day, the Facebook page 'Syrian Revolution 2011', based in London – a page that would become a kind of clearinghouse of video footage and audios of the protests and subsequent violence in Syria – posted pictures of demonstrations in Berlin, Paris, Helsinki, Nicosia, Cairo and Istanbul in support of the protestors. On Friday, 18 March, protests across the country intensified, and amateur video footage of the protests was posted on YouTube and Facebook.

Since Friday is the day on which Muslims are encouraged to participate in noon prayers at their communal mosque, for years mosques have been used across the Muslim world as a natural gathering point, off-limits to security forces, for preachers to preach fiery sermons and for protestors to launch demonstrations. And this is the pattern that emerged in Syria, too.

Anti-regime social media sites dubbed 18 March 'Friday of Dignity'. The practice was to become a recurring one: Fridays labeled in this way would galvanize protestors and draw attention to particular issues of importance to the opposition. People were beginning to chant against the president's cousin, Rami Makhlouf, considered the wealthiest man in Syria, as a symbol of the regime's corruption and nepotism, as well as of the unequal distribution of wealth. Over the next week, Baath party headquarters, governors' offices, police stations, security offices and SyriaTel buildings were attacked in a number of cities, including the major port city of Latakia in northwestern Syria, an area close to the heaviest concentration of Alawites in the country and near the home of the Assad family. In Deraa people were recorded chanting 'God, Syria, freedom'. Friday, 25 March was labeled the 'Friday of Glory' by online sites; it saw the largest protests to date, numbering in the tens of thousands, according to various reports.

As the protests increased and intensified, so did the government response. As a result, with each passing day more and more demonstrators were killed. And even though the protests were largely peaceful, as was demanded by the various opposition groups that were coalescing within and outside the country, some government forces were also killed by elements who were either protecting themselves or taking advantage of the situation for personal gain. Indeed, one of the problems in accurately describing the protests and the government response was the lack of direct information. Usually every report from any reputable source had a qualifying rider that went something like: '[So and so] cannot independently verify or confirm opposition or government reports of those killed or wounded because access to the country is limited.'[9] This is largely the Syrian government's own fault, because by April most journalists had been summarily told to leave the country – this a country in which access to real information was limited to begin with. The social media sites were almost all anti-regime, so images, testimonials and reports were certainly spun in a way that bolstered their viewpoint and goals. On the other hand, the government's news sites were, by most accounts, even more skewed than usual to best reflect its objectives and the vision it wanted to present to the Syrian population and abroad. The truth probably lay somewhere in the middle, although most of the journalists I spoke to (who had sneaked into the country and embedded themselves in various hotspots) were virtually unanimous in maintaining that, even though there were several egregious fabrications and misinterpretations on opposition social media sites, the truth was closer to the way the opposition presented matters.

As one might expect, the government was not just going to sit around and be painted as the 'bad guy'. Soon enough, pro-government marches began. On 29 March, the day before Bashar al-Assad's first public address, reportedly hundreds of thousands of people demonstrated in Damascus, Aleppo, Homs, Hama, Tartous and other cities, in support of the Syrian president.

With disappointment over the president's speech to parliament running high, on Friday, 1 April (anointed 'Friday of Martyrs' by websites) the protests grew some more; there was a harsher crackdown that led to more deaths. In the first week of April came reports from protestors of government snipers appearing on rooftops in various cities, reportedly firing on protestors at random and at those who broke the nighttime curfew. On 8 April the government issued an announcement of its own, saying that nineteen police officers and members of the security forces had been killed in Deraa.[10] And on and on and on . . .

Importantly, there were no significant anti-regime protests in the two largest Syrian cities of Aleppo, in the north, and Damascus. That is not to say there were none – there were small, scattered protests in various quarters of those two cities, at Aleppo University and Damascus University, and especially in the outlying areas – but there was nothing remotely resembling the anti-regime protests that were held on Tahrir Square in Cairo and that in many ways brought about the fall of Egyptian President Husni Mubarak. It was generally thought at the time that, if hundreds of thousands of anti-Assad demonstrators did come together in either city, the regime's days would be numbered, as that would indicate that an important tipping point had been reached; the support of crucial pro-regime elements would have been lost and there would be no going back. Indeed, military deployments in and around Damascus and Aleppo seemed designed to prevent the protests that were simmering in the suburbs and outskirts from reaching the cities themselves, or at least their central areas. For the remainder of 2011, neither city witnessed large-scale anti-regime demonstrations, although the suburbs of Damascus frequently erupted into protest and violence. Into 2012, it did appear that the protests (and the associated government attempts to stamp them out) were creeping closer to the hearts of Damascus and Aleppo.

There were several reasons for the relative lack of protests in these two cities well into the second year of the uprising. First, both Damascus and Aleppo received a great deal of attention from Bashar al-Assad. Of course, as he lived and worked in Damascus, his presence there was felt constantly, even though, for most of his time in power, he eschewed the Assad personality cult constructed by his father. But much more than his father ever did, Bashar traveled to Aleppo and incorporated it more into the ruling structure, even including a number of Aleppans in the state apparatus. Secondly, Damascus and Aleppo received the lion's share of foreign investment, infrastructural improvement and beautification, including maintenance and improvement of tourist sites. Over the previous seven or eight years I had been able to detect steady and noticeable improvements in the look and feel of central Damascus, especially in the area around the Four Seasons Hotel, which was built with Gulf Arab money that also funded a number of other tourist-based retail and residential development projects. This largesse generated and reinforced the support of the *nouveau riche* of the upper and upper-middle classes in both cities: they were the ones that these projects were aimed at, and they were the ones who benefited. For the most part the business elites – Sunni, Alawite and Christian – also continued to support the regime, if for no other reason than that there was no viable alternative: they were hardly going to cut off their nose to spite their face by supporting opposition movements. The hand that fed them was very powerful and adept at co-opting them into maintaining the regime by offering economic, social and political incentives. In addition, as one might expect, most government employees resided in Damascus and, to a lesser extent, Aleppo (and many of the Aleppans that Bashar brought into government still had extended family and patronage networks back home), and they were given a strategically timed increase in their salaries (see above). All these factors, along with the preponderance of military and security power in the two cities, made it well-nigh impossible for the opposition throughout 2011 and into early 2012 to organize large-scale anti-regime demonstrations there.[11]

On 22 April 2011, Syria was rocked by the largest demonstrations yet, held in a number of cities across the country. This was, correspondingly, also the bloodiest day yet: reports from human rights groups claimed that over a hundred people were killed, although government estimates were lower and focused more on the security personnel who died at the hands of 'terrorists' and 'armed gangs'. The government intensified its crackdown on the protestors on 25 April, when tanks rumbled into Deraa, which continued to be a focal point of protests against the regime (and of the government's attempts to quash them). The nearby border with Jordan was closed off, and the city had its water, telephone and power lines cut. Frustration with the regime mounted, and calls for Bashar al-Assad's removal became more common. As one Deraa resident pleaded, 'Let Obama come and take Syria. Let Israel come and take Syria. Let the Jews come. Anything is better than Bashar Assad.'[12]

By 28 April there were reports and videos that appeared to show Syrian soldiers wounded by government security forces after refusing to fire on protestors. There was speculation that some soldiers were deserting. As usual, this could not be independently verified, but this sort of news story started to multiply. Of course, the opposition sites amplified such reports to give the impression that the Syrian military might be on the verge of turning against its masters and to encourage more desertions. Such defections did occur, leading to the formation by the summer of a semi-organized opposition fighting force called the Free Syrian Army. On the whole, however, the military and security forces, particularly the upper echelons, remained loyal to the regime.

In the last week of April, two parliamentary deputies and a leading religious figure resigned their positions. All three were from Deraa. Shaykh Rizq Abd al-Rahim Abazeid, the mufti of the Deraa region, quit with the statement: 'I cannot tolerate the blood of our innocent sons and children being shed.'[13] The two members of parliament who resigned were Nasser

Hariri and Khalil Rifai. Hariri said: 'If I cannot protect the chests of my people from these treacherous strikes, then there is no meaning for me to stay in the People's Assembly. I declare my resignation.'[14] Opposition elements commented that, as parliament had very little real power, the resignations were largely symbolic, but they hoped the move might lead to other, more significant, resignations by government officials. On the whole, this did not happen; nor were there Syrian diplomats asking for asylum in the countries in which they served. This was markedly different from what happened in the Libyan uprising, where, fairly early on, there were important defections by government officials, diplomats and military officers. Not only did this once again reveal a certain degree of loyalty to the regime and a lack of viable alternatives in Syria (in contrast to Libya), but I believe it also reflected the fear factor: no doubt there were those who wanted to defect but were afraid of the potential lethal repercussions for family members in Syria if they did.

Despite all this, there still seemed to be a glimmer of hope that the regime would come to its senses, genuinely engage in serious political reform, and return the army to its barracks. In late April, one prominent Syrian exile opposition group, the National Initiative for Change (many of whose members would appear in larger and better organized opposition groups later in the crisis), issued a final call for a peaceful transition. The statement, in a way turning Assad's own words regarding the prospects for 'chaos' against him, rather prophetically declares:

> Syria today only faces two options; either the ruling regime leads itself in a peaceful transition towards democracy – and we are very doubtful to the desire or will of the regime to do so – or it will go through a process of popular protests that will evolve into a massive and grassroots revolution that will breakdown the regime and carry Syria through a period of transition after a wave of violence and instability. There Syria is at a crossroads; the best option is for the leadership of the regime to lead a transition to democracy that would safeguard the nation from falling into a period of violence, chaos and civil war.[15]

The call for change included the usual demands for broad-based political reform and was fairly moderate, considering the growing cycle of violence. It did not directly call for Assad to step down, instead saying: 'If the President does not wish to be recorded in history as a leader of this transition period, there is no alternative left for Syrians except to move forward along the same path as did the Tunisians, Egyptians and Libyans before them.'

Incredibly, in what seems to have been a blatant attempt to separate the military from the regime (as happened in Egypt), the statement singled out two Syrian military leaders by name: 'the only institution that has the capability to lead the transition period would be the military, and especially the current Minister of Defense General Ali Habib and the Chief of Staff General Dawud Rajha. Both individuals represent a background that Syrians can positively relate with that enables them to take a key pivotal role during the transition process'. I remember thinking to myself at the time that this practically guaranteed their removal, and (at worst) could be their death sentence. Not unsurprisingly, then, Ali Habib was found dead at his home on 8 August, the day after he was dismissed as minister of defense. The state-run Syrian Arab News Agency (SANA) reported that he had been in declining health. I suspect he did not die of natural causes.

The protests into April were still mostly haphazard and not terribly well coordinated at the national level, as there were no overarching opposition organizations inside or outside the country, but only an amalgam of groups, many of which were simply carry-overs of opposition elements that preceded the uprising. The traditional opposition in Syria, such as the signatories to the Damascus Declaration, was caught somewhat off guard by the protests. These people tended to be older and out of touch with the youthful protestors, especially in the application of social media technologies. As they had been weakened over the years, with several prominent figures still in prison, they could largely only observe the dramatic course of events from the sidelines, although many would play an important role in mediating between various opposition groups, as well as in assisting with the media image of the protestors.

On the whole, the protests seemed to be more like spontaneous outbursts, enhanced by social media networks, and still reflected local concerns rather than national agendas. They tended to concentrate in areas where there were clear Sunni majorities and that were not bastions of the regime: the Houran Governorate (where Deraa is located) was volatile, as was the Homs Governorate, whereas the Latakia, Tartous and Sweida Governorates, where there are strong minority populations (Alawite in the first two, Druze in the third) for the most part remained supportive of the regime. But, importantly, protestors were beginning to become more adept at maneuvering around the security forces. The situation in many Syrian towns and cities developed into an increasingly sophisticated game of cat-and-mouse between protestors and government forces. Typically, protestors would set up spotters at all entrances to a neighborhood and on rooftops, to keep watch for security. Once they gave the green light, what seemed like spontaneous outbursts of activity – yet were obviously planned – broke out in the adjacent streets, usually at night. These protested against the regime and celebrated a bit of freedom of expression, all the while accompanied by music and anti-regime chants, in an almost festival-like atmosphere. The demonstrations tended to be short-lived, usually lasting only ten or fifteen minutes before the spotters warned of approaching security forces. Everyone then began a mad dash for their homes or their predetermined hiding places. The next night, the whole thing would be repeated.

Regime schizophrenia

Into May and June 2011 the regime continued to engage in a schizophrenic response to the protests. While continuing to make some concessions and announce reform measures, the military and security forces intensified their crackdown in cities across Syria that were hit by demonstrations. To the outside observer, this approach may seem contradictory and indicative of fissures within the ruling elite on how to respond to the crisis. On the other hand, from the perspective of Bashar and his inner circle, it could be seen as two sides of the same coin: in a way that came to be expected of the Assad regimes – old and new – it was something of an axiom of power politics that one offers concessions only from a position of strength, never from a position of weakness. Therefore, while there was a practical side to the Assad approach, in terms of repressing the unrest, it also clearly indicated that the regime wanted to portray itself as only making concessions and offering reform measures from a position of strength. As such, there were numerous indications that the regime was hunkering down for the long haul, in order to deliver a knockout punch to the opposition – or, at the very least, to wear them down.

The regime continued to paint the uprising as a foreign conspiracy tied to Syrian armed gangs, Islamic terrorists, criminals and thugs. It moved almost entirely toward the narrative of armed gangs, supported by enemies from the outside with their own pernicious anti-Syrian agendas. Even if the exaggerated claims of government brutality made by opposition groups and by the inadequately informed Western media are filtered out, it is clear that the military and security forces were employing excessive force against protestors, many of whom were completely innocent of anything other than peaceful protest. As a result, Damascus was losing the propaganda war internationally, and even domestically, and any pretense of reform or dialogue was seen as disingenuous or simply as delaying tactics. As Peter Harling of the International Crisis Group wrote in late April:

> In more parts of the country than one can count, protestors now face only the most brutal, repressive side of the regime. For those who mourn the dead and know them not as saboteurs and traitors, but as relatives, neighbors, and friends, there is nothing left to discuss. Slowly but surely, these ink spots of radicalized opposition are spreading and joining in an increasingly determined and coordinated movement to topple the regime.[16]

The Manichean nature of the evolving contest between the government and opposition forces seemed to be confirmed in a rather strange interview that Rami Makhlouf, the forty-two-year-old cousin of the president, brother of one of the intelligence chiefs, and Syria's richest businessman, gave to the *New York Times* in May.[17] In 2008, during the Bush administration, the United States had slapped sanctions on him personally, accusing him of manipulating the judicial system and using Syrian intelligence to intimidate rivals and thus enhance his business empire. As mentioned above, as the prime example of corruption and nepotism, Makhlouf became a lightning-rod for the protests.

I know Rami Makhlouf; I have spoken to him on the phone on several occasions, and he graciously hosted me for a meeting and lunch at his office in the SyriaTel headquarters in Damascus. He is a very measured individual. In my conversations with him, his words always appeared to be quite carefully chosen.

He does not necessarily speak for the regime, but his newspaper interview most likely had the approval of the regime (even if it did not like what he said after he had said it). He is someone who consistently denies having influence over Syrian policy, saying repeatedly that he is simply a businessman and 'just' the president's cousin. That said, however, it is generally thought, both within Syria and outside, that he regularly consults with Bashar, and therefore has a great deal of influence over regime policy, especially given his relatives in high places in the security apparatus. So, in other words, what he says matters, and his unusually frank interview probably reflected important regime sentiments at the time. He seemed to have as an objective in the interview to warn the international community what might happen in Syria and in the region – a regional conflagration that would have global consequences – should the regime fall: 'if there is no stability here, there's no way there will be stability in Israel. No way, and nobody can guarantee what will happen after, God forbid, anything happens to this regime.' When asked if this was a threat, he responded: 'I didn't say war. What I'm saying is don't let us suffer, don't put a lot of pressure on the president, don't push Syria to do anything it is not happy to do.' Providing a clear indication of the tenacity of the regime in putting down the protests, he went on: 'the decision of the government now is that they decided to fight . . . We will sit here. We call it a fight until the end. They should know when we suffer, we will not suffer alone.' Warning that the alternative to the Assad regime was a radical Islamist government, he stated: 'we won't accept it. People will fight against them. Do you know what this means? It means catastrophe. And we have a lot of fighters.'[18]

The next day, the Syrian government distanced itself from the interview. The country's ambassador to the United States, Imad Moustapha, had a letter to the editor published in the *New York Times* the day after the interview, clearly stating that Makhlouf was a private citizen and did not speak for the Syrian government. Ironically, on 16 June, it was announced on Syrian television that Makhlouf was quitting as head of SyriaTel and was giving up his other business activities to concentrate on charity work. He said he was going to offer shares in SyriaTel, Syria's largest phone company, to the poor, and that profits would go to the families of those killed in the uprising. He vowed not to engage in any more business that would result in personal gain.[19] At the time, it seemed to be an indication that Makhlouf had fallen out of favor with the regime – and specifically with Bashar – possibly as a result of his disastrous interview. Some viewed it as a crack in the regime's edifice and a possible portent of things to come, i.e. the crumbling of the inner circle around Bashar and, therefore, of the regime itself. As one might imagine, any statement by the person who had been called the 'Assad family banker' was not taken particularly seriously by Syrians, whether or not they belonged to the opposition. Ammar Qurabi, the head of the Syrian National Association for Human Rights, located in the United Arab Emirates, said: 'There is no transparency in his declaration because we don't know what he owns and how much money he has. It is a step designed for media consumption only.'[20] A banner unfurled during a protest in a Damascus suburb said of Makhlouf's announced retirement: 'You can't do charity with the millions you stole from us.'[21] In retrospect, it was not a portent of regime collapse. It appears to have been simply a publicity stunt that Makhlouf may have initiated himself, in an awkward attempt to rehabilitate his image. It didn't work.

The regime's security strategy – to the extent that it had one in the first few months of the uprising – seemed to be what I called at the time the 'whack-a-mole' approach. Generally, wherever serious protests popped up in a particular city or region, the elite and most loyal units of the military and security forces were sent to whack them down. This highlighted several things. First, blunt force was used as a deterrent to future protests. Reportedly, on some occasions individuals were repressed three or four times over: first by the military, then by security (one or more branches of which would follow the army into a city), and then by the so-called *shabbiha* (loosely translated as 'ghost'), which were pro-regime paramilitary or militia groups, usually dressed in civilian clothes but well-armed and apparently operating outside the norms of any military code. The left hand frequently not knowing what the right was doing, a protestor could be arrested and tortured, only to be arrested and tortured all over again by a security branch that did not know the military, police or some other branch of intelligence had already done the job.

Secondly, only certain elements of the military were deployed, because of the lack of training and proper equipment provided to the rank-and-file units that made up the bulk of the Syrian military. Thirdly, the mobility of the Syrian forces was necessary to prevent any safe zones from being created, especially on the northern border with Turkey, which could offer refuge for the Syrian opposition or military deserters, or that could provide an area of ingress for international aid, if not military intervention (as had occurred in Libya). And finally, only the most loyal forces – security or military – were utilized, which usually meant those made up mostly or entirely of Alawites. Since most of the protestors were Sunni, the regime was probably afraid that the mostly Sunni rank-and-file of the military would defect en masse, unwilling to fire on their co-religionists. This, of course, gave the unrest a sectarian coloring.

With this strategy, the regime's enforcer came into his own: Maher al-Assad, the president's younger brother, who headed the Syrian Army's elite Fourth Armored Division, as well as the Republican Guard – in essence the regime's Praetorian Guard. Over the years he had developed a reputation, not wholly undeserved, as the tough guy of the regime. Many equated his role with that of Bashar's uncle, Rifaat al-Assad, back in the days when he occupied a very similar position under his brother, Hafiz al-Assad. He it was who had led the crushing of the Muslim Brotherhood revolt at Hama in 1982. Such was Maher's reputation that many Syrians who saw videos showing a man taking potshots at protestors were convinced that the gunman was, in fact, the president's brother. More to the point, it was a reputation that Maher appeared to be in no hurry to deny, whether true or not.[22] His carefully cultivated image was that of someone to be feared. It may be that a kind of Maher al-Assad cult had developed among some of the more extreme security elements, which may have constrained his brother's ability to move against him if necessary (as Bashar's father had moved against his own brother, Rifaat, in 1983). Indeed, there were those inside and outside Syria who believed that the increasing severity of the crackdown indicated that Maher was now the one actually calling the shots. Maybe Maher had pushed aside Bashar, who was lamely offering concessions and reforms, and who had stated publicly on several occasions that he had ordered the security and military forces not to fire on civilians, when it was abundantly clear that civilians were still being shot at – and killed in increasing numbers.

Bashar was not pushed aside. This was just how the Syrian regime under the Assads reacts to such things. When a domestic threat appears, there is a push-button response of quick and ruthless repression. Survival instincts. No one really questions it. The *mukhabarat* and the elite units of the military swing into action. It was an institutional, convulsive response to perceived threat. The real story in all of this would have been if Bashar did not press that button. He probably did not fret over it too much once the initial shock of the protests wore off. This is just how things are done. It was business as usual in a *mukhabarat* state.

The Syrian regime's other important strategy to outmaneuver, if not defeat, the opposition forces – in other words, to stay in power – was to play the sectarian card. As a minority regime, the Alawite leadership had trumpeted the secular nature of its vision of society and the related protection of minorities, particularly the various Christian sects in Syria that make up over 10 per cent of the population (see Chapter 3). Also included were the Druze (mostly in southern Syria), although their relationship with the Alawites had ebbed and flowed over the years, particularly in the internecine political battles of the 1960s, during the early stages of Baath party rule. Also, although the Arab nationalist policy of the Baath party naturally sometimes placed it at odds with the non-Arab Kurdish population of Syria (located mostly in the north and northeast), the Assads were, by virtue of force or persuasion, largely able to keep a lid on Kurdish separatism. Kurdish groups were also sitting back and playing a waiting game before they committed themselves in any direction. Given previous Kurdish protests against the regime, their opposition credentials were solid, and so they would not be discredited if they chose not to actively join the opposition. On the other hand, they were mindful of the weaknesses of the Syrian opposition and of the likely retribution the government would wreak against them should it survive. Their Kurdish brethren in Iraq had paid a very high price for opposing Saddam Hussein in the 1980s and early 1990s. Syria's Kurds perhaps did not want history to repeat itself. Finally, many Kurdish parties were wary of the increasing drift toward Turkey on the part of Syrian opposition groups, particularly the soon-to-be-formed Syrian National Council (see below). The Kurds in Syria, as in other countries, have long had an antagonistic relationship with Ankara. This is rooted in the repeated attempts by Kurds in Turkey to agitate for more autonomy, as well as in Turkish opposition to almost any attempt by Kurdish populations in neighboring countries to achieve independence, which may have repercussions back home and encourage Turkish Kurds to do the same.

The fact that the government forces cracking down ruthlessly on the protestors in the uprising were predominantly Alawite only exacerbated sectarian tensions. This was not at odds with what the regime was trying to accomplish. Painting the opposition as Sunni *salafist* extremists helped secure the continued support of the sectarian communities that were of primary importance to the regime, the Christians and Alawites, even if there were those in both communities who were not particularly enamored of the Assads. They were more afraid of what might happen if Assad fell and a conservative, Sunni-dominated regime came to power seeking retribution – an unfortunately frequent occurrence in modern Middle East history in the wake of coups and revolutions.

Such a development is particularly common – and usually particularly bloody – in countries that are sectarian and in those that have not developed a deep national identity. This had happened most recently in neighboring Iraq, where Christians endured numerous horrific acts of violence perpetrated by Sunni and Shiite extremists in the aftermath of the fall of the regime of Saddam Hussein in 2003. Coptic Christians in Egypt also experienced violent acts carried out by Sunni extremists in the wake of Mubarak's fall from power. The Syrian regime's insistence that it was either 'us or chaos' resonated with Syrians who feared instability and sectarian warfare. And Syrian opposition groups were not doing enough to placate those who feared retribution; on the contrary, a number of statements by opposition elements seemed to indicate that they were bent on vengeance rather than reconciliation. Often attempts to include minorities in opposition activities were merely cosmetic. As one leading opposition figure commented, 'Nowadays they're [the opposition groups] looking for one Christian, two Alawites, three Druze, and then they say they're representative.'[23]

But it became a self-fulfilling prophecy that the sectarian card played by the regime actually helped bring about what it said it was trying to avoid – a retreat into sectarian fortresses, sectarian segregation in a number of cities, sectarian-motivated violence and the potential of all-out sectarian civil war. As Nadim Houry of Human Rights Watch commented, 'The regime in Syria presents itself as a buffer for various communities, essentially saying "if we go, you will be left to the wolves". That gives it ability to mobilize large segments of the population.'[24]

It is important to note that many Alawites are poor and felt neglected by the regime that was dominated by their religious brethren. Those who were not from the family or tribe of the Alawite elite, could find themselves struggling to eke out a living, just like other Syrians, particularly in rural areas. However, they also know that retribution does not differentiate. They remember the civil war between the government and the Sunni Muslim Brotherhood in the late 1970s, culminating in the Hama massacre of 1982. One Alawite recalled that period: 'Anything with intellect they [the Muslim Brotherhood] destroyed in those days. They killed doctors and judges. Now its goal is strife and destroying the economy, everything that is the state. They are like [former US President George W.] Bush. If you are not with us you're against us. There is a Saudi *takfiri* mobilization.'[25] The final sentence refers to Saudi Arabia's penchant for supporting Sunni extremist elements in Syria, who view the Alawites as apostates to Islam (*takfiri* coming from the Arabic word *kafir*, or 'unbeliever').

Stoking this fear, there were reports of stories and videos being circulated within the security services that showed disgusting, beyond-the-pale behavior by Sunnis against Alawites – such as a woman in Homs drinking the blood of dead Alawites, surrounded by their dismembered bodies, which had been delivered to her by armed terrorists.[26] Other stories broadcast by the government included Sunni extremists establishing Islamic emirates in areas they controlled in Syria, as well as 'evidence' of Israeli funding and arms deliveries to opposition forces.[27] It did not help matters when a prominent opposition leader in Homs, who had apparently lost family members during the government siege of his city, was caught on video participating in chants to 'exterminate the Alawites'.[28] No doubt sectarian animosities have been exacerbated by the rebellion, but footage such as this only confirmed the regime's narrative within its support base of minorities in Syria.

There were a number of incidents or events during the course of the Arab Spring in Syria that elevated the crisis to new levels – or at least that is how they were portrayed in the media. One of these was what happened to a thirteen-year-old boy by the name of Hamza al-Khateeb, who went missing from his southern village of Jeezah on 29 April. His mutilated body was returned to his family about a month later. The gruesome pictures of the poor boy were broadcast around the world, and the international outrage was not slow in coming. The Syrian government obviously denied torturing the boy: it even had a government-employed doctor examine the body, and he concluded that the deformations and scars were not consistent with torture. Regardless of who was responsible, it was clear that the Syrian crisis was the cause, and certainly most fingers pointed to the regime's security forces, which were already known from the Deraa incident to have no qualms about torturing children. Backtracking, the government announced an investigation into al-Khateeb's death, and Bashar al-Assad even visited the family. Echoing jarring, mobilizing deaths in other Arab states during the Arab Spring, chants of protest and websites grew up around the phrase 'We are all Hamza al-Khateeb'. A Facebook page was created in his name on 28 May and logged more than 67,000 supporters. As one comment read, 'There is no place left here for a regime after what they did to Hamza.'[29] If the perception of a regime is that it is ordering or condoning the torture and murder of children, it is well-nigh impossible to rehabilitate such a tarnished image.

Another moment occurred at Jisr al-Shughur, a Sunni-dominated city in northwestern Syria, on the Turkish border in the Idlib Governorate. The city had a history with the Assads: in 1980, the government carried out a brutal crackdown there that presaged the events of a couple of years later in Hama, another conservative Sunni city. Violence now broke out on 6 June 2011, with government forces entering the city. According to Syrian state reports, 120 security personnel were killed by 'armed gangs' in the largest death toll to date in any single theater of combat in the uprising. Opposition websites contended that the 120 security personnel had actually been killed by their own, when they threatened to (or actually did) defect to the opposition.[30] This is but one example of the diametrically opposed narratives offered on the same incident by the two sides, which were attempting to spin the story to their own advantage. Perhaps more importantly in the long term, the action taken along the Turkish border by Syrian forces, which were probably attempting to prevent any safe zones from developing,[31] not only greatly boosted the flow of Syrian refugees into southern Turkey, but also hastened Turkish involvement in the crisis and increased pressure on Ankara's erstwhile friend, Bashar al-Assad, to really implement the reforms that had been announced. The Syrian government's failure to do so, the increasing violence and the associated flood of refugees to Red Crescent camps in Turkey (approximately 10,000 by mid-June) would eventually alienate one of Syria's most important regional friends. Jisr al-Shughur and other towns in the area had been virtually emptied, with most of the residents fleeing to or across the Turkish border; there were reports that Syrian artillery actually shelled some of the refugee camps inside Turkey.

Bouthaina Shaaban announced on 9 May that the Syrian government had gained the upper hand in the uprising: 'I hope we are witnessing the end of the story. I think now we've passed the most dangerous moment. I hope so, I think so.'[32] Commenting on the protestors, she went on to repeat the now oft-heard refrain: 'We think these people are a combination of fundamentalists, extremists, smugglers, people who are ex-convicts and are being used to make trouble.' She said that she had been asked to meet well-known political activists in Syria, such as Michel Kilo, Louay Hussein, Aref Dalila and Salim Khayrbek in an attempt to begin a dialogue leading to political reform. Shaaban noted that this was the beginning of an effort by the government to create a national dialogue and to reach some sort of political resolution to the crisis: 'We want to use what happened to Syria as an opportunity. We see it as an opportunity to try to move forward on many levels, especially the political level.'[33]

These apparent concessions by the government were dismissed by opposition elements, which claimed that they were simply more delaying tactics. They were also not going to enter into any sort of political dialogue while army tanks were still on the streets, killing civilians. The security forces had first to be withdrawn, and the political prisoners who had been arrested since the uprising began (an estimated 10,000 by June) had to be released. They were usually held in existing prisons in terrible conditions, or else had been thrown into makeshift prisons converted from school gymnasiums, warehouses, government buildings or stadiums. As one anonymous Syrian official said, highlighting a central conundrum for the Syrian president, even assuming he was truly committed to expeditious reform: 'Assad is not capable of implementing these reforms. He's not capable. He knows if he did, it would be the end of him. He would fall.'[34]

The Syrian regime suffered another blow to its quickly deteriorating international reputation on 1 June 2011, when Human Rights Watch published a scathing fifty-five-page report on the Syrian crisis. One need go no further than its title to intuit its findings: *'We've Never Seen Such Horror': Crimes against humanity by Syrian security forces.*[35] The report detailed 'systematic killings of protestors and bystanders', as well as extensive arbitrary arrests, disappearances, torture, denial of medical assistance, executions and mass graves, among other violations. It certainly added to the debate at the time on whether or not to pass a UN Security Council resolution to refer Assad to the International Criminal Court for crimes against humanity.

Opposition matures

The Syrian regime continued its attempts to portray itself as interested in a political solution – attempts that may have been aimed more at an international audience than a local one. This was probably also an attempt to outflank exiled opposition groups that were trying to join forces. In any event, on 31 May President Assad announced, via the state-run media, the formation of a committee to set up a basis for a national dialogue. Assad also offered a pardon for all political crimes committed before 31 May 2011, including to all members of political movements, even the outlawed Muslim Brotherhood. The date of both announcements was probably not a coincidence, as a number of exiled opposition groups and individual activists were meeting at the time for a three-day conference (31 May–3 June) in Antalya, Turkey, in an attempt to form an overarching organization that could represent the opposition, especially internationally, and help coordinate efforts. The name of the gathering was the 'Syrian Conference for Change'. It was organized by the Egypt-based National Organization for Human Rights, and about 300 opposition figures were in attendance. The goal was to establish a dialogue between the various opposition groups with the aim of creating a transitional council – again mimicking what was happening at the time in Libya, with the formation of the National Transitional Council. As one prominent activist, Washington-based Radwan Ziadeh, noted: 'Everyone knows that the Syrian uprising is leaderless. We need to establish some sort of balance to move ahead. The intended outcome is for a united opposition established on the principles of greater coordination inside and outside Syria.'[36] It was worrisome to the regime, whose continued existence relied in part on the loyalty of the Sunni merchant class, that the conference also attracted the support of a number of prominent Syrian businessmen; in fact, it was funded by Ali and Wassim Sanqar, brothers who were in the luxury car distribution business in Damascus.

As a clear sign of continuing division among exiled Syrian opposition groups (and differences between domestic and external opposition elements), on the eve of the conference, Ribal al-Assad, the president's exiled cousin and head of the London-based Organisation for Democracy and Freedom, said the conference was a front for Islamic extremism. He further announced that he would hold an alternative conference based on 'freedom, democracy and religious pluralism'. He claimed that Muslim Brotherhood members at the conference were posing as moderates: 'I can assure you that none of these people represents the Syrian opposition. They are individuals that only represent themselves.' Ziadeh countered that 'We know Syrian society is very conservative. Moderate Muslims must be present.' Kurdish opposition groups boycotted the conference, while other exiled opposition elements bemoaned the inadequate planning, the lack of consultation and the hasty way in which the conference had been organized.[37]

At the conference, the opposition rejected Assad's amnesty offer, as well as the call for national dialogue. Instead, the participants announced that they were beginning the process of forging a plan for a 'new, democratic Syria' and creating committees to liaise with the international community. Ammar Abdulhamid, the Washington-based Syrian pro-democracy activist, stated that the conference 'hopes to create a representative body that can be accepted by the protestors inside Syrian that can meet their demands in terms of the opposition trying to play a role in getting their voices heard by the international community'.[38] Perhaps damping down expectations of the outcome of the conference, however, he was quick to point out that

> this is not going to be any kind of government in exile, simply a group of people who are willing to represent the movement internationally because the world cannot engage in a revolution that does not have any recognizable representatives. Our hope is to fuel that kind of body on an interim basis until such time that the Syrian people can freely elect a

> transitional council inside the country that can lead the country to democracy.

Although disagreements and divisions persisted, this meeting served as a launch-pad for what would become the Syrian National Council (SNC), formed in the autumn of 2011. Although still riven by disputes, by the end of 2011 the SNC had become the generally recognized and legitimate Syrian opposition organization, at least in the international arena.

One of the more interesting aspects of the growing opposition to the regime was the development of homegrown activists, particularly the loosely organized groups that called themselves the Local Coordination Committees (LCC). Made up largely of tech-savvy youth, they emerged and have continued to play a very important role in the uprising. The exiled opposition – and any post-Assad government – must take the LCC seriously: although (for obvious reasons) largely anonymous during the uprising, they it was who led the protests against the government on the ground, risking life and limb; and they it was who battled and outwitted government forces to a virtual standstill. They and their supporters would not look kindly upon exiled opposition leaders scooping up the rewards for what they rightly earned. On the LCC, Anthony Shadid of the *New York Times* wrote:

> Their success has stemmed from an ability to stay decentralized, work in secret and fashion their message in the most nationalist of terms. But that very success has made them a mystery to the Syrian government, which prefers to work with more recognized opposition figures . . . The youthful demonstrators who make up these coordination committees have bridged divides of sect, religion and class to try to formulate a leadership. As in Egypt, they were able to build on years of local dissidence that had already created informal networks of friends and colleagues. Across Syria, as many as 35 activists who are acknowledged as committee leaders try to communicate by Internet chat room each day . . . One who identified himself as a 23-year-old civil engineering student . . . said he spent 15 hours a day online. 'We live and work in the virtual world, not the street,' he said.[39]

As with the exiled opposition, there have been some bitter divisions between various LCC in different cities across Syria – many of them have differing agendas, based on local circumstances. Nevertheless, the LCC proliferated and, according to many, became the driving force behind the uprising on the ground.

Assad kept trying to seize the initiative as a reformer, despite the death of over 1,100 Syrians in the first two and a half months of the uprising, as reported by UN human rights organizations. On 20 June, in a Damascus University auditorium that was packed with pro-regime supporters, the Syrian president delivered his third public address on the crisis. Since the speech was broadcast by Syrian television, it was an 'address to the nation'. This speech was less arrogant and bombastic than his two previous public addresses. While a little more forthcoming on the need for reform, it still contained the same rationale for the causes of the uprising. Assad said he was 'working on getting the military back to their barracks as soon as possible', but then warned that the government would 'work on tracking down everyone who shed blood or plotted in shedding the blood of the Syrian people, and we will hold them accountable'.[40] He again blamed armed gangs and conspiracies for the violence: 'There are those who are distorting the image of the Syrian nation abroad, and they wanted to open the gates and even called for foreign intervention. They tried to weaken the national political position. There are those who are killing [in] the name of religion and want to spread chaos under the pretext of religion.' He went on to compare the conspiracies to 'germs' that cannot be 'exterminated'.

Assad tried to focus more on reform, raising the possibility of amending Syria's constitution and entering into national dialogue: 'It is not a dialogue of the opposition with the government . . . but it should be a dialogue that will include all fabrics of Syrian society.' He promised to reform 'what had been damaged', although he admitted this would take time: 'For us the reform process is an absolute conviction that will be in the best interest of the nation and the citizen. We can't jump into the unknown. We are working on building the way to our future.' He also urged Syrian refugees in Turkey to return home: 'The military is there for the sake of their security, the safety of all citizens and their cities.'

The opposition was quick to dismiss the president's speech, saying that, once again, the proof of the pudding was in the eating: these were empty promises, since he had said many of the same things before, without actually implementing them. By focusing once again on foreign conspiracies and armed gangs as the causes of the uprising, he denied – yet again – the real socioeconomic and political roots of the crisis and the legitimate needs and demands of the protestors. As one protestor's sign read after the speech: 'If we are all germs, are you the head of all germs?'

A potentially interesting development regarding political reform in Syria resulted from this latest speech. A new political party law was drafted by the government and posted online for public debate, with the intention that it should be ratified in parliament in August. The law would end the one-party rule of the Baath (which at the time had about 2.8 million members, in a country of 22 million). Since the early 1970s there had been a 'loyal opposition' in parliament – the National Progressive Front, an umbrella organization that consisted of a number of left-wing parties. But the Baath party was overwhelmingly dominant. Article 8 of the Syrian constitution even stated that the Baath party was the 'leader of state and society'. The new party law would create a multi-party system, acknowledging that the goal of political pluralism is to create a rotating system of power in the executive and legislative branches of government. There were, however, a number of restrictions, mostly aimed at blocking any religious, ethnic or regional parties (such as a Muslim Brotherhood or a Kurdish party). In order for a party organizer to acquire a license, he or she had to be over twenty-five years of age and to have attracted at least fifty founding members. All the members of the party had to be resident in Syria, and it had to draw its membership from at least 50 per cent of the Syrian governorates. A party needed to have 2,000 members at the time of application, as well as an identified headquarters. A Party Affairs Committee, chaired by the minister of the interior (in itself something of a red rag to a bull!), would approve or reject a party's application, according to certain procedures. There were also rules regarding donations, funding and equal access to the media.[41] As before, skepticism was rife both inside and outside the country: people would believe it when they saw it.

As promised, in one area at least, in early July the regime did gather together a number of leading figures in the country, including academics, youth leaders and known democracy activists, to engage in a 'national dialogue'. It was chaired by Farouk al-Sharaa, Syria's vice president and a Sunni, originally from Deraa. Sharaa was well-respected in the country as a senior statesman, and he was known as one of the few in the upper echelons of the leadership who acted in the interests of the country and was not corrupt. In his opening remarks, he hailed the meeting, held at Damascus University, as a step towards creating a democratic nation: 'We hope that at the end of this comprehensive meeting to announce the transition of Syria to a pluralistic democratic nation where all citizens are guided by equality and participate in the modeling of the future of their country.'[42] One of the activists at the meeting insisted that 'The bloodshed needs to stop.'[43] To which the Syrian vice president responded: 'We have to admit that without the big sacrifices that were presented by the Syrian people, from the blood of their sons, civilians or military in more than one province, city and town, this meeting wouldn't have happened.'[44]

But the meeting was not followed up by any more serious national dialogues. One high-level Syrian official told me that the government had 'really messed up the whole thing'. Longtime democracy activists, such as Michel Kilo and Louay Hussein, admitted that they could not (and did not want to) speak for the protestors: 'Representatives of the street should contribute to this dialogue themselves.'[45] Another activist, Nabil Samman, argued that picking and choosing with whom to engage was self-defeating on the part of the government: 'Everyone has to be invited to the dialogue: writers, tribal leaders, human rights activists . . . all.' This was one of the main problems with the government's attempt at national dialogue: it was seen, perhaps rightly so, as yet another delaying tactic, or even as a cynical attempt to separate the 'acceptable' opposition elements from the unacceptable ones inside and outside Syria. The meeting denied a place to the LCC and others who had been assuming the larger burden of the protests. Accordingly, during the meeting, protestors held nationwide 'No Dialogue' marches.

Furthermore, many opposition elements – Syrian residents and exiles – had already determined that the Assad regime must go – it was past the point of compromise. In their opinion, no dialogue could possibly work with a regime that would, under no circumstances, go any further than Egyptian President Husni Mubarak had done in his own country – i.e. allow 'a ruling party that tolerates feeble but legal opposition parties, a measure of freedom of expression and a critical press, a loud but ineffectual Parliament, and security services that may undergo some reforms but are still riddled with corruption'.[46]

The largely Sunni city of Homs – an industrial hub, the third-largest city in Syria and the original home of Asma al-Assad's family – descended into vicious daily warfare between protestors and government forces, and soon became the epicenter of the uprising. The violence escalated throughout the country, the different sides hardened their positions, and any serious thoughts of national dialogue receded.

The social network

The role of the social media in the protest movements in Tunisia and Egypt has been well documented.[47] Since nothing breeds imitation as much as success, social media networks also played an important role in the Syrian uprising, mobilizing opposition activity through such popular media sites as Facebook, Twitter and YouTube. Indeed, the use of these social media sites has in itself been revolutionary, transforming sporadic acts of civil disobedience into nationwide demonstrations.[48] The primary advantage of social media is that they are largely uncensored and anonymous, thereby better protecting opposition elements that use them.

With social media, authoritarian governments could not control the stream of information as they had done in the past; indeed, the information could be shaped and spun in a way that benefited the opposition and that cast the Syrian regime in as negative a light as possible – much as the state-controlled media had been used by the government for decades to shape and spin information to its advantage. First and foremost, social media generated a freer flow of information about the uprising that could not be controlled by the state. As Radwan Ziadeh commented:

> The social media networks have played crucial roles in showing the world what is going on in Syria. Since Day One, the Syrian government has banned any media presence and kicked out all the reporters. This is how every Syrian citizen became an activist, and, at the same time, a journalist. This is the perfect model of citizen journalism. It has empowered more young activists[.][49]

Dissidents used popular media outlets such as Facebook and Twitter to organize opposition activity. A number of social media websites, such as 'Syrian Revolution 2011' and 'Syrian Revolution News Round-ups' were created to coordinate protests throughout the country and to act as clearing-houses for information and updates on the uprising. The sites have been used by the opposition to show to the country and the world the atrocities perpetrated by government forces in brutally suppressing the protests, including footage of the mutilated body of thirteen-year-old Hamza al-Khateeb. Such videos have galvanized the opposition, leading to larger and more vocal protests. Government filtering of information is no more. In a way, the social media have allowed ordinary citizens to counter the decades of censorship in Syria, inspiring an attitude of defiance among tech-savvy youths that will most likely be impossible to rein in again.[50] The social media have allowed people to escape the culture of fear.

Ironically, it was the self-described computer nerd, Bashar al-Assad, who, as chairman of the Syrian Computer Society in the 1990s, accelerated the Internet's penetration in Syria, thus providing the technological foundation for the opposition in its attempt to unseat him. The major Internet providers in Syria were state-controlled, though there were a few private companies. The country's two largest providers were SyriaTel, the head of which was Rami Makhlouf, and the government-controlled Syrian Telecommunications Establishment (STE). Over the years, the state generally placed greater emphasis on telecommunications *security* than on quality of service, and there was a fairly sophisticated system of media surveillance acquired from foreign software companies in Iran, Italy, Canada and the United States.[51] According to one report:

> In 2006, Reporters Without Borders ranked Syria among the 13 enemies of the Internet, and in 2007 described Syria as the biggest prison for cyber dissidents in the Middle East because of the number of arrests and the frequency of mistreatment of online activists. In 2009, the Committee to Protect Journalists ranked Syria third in a list of the ten worst countries in which to be a blogger, given the arrests, harassment, and restrictions that online writers in Syria have faced.[52]

So, even though Syria seemed to be opening up to the outside world via the Internet, cyber technology was also utilized to track down real and suspected dissidents. This function came to the fore between 2000 and 2007, when Internet usage in Syria soared by over 4,900 per cent, thanks to the new private media outlets authorized by Assad in 2001.[53] In a way, the heightened surveillance and security precautions undertaken by the regime helped young people develop the technical skills to evade surveillance and gather information. By 2011, Syrian youth had acquired a great deal of online experience and was well practiced in the art of evading the watchful eye of the security forces.

In 2007, Facebook was banned by the Syrian government, which claimed that it was being used as a 'conduit for Israeli penetration of Syrian youth', although dissidents believe the decision was taken to block civil society activists from forming organizations and social networks beyond the reach of the regime.[54] Tech-savvy youths, however, were able to work around this by using international proxy servers. Indeed, a mobile phone video in 2010 of schoolchildren being beaten by teachers went viral, embarrassing the Syrian government.[55] It was a portent of things to come. Interestingly, the ban on Facebook and other social media sites was lifted by the government in early February 2011. Skeptics figured at the time that it was not really a government concession, but rather an attempt to more easily monitor dissident activity – especially considering the fact that Syria had most likely acquired cyber-surveillance technology from the Iranians (who have some of the most sophisticated technology of this sort in the world, developed over many years of using it to suppress dissent in their own country).

Unable to control the stream of information, the Syrian government watched helplessly as a wave of 'virtual activism' over Facebook, Twitter and YouTube fueled the uprising. Images of torture, killings and brutality by government forces were posted, as were videos, interviews, guerilla art, anti-regime music and opposition commentaries, a good portion of which could be seen and heard in real time. What could have become routine news instead became a drama of life and death; of freedom versus tyranny.

Because of the anonymous nature of social media sites, there is also the potential for abuse by opposition elements – or even just people who want to create a sensation. After all, those interested in the fall of Bashar al-Assad are hardly going to display any positive videos of Syrian soldiers. Videos can be cleverly edited, and unattributed information can appear in any format. One notable case in summer 2011 involved a blog entitled 'Gay Girl in Damascus', supposedly organized by lesbian blogger Amina Arraf. Her writings captured the attention of thousands inside and outside Syria as an example of a downtrodden minority fighting back. When the blog suddenly went silent, word spread on social media sites that she had been arrested, and worldwide outrage ensued. After about a week, it emerged that 'Amina Arraf' was actually Tom MacMaster, a forty-year-old male postgraduate at the University of Edinburgh in Scotland. It was an elaborate hoax that served as a warning and a timely reminder that accurate information on the Syrian uprising was hard to come by.

Tendentiousness was common. As mentioned earlier, the Syrian government had only itself to blame for this, as it generally prevented the international press from freely reporting inside Syria. That said, a number of professional journalists and photographers did manage to slip into the country, usually from Lebanon. They bravely embedded themselves on the front lines of the uprising, but several were killed in the fighting. As some have pointed out, however, 'the Internet . . . is a natural playground for the dissemination of disinformation'.[56] Toward the end of 2011, even Stratfor, a geopolitical risk-analysis group based in Austin, Texas, whose reports during Bashar's presidency had tended to reflect Washington's negative attitude toward Syria, questioned the veracity of opposition information: 'most of the opposition's more serious claims have turned out to be grossly exaggerated or simply untrue, thereby revealing more about the opposition's weaknesses than the level of instability inside the Syrian regime'.[57] While certainly not denying the violent actions carried out by the Syrian regime, it cautioned the US government against making important foreign policy decisions based on one set of observations.[58]

The Syrian government tried to fight back in this cyberwar. It created a special division of computer specialists called the Syrian Electronic Army (SEA). The purpose of the new agency was to track dissidents, post pro-regime materials, attempt to block or shut down social media sites and web pages that were critical of the Syrian government, and prevent sabotage by cyber dissidents.[59] It appeared to be another form of cat-and-mouse between the protestors and the government, as security forces and the SEA would close Internet sites, and just as fast the cyber dissidents would find new ways to post information. And – just as in the cat-and-mouse games on the streets of villages, towns and cities across Syria at the time – the government forces were on their heels. Complicating the Syrian government's efforts is the support the Obama administration began to give to Syrian cyber activists as the crisis wore on. They are reportedly receiving US assistance outside of Syria in the form of 'training in computer encryption, circumvention of government firewalls and secure use of mobile phones' by way of federally-funded nonprofit organizations.[60] The modus operandi for this process was originally established via the State Department in 2008 with China as the target. As a result, a rebel's computer and tech knowledge may be as or more important than his or her weapons.

As Lebanon-based cyber activist, Rami Nakhla, said: 'You can't quash an uprising if millions of people are acting like their own independent news stations.'[61]

CHAPTER 7

The International Response

The international reaction to the uprising in Syria and the Syrian government's policies in response evolved as the situation itself evolved. The initial reaction from practically every international actor who had a 'dog in this fight', so to speak, was guarded and muted. It was almost as if everyone hoped the burgeoning crisis in Syria would just fizzle out and go away, so that there would be no need to make any difficult decisions regarding the proper response. Unfortunately, the uprising did not just go away, and the major regional and international players in the unfolding drama did indeed have to make some difficult decisions.

But, in contrast to Libya, there was no clear-cut answer and no definite direction – even as the violence became inexorably linked to the question of what the international community would, could or should do. By autumn 2011, though – if not earlier – it was apparent that the Syrian crisis had in many ways become a function of what, in recent years, had emerged as a regional cold war between Iran and its allies (first and foremost Syria, but also Hizbullah-led Lebanon and, to a lesser degree, Shiite-led Iraq) and Saudi Arabia and its allies (especially Qatar and likeminded countries such as Israel, the United States, and, after the uprising, Turkey). The crisis in Syria also saw the rebirth of what appeared to be a new Middle Eastern cold war at the international level, between a US-led bloc that included the European Union, and a Russian-led bloc, which included China and emerging powers such as India, Brazil and South Africa (the so-called BRICS countries).

The hesitancy with which the international community acted toward the regime of Bashar al-Assad, despite evidence of growing and indiscriminate violence perpetrated against largely peaceful protestors by government forces, can be attributed to what one article in May 2011 called 'the Doomsday scenario if Syria fails'.[1] Simply put, no one wanted to see another post-Saddam Iraq – i.e. chaos and instability in a country due to the precipitate removal of the central authority that had held it together. Indeed, it was thought at the time that Syria could even be worse.

The concern, of course, was that Syria, like Iraq, is both ethnically and religiously sectarian. Also like Iraq, an authoritarian minority sectarian regime had a chokehold of power at almost every level. Nor were there any well-developed political institutions or civil society to fill the vacuum that would be created by the removal of the ruling regime. As one scholar at the American University of Beirut noted in a *Washington Post* article, 'If the regime collapses you will have civil war and it will spread throughout the region, engulfing Lebanon, Iraq, Saudi Arabia and beyond.'[2] According to many, the entire balance of power in the region was at stake. Rami Khouri, also based in Lebanon, compared the situation to the 2008 US government bailout of bankrupted financial institutions, saying that Syria was like a bank that is too big to be allowed to fail. He went on: 'the specter of sectarian-based chaos within a post-Assad Syria that could spread to other parts of the Middle East is frightening to many people'.[3] Or as Josh Landis stated at the time, 'Syria is the cockpit of the Middle East, and a struggle for control of Syria would be ignited.'[4] I also chipped in: 'for the Obama administration, the last thing they want, just at the time they're withdrawing from Iraq, is a destabilized Syria that would lead to an open season for jihadis to cross the border into Iraq'.[5]

The biggest fear was that the chaotic collapse of the Syrian state could lead to outside intervention or could precipitate regional war, perhaps even another Arab-Israeli war. The latter emerged from concerns that – much as Saddam Hussein had tried to do in the 1991 Gulf War – a desperate Assad regime could initiate hostilities with Israel in a last-ditch attempt to get the country behind the government and to turn a failing domestic situation into an Arab-Israeli conflict. This could lead to the involvement of Iran or its proxies (particularly Hizbullah) in the conflict, providing backing for Syria. And, just as a conflicting alliance system in World War One turned a bilateral conflict into a global one, so could this, with Saudi Arabia and its allies joining the West in an anti-Iranian coalition.

Intervention by Turkey in northern Syria to protect its interests would be a very real possibility; while, from the east, Iraq – and, by extension, Iran – could seek to safeguard its interests by attempting to maintain a friendly (or at the very least non-threatening) regime in Damascus. The instability in Syria could then spill over into neighboring Lebanon, Iraq and maybe even Jordan, and there could potentially be a ripple effect of internal instability (if not outright civil war) in those countries. The United States would be compelled to become directly engaged in this tsunami, either getting caught up in the tidal wave, or trying to clean up the mess – either of which would be expensive in political capital, resources and probably lives. The domestic repercussions in the United States – particularly with a presidential election looming – would be monumental, as there would be little appetite there for a third full-blown military engagement in the Middle East in a decade. On the other side of the equation, the Middle East is quite tired of US military intervention, and an already negative opinion of the United States in the region would gain further currency.

Maybe now one can understand the doomsday scenarios applied to Syria in the early stages of the uprising, as well as the measured response of the international community. If only Assad would actually implement the long-promised reform, end the violence and engage in dialogue with the opposition, all would be well. The uprising would fade away, the most extreme opposition elements would be marginalized, and Syria would morph into something resembling a democratic, open society – at least enough to divert the gaze of a wary international community toward something else. Most of all, Syria would not fall apart.

The best – or perhaps the least confusing – way to cover the international reaction to the crisis in Syria during its first six months or so, when state policies on the uprising became better defined and more developed, is to conduct a roll call of the relevant parties and to examine the varied interests, motivations and constraints regarding the policies that each actually adopted vis-à-vis Syria. The parties will be grouped into those that were generally supportive of Assad's Syria and those that were arrayed against it and were supportive of the opposition. The international response *after* the first six months of the uprising, including the role of the United Nations and the Arab League, will be picked up in the remaining chapters.

Pro-Assad

Iran

On the surface, Iran and Syria would appear to be less than ideal allies. Syria, as we know, is a predominantly Arab state that has been ruled by a party that is staunchly secular. Iran, on the other hand, is mostly Persian and is ruled by a theocratic hierarchy as an Islamic republic. And even though the Alawites are considered in scholarly circles to be an offshoot of Shiite Islam, in practice most Shiites (particularly of the mainstream 'Twelver Shiite' strain that is dominant in Iran) consider the Alawites heretical. But this alliance – Syria's most important of the last decade – is strategic, and the best explanation for it lies in the old Arab proverb 'the enemy of my enemy is my friend'. That 'enemy' was Saddam Hussein's Iraq. The alliance began soon after the Iranian Revolution of 1979 and was nurtured by Syria's support of Tehran against Iraq in the 1980–88 Iran–Iraq War (in which Syria was the only Arab state to support non-Arab Iran against Arab Iraq). Of course, it was in part the hostility between Damascus and Baghdad that led to Hafiz al-Assad's decision to participate in the US-led UN coalition that evicted Iraq from Kuwait in the 1990–91 Gulf crisis and war.

Iran's relationship with Syria allowed Tehran to extend its influence into the heartland of the Middle East, and particularly right into the middle of the Arab-Israeli conflict, through its extensive support for the anti-Israeli Islamist groups Hizbullah in Lebanon and Hamas in the Palestinian territories. Its ability to do this has been important for Iran in terms of extending its regional leverage and footprint. In the region, it also claimed that its 1979 revolution had been *Islamic*, not simply Iranian – i.e. its significance as an agent of change in the region did not stop at the Iranian border. In tough economic times, this position – on an issue that was of importance to many Iranians – won the regime points domestically.

Iran's support offered Damascus strategic depth, especially when it was vulnerable. As we have seen, Syria's policies often set it at odds with other states in the Middle East. It did no harm to have a powerful friend, especially one on the other side of the Arab state that had been most problematic to Syria since the 1970s: Iraq under Saddam Hussein. It also did not hurt to add more friends when the Soviet Union imploded in the early 1990s. Hafiz al-Assad was always one to hedge his bets, even flirting with the United States following the 1991 Gulf War and getting tantalizingly close to a peace treaty with Israel. But Iran and its assets provided Syria with what the Syrian leadership felt was much-needed bargaining power in any negotiations with Israel over the Golan Heights and in any discussions with Washington. In addition, Iran's sponsorship of Hizbullah (in terms of military and financial support) often reached the Shiite Islamist group via Syria, which provided Damascus with an important ally and asset in politically sectarian Lebanon – a country of supreme importance to Syria (which will be discussed below). The Iranian-Syrian alliance, one of the most important in the Middle East, would not be easily broken.

Over time there also developed an economic dimension to the relationship, particularly as investment opportunities, tourism and trade developed between the two countries, and as discounted oil from Iran was shipped into Syria, allowing Syria's oil companies to export the country's meager oil supplies at market price and the country to pocket the difference. The economic relationship, however, has tended to be one-sided, especially in the tourism sector: thousands of Iranians undertake religious pilgrimages every year to Syrian Shiite shrines, but relatively few Syrians visit Iran.

But there have also been some noticeable differences over the years, such as Iranian frustration with Syria's willingness to negotiate a peace treaty with Israel, or Syria's frustration over what its leadership often believed to be too much Iranian interference in Iraqi affairs, especially after the fall of Saddam Hussein and the installation of a Shiite-dominated government in Baghdad. In addition, the improvement in Syrian-Turkish relations over the last few years has allowed Turkey to enter Syria not only economically but also culturally, with such things as the popular Turkish soap operas that are translated into Arabic. Iranian shows are not nearly as popular, and the Turks have the advantage of a shared border, a shared heritage going back to the days of the Ottoman Empire, intermarriage, and the fact that Turkey is predominantly Sunni, just like Syria. The form of government in Ankara – secular Islamist – also appeals to more Syrians than does Iran's theocratic form of government.[6] Indeed, underneath the Saudi-Iranian tussle, there is a growing competition between Turkey and Iran over Syria. None of these differences and shifting strategic alliances, however, was too great to overcome the shared strategic interests for the time being between Damascus and Tehran.

Under Bashar al-Assad, Iranian-Syrian ties deepened. From the point of view of Damascus, in part this was out of sheer necessity: under great pressure from the United States following the US-led invasion of Iraq in 2003, and particularly following the Hariri assassination (when Saudi Arabia and France could be added to the anti-Assad list), Syria desperately needed Iranian support to stay afloat. This meshed with Iranian interests at the time: Tehran was under increasing pressure from a variety of quarters over its alleged 'weaponizing' of its uranium enrichment program in its nuclear power facilities. There was a tangible and growing concern that Tehran could develop nuclear weapons. As the pressure increased and there was serious talk of possible Israeli or American pre-emptive airstrikes to take out the facilities, one card that Iran had up its sleeve was the deterrent effect of unleashing Hizbullah on Israel, should it be attacked. This would, at the very least, indirectly involve Syria in supplying weapons to Hizbullah; it would probably also lead to direct Israeli-Syrian military conflict. Syria was a vocal proponent of Iran's nuclear program. Damascus repeated Tehran's mantra that the program was for peaceful purposes, and pointed out the inconsistency in the international anti-Iranian consensus that Israel had a nuclear weapons capacity of several hundred warheads (according to most estimates), yet was not a signatory to international non-proliferation agreements.

When the uprising began in Syria, Iran tended to parrot Syrian government pronouncements that the trouble was due to pernicious external forces and an international conspiracy. Certainly, from the very beginning Tehran believed it was a conscious attempt by the United States, Israel and their allies to weaken the Iranian hand by fomenting a rebellion that might overthrow Iran's closest ally in the Middle East. Ayatollah Ali Khamenei, Iran's supreme leader, stated in June: 'In Syria the hand of America and Israel is evident. Wherever a movement is Islamic, populist, and anti-American, we support it.'[7] Another Iranian official commented: 'Having lost Egypt, the US has targeted Syria.'[8] Finally, Iran's former ambassador to Syria, Ahmad Mousavi, supported the conspiracy theory: 'Current events in Syria are designed by the foreign enemies and mark the second version of the sedition which took place in 2009 in Iran. The enemy is targeting the security and safety of Syria . . . [The protestors] are foreign mercenaries, who get their message from the enemy and the Zionists.'[9] There were credible reports that Iran was providing Syria with substantial assistance, particularly in surveillance technology to monitor email, mobile phones and the Internet, in order to combat the social media roots of the uprising and fight back against cyber warfare conducted by opposition groups.

In addition, it appears that Iran sent elements of its Revolutionary Guards (the elite Quds Force), possibly supported by Hizbullah units, to train Syrian forces in how to quell protests, skills the Iranian government honed when putting down its own popular uprising after what most believed to have been a fraudulent presidential election in 2009. The irony of Iran supporting the Egyptian and Tunisian protestors against pro-Western governments, yet supporting the Syrian government's brutal crackdown was not lost on anyone who cared to notice. However, there was enough of this cynical irony to go around, as the United States, Saudi

Arabia and other Gulf Arab states supported the Syrian protests (and others in the Middle East), yet turned a blind eye to protests in the Gulf Arab state of Bahrain, home to the US Persian Gulf carrier fleet, where an uprising was violently put down by Gulf Cooperation Council forces, supported mainly by Saudi Arabia. So we need to dispense with any thoughts of ideological consistency: as usual, the actors in this play were acting first and foremost in accordance with their perceived national interests.

What is interesting about the Iranian position is not that Tehran strongly supported Syria: that was only to be expected. The surprising thing is that, as the violence in Syria escalated in the summer of 2011 and into the autumn, Tehran – and Hizbullah – seeing the real possibility of a vital ally falling from power, began openly to encourage Bashar al-Assad to implement the necessary reforms in order to stem the tide of protest; they urged the Syrian government to curtail the violence and deal calmly with the opposition. There were also reports that Iranian officials were making contact with opposition forces inside and outside Syria, possibly hedging their bets in the crisis.

It had been seen in Egypt, Tunisia and even Libya that there was no guarantee that the new political landscape would be pro-Western: if anything, the new governments adopted more anti-Western and anti-Israel attitudes than had their predecessors. Tehran therefore figured that, even if Assad should fall, a new Syrian government need not necessarily be anti-Iranian and would not necessarily sever the relationship entirely. In addition, even if the West intervened militarily in Syria to accelerate the fall of Assad, Iran only had to look at Iraq to satisfy itself that Western military intervention did not guarantee a pro-West government in the long term: in the aftermath of the withdrawal of US troops, Iraq certainly has a strained relationship with Washington, and Iran is probably the most influential player in Iraqi politics today. Unfortunately for most Syrians, what began as an indigenous Syrian crisis that begged for a Syrian solution has become bound up with the most important geopolitical fissure and hotly debated topic in the Middle East: Iran.

Lebanon/Hizbullah

For a host of reasons, Lebanon is important to Syria. Under both Hafiz and Bashar al-Assad, it has been imperative that the country should remain within Syria's sphere of influence. First and foremost, from the perspective of Damascus, Lebanon must not fall under the control of an anti-Syrian government or forces. That is why Syria fought hard and did what it could to help push the Israelis back after the Jewish state's invasion of Lebanon in 1982. To Syrian leaders ever since independence, any sort of pro-Western, pro-Israeli and/or anti-Assad government in Beirut would smack of a flanking operation against Syria – a country that is bounded to the north by a (for most of this period) hostile member of NATO, Turkey; to the south by Israel and the pro-Western Jordanian monarchy; and, from 1963 to 2003, by a rival Baath party regime to the east, in Iraq. It was also important to have a friendly government in Beirut, in order to prevent clandestine anti-Syrian activity by Syrian exiles. As the Baath party engaged in a good bit of its own clandestine activities against successive Syrian regimes prior to the Baath coup of 1963, its members were only too aware of how Lebanon could be used by opposition elements.

Prior to the exit of Syrian troops in April 2005, following the Hariri assassination, Lebanon also provided Syria with an alternative labor market, generating approximately $2 billion a year in remittances and employing up to about a million Syrians, thus relieving the pressure on the Syrian economy to provide jobs. For most of the period under the Assads, the banking and finance sector was state controlled, and many Syrians took to keeping their money in the private banks of Lebanon, where market-oriented investments could be made beyond the watchful eye of Damascus.

Hizbullah ('Party of God'), the largest Shiite political party and militia in Lebanon, became that much more important to Syria following the withdrawal of Syrian troops in 2005. By the late 1990s, Hizbullah had easily the strongest military presence in Lebanon. It added to its reputation by directly taking on the Israelis on multiple occasions, first helping in 2000 to drive Israel out of southern Lebanon (which Israel had occupied since the 1982 invasion), and then essentially fighting the Jewish state to an impressive standstill in the 2006 Israeli-Hizbullah war. Indeed, Hizbullah's leader, Hassan Nasrallah, was the most popular figure in the Middle East following the 2006 conflict – and Bashar rode his coattails to increase his own popularity in Syria and the region, as one of the mainstays of the axis of resistance (Iran, Syria, Hizbullah and Hamas) to what was thought to be Israeli and American designs on the region. By the end of 2008, Hizbullah's dominant military position in Lebanon was matched by its political dominance, and by 2011 it had the foremost position in the Lebanese government. Hizbullah's position allowed Syria to maintain its influence in Lebanon (although there seemed to be some question as to who was the more dominant in the relationship, with Syria almost seeming to be the subservient partner). However, Syria's role as the supply route for Hizbullah still provided Damascus with a considerable amount of leverage.

Although a number of traditionally anti-Assad and anti-Syrian groups and individuals in the fissiparous political environment of Lebanon voiced their support for the protestors and against the Syrian government's crackdown, the official government stance, as directed by Hizbullah and its political allies, supported the Assad regime (as did its benefactor, Iran). However, perhaps taking its cue from Tehran, Hassan Nasrallah, while vociferously supportive of Assad, also took time at the end of summer 2011 to recommend that the Syrian government should implement the reforms announced in order to quell the protests. No doubt, like Iran, Hizbullah was hedging its bets in Syria, establishing contacts with opposition elements just in case Assad should fall, since it is vitally important for it to maintain its lifeline to Iran through Syria.

Yemen, Algeria and Iraq

The leaderships in Yemen and Algeria do not necessarily support either the regime of Bashar al-Assad or the government crackdown, but they did not leap on the anti-Assad bandwagon – primarily for reasons of self-preservation. When the Arab League began to take measures against the Assad regime in autumn 2011, Yemen and Algeria either voted against such measures (as Iraq and Lebanon regularly did) or abstained, or else provided only lukewarm support. The reason is simple. The Yemeni president, Ali Abdullah Saleh, was also up against the Arab Spring wall, as his country was one of the first to experience anti-government protests and demonstrations. Saleh also cracked down on demonstrators and tried all the tricks of the trade to stay in power, despite Saudi Arabia's repeated attempts to ease him out and arrange a peaceful transition – a methodology that Saudi Arabia and other Arab League members would try to employ later on in Syria. The Yemeni president did not want any sort of precedent set in the Arab League or the international community toward Syria that might be applied to him and his country. Now that Saleh has finally stepped down, it will be interesting to see where Yemen's new leadership stands on Syria.

Algeria has been similarly tepid in its response to the Arab Spring, not just the situation in Syria. It is a secular state that emerged in the 1960s (not unlike Syria). Its leadership realized that most of the Arab regimes that fell or came under pressure during the Arab Spring were the secular republics, rather than the monarchies. Thus, and considering the fact that Algeria had experienced a bloody civil war in the 1990s between largely secular supporters of the government and Islamist dissidents, the Algerian leaders felt they had to tread very carefully in terms of their positioning on Syria, so as not to incite domestic unrest of their own, but also not to support actions that might be used against them.

With regard to Iraq, the Assad regime did a good job of cultivating important relationships with a wide spectrum of Iraqi political groups following the US-led invasion of 2003. Despite some flare-ups every now and then between Syria and Iraq (primarily over terrorist attacks in Iraq that may have been carried out by groups entering the country from Syria), the relationship between the two countries had improved steadily. Over a million Iraqi refugees who escaped the chaos of post-invasion Iraq moved to Syria for a number of years and were, for the most part, welcomed and integrated into Syrian society. These are contacts that the Syrian government nurtured in a way that perhaps paid dividends when the uprising broke out and Syria became more isolated internationally.

As they share a 400-mile border, Syria and Iraq have also enhanced trade relations in a number of areas over recent years, and an Iraqi oil pipeline that traverses Syria and that had been effectively shut down since 2003 was finally reactivated. Also, as Iran extended its influence with the Shiite-led government in Baghdad (especially as the American presence dissipated), the Iraqi government naturally looked to have at least a cordial relationship with Damascus. Iraqi (and Lebanese) support – or at least not their opposition – has prevented unanimous backing for Arab League measures against Assad, a symbolic victory of sorts. More importantly, it has given Syria trade outlets on its eastern and western borders, and, from a strategic point of view, has meant that it is not surrounded by hostile governments. The leadership in Baghdad, though, does not want to place all its eggs in the Iranian or Syrian basket, and thus it voted for the Arab League-sponsored UN General Assembly resolution in February 2012, which condemned the violence in Syria and called for a political transition, with Assad stepping down. Although Damascus was obviously displeased with this, it was a fairly safe vote for Baghdad, since General Assembly resolutions carry far less weight than UN Security Council resolutions.

Hamas

It is not so easy to place Hamas under the 'Pro-Assad' heading because, for most of 2011, it was noticeably reticent on Assad and the situation in Syria; that would seem to indicate that it did not support the Syrian regime. Also, by early 2012, the Hamas leadership, as articulated in statements by Prime Minster Ismail Haniyya, had clearly adopted a position in support of the protestors and against Assad. On the other hand, Syria has been a strong backer of Hamas, the Palestinian Islamist group that controls the Gaza Strip, since its inception in the late 1980s. Aside from the mainstream Fatah faction (with which it has had a mercurial relationship over the decades), Syria has strongly supported a number of other Palestinian groups, both Islamist and secular: Islamic Jihad, the Popular Front for the Liberation of Palestine (PFLP) and the PFLP-General Command. Over the years, Damascus became the headquarters of these groups (or at least hosted their political offices). From the Syrian perspective under the Assads, support for such groups gave Syria additional leverage against Israel that could be utilized in any negotiations over the return of the Golan Heights. Hafiz al-Assad also supported these groups as an alternative to the longtime PLO chairman, Yasser Arafat (and his Fatah faction), with whom he had frequent tussles for influence and control over the Palestinian movement.

Once the uprising intensified in Syria, Hamas withdrew all its members and their families, although it continued to maintain a political office there. It was in a difficult position: it was grateful to the Syrian regime for its backing over the years, but it is also an organization born of the Muslim Brotherhood, which is Sunni. While Hamas points out that it has no relationship with the Syrian Muslim Brotherhood, Syria is 75 per cent Sunni, and most of those Syrians protesting are Sunni. In addition, most of the Palestinian refugees in Syria and those Palestinians integrated into Syrian society are Sunni, and a number of those have taken to protesting against the regime. Commenting on the problem, one Hamas official stated:

> Hamas has a different position than Hizbullah. We are Sunni, we have the support of the people . . . If we lose the support of Iran and Syria, it will affect us deeply – but it's not a strategic loss. This is different from Hizbullah. If Hizbullah loses the support of Syria it might be the end of Hizbullah. From the first day we declared that we were thankful to the regime – which supported the [Hamas] resistance during some very difficult periods we went through – and at the same time we admire people getting their freedom, reform and prosperity.
>
> Hamas' Khalid Meshaal tried to advise Bashar al-Assad to reform . . . offering to mediate between the regime and its people. He also met Hassan Nasrallah of Hizbullah to ask him to take his plan to Assad. But these mediation attempts failed.[10]

Apparently practicing what they preach, in summer 2011 Hamas officials ordered the suspension of all pro-Assad rallies in the Gaza Strip; it was then reported that Iran had cut off funding to Hamas.[11] Unlike Hizbullah, Hamas seems to have decided to sever its ties with the Assad regime.

There were two interesting events involving Palestinian refugees in Syria, one in May and the other in June 2011; both were likely to have been related to the uprising in Syria. For the annual remembrance of what Palestinians term *al-Nakba* ('the catastrophe') – the creation of the state of Israel on 15 May 1948 – hundreds of Palestinians from refugee camps in and around Damascus were bussed to the demilitarized zone separating Syria from Israel on the Golan Heights. They breached the fences on both sides, actually entering Israeli-held territory. Israeli forces, caught somewhat off guard, opened fire and killed between four and twelve Palestinians (the figure varies depending on the source). Something similar happened on 5 June, the anniversary of the outbreak of the 1967 Arab-Israeli war: on this occasion, at least a dozen Palestinians were killed by (rather better prepared) Israeli forces.

Palestinian demonstrations are common throughout the Arab world on these two dates, particularly 15 May. However, it was unprecedented for Palestinians to be transported (no doubt in Syrian government-supplied vehicles) to the Golan and to breach the defenses. Quite the reverse: the Syrian-Israeli ceasefire line along the Golan, negotiated as part of a US-brokered disengagement agreement after the 1973 Arab-Israeli War and monitored by UN forces, had been assiduously observed. In thirty-seven years, there had been nary a gun fired in either direction. This has been one of the real success stories of UN peacekeeping. Thus, there was strong speculation that the Syrian government had used the Palestinian issue in an attempt to deflect attention from its domestic difficulties, possibly trying to manufacture Arab-Israeli hostility in order to rally the Syrian populace behind the regime. Since one of the main intelligence branches in Syria deals almost exclusively with Palestinian issues, it is impossible that the Syrian government did not know about, and approve of, Palestinian actions in the Golan. It seems to have been a fairly transparent and cynical act on the part of the Syrian government. As of the time of writing, there has been no repeat incident; but it certainly highlights how the instability in Syria could lead to heightened Arab-Israeli tensions, if not conflict.

Russia (and China)

Russia, of course, has had a long-standing and close relationship with Syria, dating back to the superpower Cold War days of the Soviet Union, when Damascus was more often than not allied with, and supported by, Moscow. The relationship had economic, political and military dimensions, and these continued under Bashar al-Assad. That said, over the years Syria's orientation toward the Soviet Union/Russia has been driven more by necessity than choice. Indeed, Hafiz al-Assad only signed a Treaty of Friendship and Cooperation with Moscow in 1980, after the 1979 Egyptian-Israeli peace treaty. Having in this way secured its southern flank against Egypt, the Jewish state could (from the point of view of Damascus), focus its attention northwards, toward Syria and Lebanon. This made Syria feel strategically very vulnerable.

It is not surprising, then, that Russia should have backed Bashar al-Assad when the uprising broke out in March 2011, or that it continued to lend strong support to the Syrian government well into 2013. There are many reasons behind Russia's support for the Assad regime. First, there is a long history of mutually supportive relations; this cannot easily be dismissed or reversed, and there is a degree of institutional inertia keeping the relationship relatively close. There is also bureaucratic momentum in both Moscow and Damascus, with officials in both capitals having a vested interest in maintaining close ties. Next, and at a more practical level, Russia has significant commercial interests in Syria: in 2009, the total investment of Russian companies in Syria's tourism and energy sectors, as well as in infrastructure projects, totaled approximately \$19.4 billion.[12] More importantly, at a time when Russia's defense industry has lost billions of dollars' worth of military contracts with Iran (due to sanctions) and with Libya (due to the overthrow of its regular customer, Muammar al-Gadafi), Syria provides an important outlet for weapons sales: the total amount of sales over the previous decade was about \$1.5 billion, making it Russia's seventh-largest buyer.[13]

Strategically, Syria is important to Russia because the Syrian port city of Tartous is Moscow's last naval base in the Mediterranean, and the facilities were recently upgraded by Russian technicians, indicating Moscow's long-term intention of maintaining access to the port.[14]

Incidentally, China, too, has increased its trade with Syria over the past decade, by 2010 becoming Syria's third-largest importer, according to data from the European Commission.[15] As a Jamestown Foundation report assessed matters in 2010:

> Beijing's renewed interest in Damascus – the traditional node of the ancient Silk Road . . . indicates that China sees Syria as an important trading hub . . . China and Syria gave each other understanding and support on issues concerning each other's core and major interests . . . China showed consistent understanding and firm support for Syria's position on the Golan Heights while Syria remained committed to the one China position and rendered China staunch support on matters related to Taiwan, Tibet, Xinjiang and human rights.[16]

In a diplomatic sense, for Russia, Syria's geo-strategic centrality in the Middle East gives Moscow one of its few remaining areas of ingress into Middle East affairs, providing it with some diplomatic leverage (much of which had been lost following the collapse of the Soviet Union). It has often been said of Russia's leaders over the past twenty years – and certainly of Vladimir Putin, Russia's prime minister or president over the past decade – that they have wanted to regain at least some of the super-power status the country lost. And Syria provides just such an opportunity, especially in an area – the Middle East – that remains strategically important to Moscow.[17]

As part of its desire to regain lost diplomatic status and to carve out a bigger role in international affairs, Russia has, more often than not in recent years, been on opposing sides to the United States and its Western allies in global organizations, such as the United Nations. More specifically, with regard to the situation in Syria, Russian leaders felt duped by the UN Security Council resolution that was passed in May 2011 on Libya. UNSC resolution 1973 established a no-fly zone over Libya and authorized 'all necessary measures' to protect the Libyan civilian population.

The resolution passed by ten votes to zero, with five abstentions (Russia, China, India, Brazil and Germany). The abstention appeared to cause a rift between Russian President Dmitry Medvedev (who supported the abstention) and Prime Minister Putin (who had wanted to veto the resolution).

As the Syrian situation developed, Putin's position became more dominant in Russian policy-making circles and led to a hardening of Moscow's position in support of the Assad regime. Moscow came to believe that what was intended as a protective measure to safeguard civilian lives in Libya was interpreted liberally by the United States, Britain, France and other interested parties, giving carte blanche for NATO military intervention that proved the key to the Libyan rebels' overthrow of Gadafi. Russian leaders do not want to see any repeat of this in Syria, and that is why they have been so sensitive to the specifics of the language in proposed UN resolutions condemning Syria. They – and the Chinese – also do not want to see any UN resolutions that might authorize or lead to military intervention or economic sanctions based on human rights abuses (as has been consistently proposed in the case of Syria). In this regard, Beijing and Moscow do not want to see precedents set that might possibly be used against them in the future.

Moscow also perceives a great deal of hypocrisy and double standards on the part of the West, and especially the United States, regarding human rights abuses and repressive regimes. In the minds of many, while Palestinians suffer under Israeli occupation, the West largely sits and does nothing. Russian leaders point out that, even as Washington was pressuring Syria, the US State Department quietly lifted a ban on military aid to Uzbekistan, which is ruled by a repressive authoritarian regime that killed a number of homegrown protestors a few years ago.[18] But Uzbekistan is important to the United States in terms of supply lines for NATO troops in Afghanistan. As noted above, Washington also stayed largely quiet when the minority Shiite ruling regime in Bahrain violently put down protests in the capital city of Manama, yet at the same time the White House was championing protestors in Tunisia, Libya and Egypt. As one scholar has noted, it is for just this reason that 'Russian policymakers have developed an allergy to Western leaders' moralizing'.[19]

Finally, the Kremlin does not want to see instability in the Middle East that could lead to a region-wide war or a shift in the balance of power that could have deleterious effects on Russia's position in the region (and even in Russia itself). According to Russian scholar Dmitri Trenin:

> The Russian government is openly conservative; it abhors revolutions. This, however, is more than a self-serving ideological stance. When the Kremlin . . . looks at the Arab Awakening, they see democratization leading directly to Islamicization. Revolutions are bad enough, in the Kremlin's view, but attempts to interfere in other countries' civil wars can only make things worse.[20]

The Kremlin also sees the West's attempts to remove Assad more as a way of weakening Iran than of helping the Syrian people rid themselves of a tyrant. If this is the intention – and it is certainly seen as such by Iran and its allies – then it could in itself catapult a domestic crisis into a region-wide conflict. For this reason, too, Moscow has been consistent in supporting a largely Syrian solution to a Syrian problem.

As early as May 2011, Russian President Dmitry Medvedev joined international calls for President Assad to embrace reform; but he stated that his country did not favor sanctions against Syria, as these would only serve to exacerbate the situation and hurt the Syrian people. This was still at a time when most of the international community was hoping Assad would implement real reform, call off the dogs, and allow the growing crisis to safely subside. Even in early August, the Russian foreign ministry's chief of the Middle East department stated that his country was not categorically against the adoption of a UN resolution on Syria, but that it should refrain from sanctions and other forms of pressure: 'if there are some unbalanced items, sanctions, pressure, I think that kind of pressure is bad because we want less bloodshed and more democracy'.[21] As Medvedev's special envoy to the Middle East, Mikhail Margelov, stated in late June 2011: 'Leaders come and go, politicians come and go, but for Russia there remains a single reliable and trusted friend, the Syrian people.'[22]

This apparent equivocation reflected two things: 1) the Russian leadership was hedging its bets and wanted to maintain good relations with all sides of the conflict in both Libya and Syria; and 2) Moscow had made a concerted attempt throughout much of the 2000s to raise its profile in the Middle East, and particularly to improve its relationships with Sunni countries in the region, such as Saudi Arabia, Qatar, Turkey, Jordan and the United Arab Emirates, even entering into a number of economic and military agreements with these states.[23] Openly supporting the Syrian regime jeopardized the progress Russia had made in this regard. Moscow strove to maintain these relationships, and at the same time it continued to back Damascus. At times this meant that Moscow seemed to be talking out of both sides of its mouth. But later on, in August, as the United States and the European Union began to call for Assad to step down, Moscow came to take a more strident stance in opposition to this. A Russian Foreign Ministry official commented at the time: 'We do not support such calls, and we think that President al-Assad should be given time today to implement all of the declared reform processes.'[24] This general position would come to characterize Russian policy to this day as will be detailed in the following chapters.

Anti-Assad

Turkey

Syrian-Turkish relations have shifted dramatically over the years – and they again shifted dramatically during the uprising in Syria. The relationship between Damascus and Ankara had been antagonistic for many years before Bashar al-Assad came to power. A number of issues separated the two countries: water-sharing; the Hatay/Alexandretta territorial dispute; Syrian support for Kurdish separatist groups in Turkey (mostly the Kurdish Workers' Party, the PKK); Turkish membership of NATO while Syria was a client-state of the Soviet Union; strong Turkish-Israeli ties that began to develop in the 1980s; and historical antagonisms going back to the days when what is today Syria was part of the Ottoman Empire. The animosity started to dissipate in the last years of Hafiz al-Assad, when, in response to Turkish threats to intervene militarily in Syria if Damascus did not stop supporting the PKK, the Syrian president decided that discretion was the better part of valor: he did indeed end Syrian support for the PKK, and turned its leader, Abdullah Ocalan, over to the Turks. Following this, economic ties improved; there were agreements on the sharing of power generation grids, as well as productive talks on water-sharing of the river Euphrates, which flows from Turkey downstream into Syria.

Under Bashar al-Assad, Syrian-Turkish relations improved tremendously, especially after the Islamist-oriented Justice and Development party, led by Prime Minister Recep Tayyip Erdogan, came to power in Ankara in 2003. The development of this relationship was, in my opinion, Assad's signal foreign policy accomplishment during the first decade of his rule, and the Syrian and Turkish leaders even appeared to become good personal friends. For Turkey, developing a good relationship with Syria was part and parcel of its 'zero problems' (with its neighbors) policy, which also allowed Ankara a prime area of economic and diplomatic ingress into the heartland of the Middle East. The developing relationship had obvious economic benefits for both countries, especially in the tourism sector and in cross-border trade. In 2010 this trade amounted to $2.5 billion: between 2009 and 2010 Turkish exports to Syria increased by 30 per cent (to $1.8 billion) and Syrian exports to Turkey doubled to $662 million.[25] For Syria, it was vital to make up for some of what was lost economically by the diminished Syrian presence in Lebanon following the troop withdrawal of 2005. More importantly for Assad, it gave Damascus an important diplomatic outlet in the wake of the US-led attempt to completely isolate Syria after the Hariri assassination. This opportunity arose with a leader, Erdogan, who had become one of the most popular statesmen in the Middle East and the Islamic world, and with a country, Turkey, that had rather distanced itself from the West and the United States in the wake of Ankara's refusal to allow the US-led coalition to use Turkish territory as a transit area for troops in the 2003 invasion of Iraq, that had downgraded its relationship with Israel and expressed fervent support for the Palestinians, and that had improved its ties with Iran and with other emerging powers that did not march to the same tune as Washington.[26] It was a foreign policy triumph for Bashar.

But the Syrian uprising – and more to the point, the brutal crackdown by the Syrian government – led to a breach in the relationship. By autumn 2011, Bashar's erstwhile friend in Ankara was calling for the Syrian president to step down. The tone became quite hostile as the violence increased and as more Syrian refugees flooded into Turkey. Perhaps more than any other leader, Erdogan was hoping that Assad could right the Syrian ship of state quickly, and could peacefully subdue the protests, so that an important relationship – one that he had personally cultivated – would continue, along with all the economic and strategic benefits. He also did not want to be placed in the difficult position of having to choose whether to stick with Bashar or to cut the ties with him (though soon enough he found himself in that very position). As early as April 2011, Turkish officials, including Erdogan, were promising to push Assad to implement reforms; and by May, the Turkish prime minister was warning the Syrian government to stop the violence and not replicate what had happened at Hama in 1982.

In June 2011, following the Syrian seizure of Jisr al-Shughur (near the Turkish border) from opposition forces, Erdogan called the behavior of Maher al-Assad (who is believed to have commanded the Syrian forces there) 'brutish and inhuman'. This angered Syrian officials, who were obviously accustomed to unabashed Turkish support.[27] Erdogan went on to issue a statement condemning the violence, and he indicated that he would support a UN resolution against Syria. Also in June, following his party's victory in parliamentary elections, Erdogan stated in a speech that Turkey would 'become much more active in regional and global affairs . . . We will call, as we have, for rights in our region, for justice, for the rule of law, for freedom and democracy.'[28] This may have been the moment when Erdogan began to emphasize a pro-democracy foreign policy rather than the 'zero problems' one.[29] It was reported in July that the Turkish government had delivered a sternly worded letter to Assad, imploring him to implement reforms and to fire strongman Maher al-Assad.[30] This is exactly the type of thing that would infuriate the Syrian leadership, including Bashar. They do not like to be told what to do – or even to have something strongly suggested. There is an almost convulsive reaction to this, especially as they see themselves and their country as a leading light in the region, not the stepsister of a more powerful neighbor (even though Damascus was clearly the junior partner in the relationship).

On 1 August, Turkish President Abdullah Gul called on the Syrian government to stop the violence and to institute reforms, saying that the use of heavy weapons against civilians (at that time in Hama) had given him a 'deep shock'. On 7 August, Erdogan stated that his 'patience is running out' with the Syrian regime, and said the Syrian situation was also a Turkish domestic issue, on account of the 530-mile shared border.[31] Turkish Foreign Minister Ahmet Davutoglu had six hours of meetings with Syrian officials on 9 August (including a two-hour meeting with Assad), during which he strongly urged Damascus to take concrete steps to end the violence. In response, the Syrian president stated (through the SANA news agency) that his forces would not 'relent in pursuing terrorist groups in order to protect the stability of the country and the security of the citizens. But [Syria] is also determined to continue reforms . . . and is open to any help offered by friendly and brotherly states.'[32] On 15 August, Davutoglu demanded that the Syrian government's violent crackdown end 'immediately and without conditions or excuses . . . or there would be nothing more to discuss about steps that would be taken'. A couple of days later, he said

> the bloodshed has to stop . . . the military operations have to stop. If the operations continue in Syria and . . . become a regional problem, Turkey can naturally not remain indifferent. We do not want foreign intervention in Syria but we do not accept and will not accept any operations against civilians.

He closed by saying that he had told Assad this was Turkey's 'final word' on the situation.[33]

On 28 August, President Gul went even further: 'We have reached a point where anything would be too little, too late. We have lost our confidence. There is no place for totalitarian regimes and one party governments. Clearly, the leaders of these countries will take the initiative or they will be changed by force.'[34] By late September, Erdogan had taken sides against Assad. The Turkish leader, who had become so popular in the Middle East and had come to back the protestors and rebels in Tunisia, Egypt and Libya, obviously concluded that he could not jeopardize his or his country's standing in the region – one that he had so assiduously built up over the years – by sticking with Assad any longer or even by hoping that the Syrian leader would at last see the light. Too much blood had been spilled in Syria, and the strong general consensus in the region by that time was that Assad would have to go. As Mark Haas writes,

> The key reason for this shift was the realization that non-ideological foreign policies were hurting Turkey's interests by squandering its large reserve of soft power throughout the Islamic world. Turkey is extremely popular because of its commitment to democracy and Islamic identity. Not supporting popular protests . . . would have been a major blow to this popularity by demonstrating Turkey's hypocrisy and selfishness.[35]

Erdogan met President Obama on 20 September on the sidelines of the UN General Assembly meeting in New York, and the two leaders agreed that both countries would have to 'increase pressure' on the Syrian regime.[36] In the following days, Erdogan announced that Ankara had cut all relations and contacts with Syria and was considering sanctions. He also announced that Turkey would be enforcing an arms embargo on Syria and would intercept any weapons deliveries to Syria by ship. Not surprisingly, Iran started to become much more critical of Turkey, even to the extent of blaming Erdogan for the unrest in Syria and promising 'consequences' if he did not mend his ways.[37] The so-called emerging Turkish-Iranian 'axis' was short-lived indeed.[38]

From autumn 2011 onward, Turkey would continue to take active steps, short of military intervention, to topple Bashar al-Assad. Among other things it continued to organize diplomatic pressure, played host to Syrian opposition groups and allowed safe havens and operation zones for the armed Syrian resistance known as the Free Syria Army. The relationship had come full circle.

Saudi Arabia/Qatar

As with the other countries on the anti-Assad list, Saudi Arabia began with a cautious approach toward the uprising in Syria, hoping that the Syrian president would enact the necessary reforms to stem the unrest, and at the same time (perhaps prudently) waiting to see how things developed. It would be difficult for the Saudi leadership to come out openly in support of the protestors when it was carefully watching for any signs of protest in its own less-than-democratic country. In fact, at this time it was pouring billions of dollars into social services and other benefits for the Saudi population, in what many described as a 'national bribe'. Riyadh had also forcefully backed its ally in Bahrain – a Sunni monarchy ruling over a majority Shiite state – in violently stamping out protests in Manama. Furthermore, the Saudis were interested in maintaining stability in the Middle East – especially given what had already happened in the Arab Spring with their friends in Tunis, Cairo and the Yemeni capital Sanaa – partly in order to prevent the Iranians from gaining any advantage by fishing in troubled waters.

Saudi-Syrian relations had deteriorated dramatically following the 2005 assassination of Rafiq Hariri, to whom the Saudi monarchy was close. The animosity was palpable, with insults flying back and forth between Damascus and Riyadh, and a sort of cold war between Saudi Arabia (along with its allies in Lebanon) and Syria (along with its allies in Lebanon, plus Iran). Syria also accused the Saudis of financially backing anti-Assad *salafists* in Syria itself and in Lebanon.

By 2008, however, the relationship had begun to improve markedly, highlighted by a Qatari-brokered power-sharing deal on Lebanon, negotiated directly with the Syrians (the so-called Doha Agreement). Assad and Saudi King Abdullah paid visits to each other's countries and seemed to agree to disagree on certain items; ultimately they believed that working to prevent Lebanon's disintegration into sectarian chaos was in everyone's best interests.

However, as the violence became more pronounced in Syria, the Saudis (like the Turks) found it increasingly awkward to maintain a cordial relationship with Damascus and to remain silent on the subject of the rising death toll. The Saudis would adopt a more behind-the-scenes role, with the Qataris more out front; but when it became clear to Riyadh that Assad was probably not going to last, King Abdullah was compelled to take a stand against Damascus. Once it appeared that Assad was on his last legs, the Saudis (and others) began to focus on the potential benefits, primarily reduced Iranian influence in the Middle East. In early August, the Saudi-dominated Gulf Cooperation Council released a joint statement condemning the violence in Syria and the excessive use of force by Syrian troops. On 8 August, King Abdullah became the first Arab head of state openly to condemn the Syrian government's actions, when he warned Assad that Syria 'will be pulled down into the depths of turmoil and loss' if it did not enact serious reform. He called on Assad personally to stop the 'killing machine'. Saudi Arabia, along with Kuwait and Bahrain, then recalled its ambassador from Damascus.[39]

Qatar's role in all of this – and that of its charismatic emir, Shaykh Hamad bin Khalifa al-Thani – is very interesting. As with the Turks and the Saudis, the Qatari-Syrian relationship had been quite cordial and productive in Middle East diplomatic circles in the years prior to the Arab Spring, and Doha had invested heavily in the Syrian economy. Indeed, it was quite frequently mentioned that, with the diminishing diplomatic clout of the United States in the wake of the Iraqi quagmire, the Qataris (and the Turks) had largely taken up the diplomatic slack in the region. And with the influential pan-Arab satellite news channel Al-Jazeera located in Doha, Qatar's soft power in the Middle East had become a force to be reckoned with: cross the Qataris and you did so at your peril, because all of a sudden you might find yourself on the sharp end of Al-Jazeera reports and broadcasts (despite the Qatari government's claims not to pressure Al-Jazeera to slant stories in the direction of Qatari policy). Nevertheless, the Syrian government expelled all Al-Jazeera personnel from Syria fairly early on in the uprising, accusing the news channel of biased reporting. Since Qatar hosts a huge US air base, the Syrian government was quick to call the Qataris lackeys of American and Israeli interests.[40]

From early on, Doha adopted a very active and public role in the Arab Spring. It played a direct role in supporting the Libyan rebels fighting to overthrow Muammar Gadafi, and in financing, arming and training the Libyan opposition. Doha particularly supported Islamist groups among the opposition elements in Tunisia, Egypt, Libya and elsewhere. This got to the point where concern was expressed by many in the West and the Middle East that the Qataris were (wittingly or unwittingly) facilitating the rise of radical Sunni Islam, in line with Wahhabism, Qatar's Saudi-inspired brand of hardline Sunni Islam. Others claim that Qatar is most interested in expanding its influence, and has simply recognized the growth in power of Islamist groups in the wake of the Arab Spring. As one scholar noted, 'Qatar is a country without ideology. They know that the Islamists are the new power in the Arab world. This alliance will lay the foundation for a base of influence across the region.'[41]

It is difficult to pinpoint when and why Qatari-Syrian relations took a nosedive. There were problems evident even before the Arab Spring, mostly over the issue of Iran, as Shaykh Hamad began to assume a prominent anti-Iranian role in the Arab world. There was also some disillusionment over Assad as the Syrian crackdown intensified, and perhaps anger – à la the Turks – that Damascus was not listening to the advice of Qatar. In addition, like Saudi Arabia and Hamas, Qatar could not continue to support a regime that was seen to be killing innocent protestors, most of whom were Sunni Muslims. As with everyone on the anti-Assad side of the ledger, as the violence escalated in Syria and it became clear that Assad had to go, Doha (which perhaps realized the score earlier than most) began to assume even more of a leading role in the diplomatic charge against Damascus, particularly within the Arab League; indeed, on 17 July – earlier than any other Arab state – Doha recalled its ambassador to Syria and closed its embassy in Damascus.

The Syrian government clearly perceives Saudi Arabia and Qatar to be behind the increasing regional pressure on Damascus. A high-level Syrian official I met in Europe in December 2011 responded thus when I asked what he would like to say to President Obama or Secretary of State Hillary Clinton: 'Get the Saudis and Qataris off our backs!'

Israel

The Israeli government of Prime Minister Binyamin Netanyahu remained largely silent regarding the situation in Syria – as it did on other manifestations of the Arab Spring. There were primarily two reasons for this: 1) anything the government might officially say could be used in turbulent Arab countries in a way that ran counter to Israeli interests; and 2) before responding in any sort of definitive fashion, Israel was waiting to see how things shook out from the regional changes in the Middle East.

With the onset of the Syrian uprising, a debate ensued among Israeli officials regarding the best outcome – in the full knowledge that they could not (and would not) do much to affect that outcome. There were those who believed it was better to have the 'devil you know' in Damascus, rather than an unknown quantity or, worse yet, instability and civil war on Israel's border that could morph into an Arab-Israeli conflict. If chaos did result in Syria, Israelis were worried about what might happen to Syria's large Scud missile arsenal, its advanced surface-to-air systems and its chemical weapons. Despite Bashar al-Assad's occasional virulently anti-Israeli rhetoric, he had been quite measured in his response to such Israeli actions as the 2007 bombing of a suspected nuclear reactor in Syria or the 2008 assassination in downtown Damascus of the notorious Hizbullah terrorist mastermind Imad Mugniyeh (though his assailants were unknown, most people suspected them of being Israeli). Syria under Bashar al-Assad had also engaged in direct peace negotiations with the Israelis (brokered by Turkey) in 2008, and, according to most reports, had come fairly close to an agreement. In other words, Bashar maintained Syria's strategic choice of peace with Israel, which had been established by his father during the 1990s Madrid peace process. Assad was predictable in a Middle East that was becoming increasingly unpredictable. And besides, even if Assad fell, the next government in Syria – secular or

Islamist – could well be more virulently anti-Israeli and more unpredictable (just look at what had happened in Egypt after the fall of Mubarak!), and could not be relied upon to sever Syria's ties to Hizbullah, Hamas and Iran.

On the other hand, there were those who, from the outset, saw Assad's fall as a net gain for Israel, in that it would automatically hurt Iran, Hizbullah and Hamas. Even if Assad was not removed in the short term, his power base would be severely weakened, and a weak Syria must be good for Israel. Indeed, perhaps this would be the best outcome of all for the Israelis. Either Assad would not come to the table to bargain over the Golan Heights from such a position of weakness (which was just fine with a very right-of-center governing coalition in Israel), or he might do so out of desperation (but with such a weak hand that Israel could dictate the terms of any agreement). Regardless, the deleterious effects on Hizbullah and Iran were the primary considerations.

What is interesting is that, even though Assad and other Syrian officials were constantly stoking the idea that the uprising was an Israeli conspiracy, Israel was the country in the region that at first remained quietest and actually counseled restraint against precipitate action toward the Syrian regime. The Israelis were mostly concerned at the time that Assad might initiate hostilities with Israel directly, or through Hizbullah, in order to deflect attention from his domestic problems – a concern that was made manifest with the Palestinians breaching the borders on the Golan in May and June (see above). But again, as with leaders in other countries, Israeli officials became more critical of Assad as the violence increased, particularly as most of the Arab world and the international community had also lined up against him – and perhaps as the Syrian situation became more of a proxy for sentiments vis-à-vis Iran and as discussion in Israel shifted toward the question of whether or not to attack Iran. At a press conference on 26 July, Israeli President Shimon Peres called on Assad to step down. By late autumn 2011, it was being leaked to the Israeli press that Minister of Defense Ehud Barak and other Israeli military and civilian officials were predicting that Assad would not be able to stay in power for long. It was almost as if there was an office sweepstake on the exact date Assad would fall.

The United States (and the European Union)

As noted in earlier chapters, US-Syrian relations had been antagonistic for most of Bashar al-Assad's tenure in power. The relationship had, it is true, grown less tense in the last year of the Bush administration, but clearly the accession to power of President Barack Obama heralded a distinct opportunity to improve matters. The Obama administration pursued a high-level dialogue with Syria, as it generally engaged in a foreign policy based on diplomacy rather than military action. The possibility of an understanding with Iran was even part of the new equation. Obama gave a landmark speech in Cairo in June 2009 that portended a better relationship between the United States and the Muslim world. Soon thereafter, it was announced that the United States would return its ambassador to Damascus (a vacant posting since the Hariri assassination in 2005). Robert Ford, an experienced Middle East diplomat, was nominated for the post in early 2010, but Republican opposition in the Senate meant that he could only finally take up his posting in December 2010 (with President Obama making a 'recess appointment').

The Syrian regime did not help the Obama administration all that much. With its usual bet-hedging foreign policy, it continued to play both sides of the fence, giving the naysayers in Washington ample opportunity to voice their opposition to any improved relationship. But the failure to confirm Ford in 2010 indicated that there were also domestic obstacles in Washington, particularly a partisan Congress, in which most Republicans rejected Obama's 'softer' foreign policy approach. They – and a number of Democrats – continued to oppose raising the level of contact between Washington and Damascus by returning the ambassador. To them, Syria was still a state sponsor of terrorism, led by a dictator. That is why Ford's confirmation was held up by the Senate. In addition, there was a web of sanctions and UN resolutions on Syria that complicated any attempt to establish a serious dialogue. The anti-Syrian inertia in Washington left over from the Bush years was quite palpable.

Still, there was hope in the Obama administration regarding Syria, and particularly its president. Thus, in common with just about every other interested party, the initial US response to the uprising in Syria was muted and cautious. There seemed to be an expectation – in retrospect, perhaps a case of wishful thinking – that Bashar al-Assad would 'do the right thing' and engage in serious reform that would stave off the protests. Like just about everyone else, the United States at first did not want to see the unrest lead to the collapse of central authority. The Arab Spring in Tunisia, Egypt, Libya, Bahrain and Yemen had been relatively well contained within the borders of each country, but there was every reason to believe that an Arab Spring in Syria would not be. The European Union states generally agreed with this assessment and approach, and basically followed Washington's lead.

On 25 March, the Obama administration issued a strongly-worded statement condemning Syria's 'brutal repression' of the demonstrations, while the State Department urged Damascus to match its words regarding reform with deeds, and to hold accountable those engaged in the violent crackdown. White House spokesman Jay Carney said the United States had called on the Syrian government to 'exercise restraint and respect the rights of the people'.[42] There seemed to be a concerted effort to pressure the Syrian government, but to refrain from openly criticizing Bashar. The administration also drew a clear distinction between the situation in Syria and that in Libya: Washington obviously did not want to give any indication that military action was being considered against Syria, at the same time as it was withdrawing troops from Iraq and was engaged in supporting NATO in its backing of the Libyan rebels.

From the US perspective, a lot was going on all over the Middle East, and the Obama administration was scrambling to react to the rapid sequence of events over the previous few months. The last thing it wanted to see was anything that might cause Syria to implode. Therefore, on 27 March Secretary of State Clinton stated that the United States would not get involved in the internal conflict in Syria, as it had done in Libya. Clinton pointed out that, in the Libyan case, there had been international condemnation, an Arab League call to action, and a UN Security Council resolution, whereas these things are 'not going to happen' with regard to Syria, in part because members of Congress from both parties saw Assad as 'a reformer'.[43] She went on:

> What's been happening there the last few weeks is deeply concerning, but there's a difference between calling out aircraft and indiscriminately strafing and bombing your own cities [in Libya] than police actions which, frankly, have exceeded the use of force that any of us would want to see [in Syria] . . . Each of these situations [across the region] is unique.[44]

By late April, the US response had begun to harden. In a statement released on 23 April that condemned the use of force against anti-government demonstrators, Obama said that the Syrian regime's 'outrageous' use of violence must 'end now'. He accused Assad of choosing the 'path of repression' and of 'seeking Iranian assistance in repressing Syria's citizens through the same brutal tactics that have been used by his Iranian allies'. For the first time he indicated that his administration was considering possible sanctions against Damascus.[45]

On 29 April, a new set of US and EU sanctions against Syria was announced. Obama signed Executive Order 13572, which imposed sanctions on Syrian officials and government-related entities responsible for human rights abuses and violence against civilians. The sanctions consisted of asset freezes, travel bans and restrictions on doing business with anyone on a list that included Maher al-Assad, Atif Najib (former head of the Political Security Directorate for Deraa) and Ali Mamluk (head of the General Intelligence Directorate), as well as the Iranian Quds Force of the Revolutionary Guard, which was suspected of lending assistance in the Syrian crackdown. The sanctions also revoked several licenses that the US government had granted for the export of equipment to Syria, particularly aircraft and aircraft parts, so desperately needed by the regime (a restriction that had been removed from the Syrian Accountability Act early in the Obama administration). Commenting on the sanctions, a US official said that no member of the Syrian leadership was 'immune' from being held accountable, and that 'Bashar is very much on our radar and if this continues could be soon to follow'.[46] A few days earlier, the State Department had issued a travel warning, advising US citizens in Syria to depart immediately while commercial transportation was still available.

On 9 May, Bouthaina Shaaban, while claiming that the government had the upper hand against the protests, also described the increasingly harsh US rhetoric and sanctions as 'not too bad' and manageable: 'this is a weapon used against us many times. Once security is back, everything can be arranged. We're not going to live in this crisis forever.'[47]

Though she stopped short of calling on Assad to step down (as many were pressing the Obama administration to do, and as it had done earlier with Egyptian President Husni Mubarak), on 13 May Hillary Clinton commented: 'Syria's future will only be secured by a government that reflects the popular will of all the people and protects their welfare.'[48]

On 18 May, as the violence continued in Syria, with an estimated 700 protestors dead, the Obama administration took the further step of adding President Assad to the list of those sanctioned for human rights abuses, along with Syria's vice president (Farouk al-Sharaa), prime minister, minister of defense, interior minister, head of military intelligence and director of the political security branch. The sanctions were announced by the Treasury Department, which froze any of the Syrian officials' assets held in the United States or in any US jurisdiction and barred companies and individuals from dealing with them. The sanctions were largely symbolic, and the importance of Assad's inclusion on the list lay not so much in what could actually be done against him as in what further measures might be taken. As an administration official noted,

> the actions ... send an unequivocal message to President Assad, the Syrian leadership, and regime insiders that they will be held accountable for the ongoing violence and repression in Syria. President Assad and his regime must immediately end the use of violence, answer the calls of the Syrian people for a more representative government, and embark upon the path of meaningful democratic reform.[49]

The EU followed suit, sanctioning individuals and government organizations in April and May, and imposing sanctions on Bashar al-Assad himself on 23 May. Again, no one was yet calling on Bashar to step down: the hope was that the pressure would convince him to implement reform and return the troops to their barracks. It was also hoped – in retrospect a rather futile hope – that perhaps the growing sanctions against the regime might produce fissures in the ruling circle that would compel it to make the necessary concessions, and possibly even to get rid of some of the more unsavory figures, such as Maher al-Assad.

Clinton stated on 1 June: 'President Assad has a choice, and every day that goes by, the choice is made by default. He has not called an end to the violence against his own people, and he has not engaged seriously in any kind of reform efforts.'[50] The pressure on Assad was certainly growing, but the United States was leaving open a crack for him. Administration officials were constantly reiterating on radio and television that every situation in the Middle East was different and had to be treated independently of each other. By now, though, there was a rising chorus of congressmen and pundits in Washington pressing the Obama administration to close that crack, pointing out the inconsistencies of the administration's actions during the Arab Spring. Emblematic of this growing frustration was a poignant comment by Robert Fisk in Beirut:

> And it is true, Obama's failure to support the Arab revolutions until they were all but over lost the US most of its surviving credit in the region. Obama was silent on the overthrow of Ben Ali, only joined in the chorus of contempt for Mubarak two days before his flight, condemned the Syrian regime – which has killed more of its people than any other dynasty in this Arab 'spring', save for the frightful Gaddafi – but makes it clear that he would be happy to see Assad survive, waves his puny fist at puny Bahrain's cruelty and remains absolutely, stunningly silent over Saudi Arabia. And he goes on his knees before Israel. Is it any wonder, then, that Arabs are turning their backs on America, not out of fury or anger, nor with threats or violence, but with contempt? It is the Arabs and their fellow Muslims of the Middle East who are themselves now making the decisions.[51]

As the death toll in Syria reached 2,000 by the end of July, according to UN human rights organizations, relations between Syria and the United States continued to deteriorate. The Syrian government claimed that over 500 of its military and security personnel had been killed by 'armed gangs'. On 8 July, the US ambassador to Syria, Robert Ford, and his French counterpart, Eric Chevallier, visited the city of Hama, a city that had been besieged by Syrian forces. The ambassadors met opposition leaders and generally observed at first hand the peaceful protests. Ford's actions were universally praised in the United States and elsewhere in the West as a courageous act that drew attention to the plight of the protestors, and in so doing helped prevent what some had been predicting: another massacre like the one in Hama in 1982. As the State Department said, it also placed the United States (and France) clearly on the side of those fighting for democracy.

The Syrian government was furious, and the foreign ministry summoned both ambassadors to accuse them of meddling in internal Syrian affairs. There may also have been a domestic political angle to it all: Congress had been increasingly critical of US policy on Syria and had called for the withdrawal of the US ambassador. Many of these members of Congress were those who had refused to confirm Ford in 2010. The administration argument for keeping Ford in Damascus was that he could stay in contact with the opposition, maintain pressure on the regime and maybe even help pry away important pillars of the regime with on-the-ground contact. The positive press that Ford received worldwide significantly reduced the Congressional pressure on him. In any event, Ford would finally be confirmed by the Senate – unanimously – in October 2011.

At the same time, the State Department summoned the Syrian ambassador to the United States, Imad Moustapha, 'to express a number of our concerns with the reported actions of certain Syrian embassy staff in the United States'.[52] Apparently, according to US officials, Syrian embassy personnel were conducting surveillance on Syrian expatriates participating in peaceful anti-Assad demonstrations in the United States. The fear was that their family members might then be in danger back in Syria – or at the very least be threatened. There were also reports of shops owned by vocally anti-Assad Syrian expatriates being vandalized; the suspicion was that the perpetrators were pro-Assad Syrian expats.

Shortly after Ford's visit to Hama, hundreds of pro-regime Syrian demonstrators marched, for several days in a row, on the US and French embassies in Damascus. The demonstrators scaled the walls of the US embassy and inflicted considerable damage, although no embassy personnel were injured. Another group of Syrians marched on the US ambassador's residence in Damascus, about two blocks away from the embassy. There, too, they scaled the walls, broke windows with rocks and used spray paint. Again, no one was injured. This is typical behavior by the Syrian government when it wants to send a message – or in this case a warning. Usually the demonstrators are government employees and include a number of plain-clothed security forces, who are directed, or sometimes even bussed, to the target site.

Secretary of State Clinton responded forcefully on 11 July, coming as close as the Obama administration had come to calling on Assad to step down. While lashing out at the Syrian authorities for not properly protecting the embassies in Damascus, she said she believed that Assad had 'lost legitimacy. He has failed to deliver on the promises he has made'. Addressing critics of the administration's foreign policy on Syria, who were eager to point to the more active US stance applied over Libya, she went on:

> If anyone, including President Assad, thinks that the United States is secretly hoping that the regime will emerge from this turmoil to continue its brutality and repression, they are wrong. President Assad is not indispensable and we have absolutely nothing invested in him remaining in power.[53]

President Obama reinforced this harder US line by telling CBS *Evening News* later on 11 July: 'You're seeing President Assad lose legitimacy in the eyes of his people. He has missed opportunity after opportunity to present a genuine reform agenda. And that's why we've been working at an international level to make sure we keep the pressure up.'[54] One senior administration official followed up the president's comments, saying that since Assad 'has shown definitively he has no interest in reform, the rationale for holding on to him has evaporated'.

The Syrian government, through Syria's state news agency SANA, denounced Clinton's remarks:

> Syria strongly condemns the statements of the American foreign minister . . . these remarks are provocative and aimed at continuing the internal tension. These statements are another proof of US's flagrant intervention in Syria's internal affairs. The legitimacy of Syria's leadership is not based on the United States or others, it stems from the will of the Syrian people.[55]

This is precisely why the Obama administration had up to now been so careful in its rhetoric regarding Assad: it did not want to play to the narrative being promoted by the Syrian government that the unrest was due to foreign interference. The Syrian government's attempt to tie Clinton's remarks into this narrative was therefore to be expected; however, by that stage, with the rising death toll and the actions against the US embassy, administration officials no longer held out any real hope for Assad. To all intents and purposes, they had turned the page.[56]

But because of limited US leverage and limited military options vis-à-vis Syria, the administration had to be careful not to paint itself into a corner, and so a delicate balance had to be struck between the rhetoric and the ability to match that rhetoric with action. This calibration was coming under increasing criticism again from Congress. In late July, at a meeting of the House Foreign Affairs subcommittee to consider the Syrian situation, State Department officials came under tough questioning from both Republican and Democratic members of Congress. Steve Chabot (Republican, Ohio) queried: 'How many must die before we have the courage to stand up and say that Assad is illegitimate and he must go?' On the other side of the aisle, Gary Ackerman (Democratic, New York) accused the administration of delaying calling on Assad to leave until it was clear he actually would: 'We're hedging our bets here on the odd chance that he's going to be able to hang on.' Of course, these differences in Washington were something of which the Syrian government was fully aware. Political commentators such as Elliot Abrams, Danielle

Pletka and Max Boot were heavily critical of the Obama administration, strongly urging a more forceful and forward-looking foreign policy against Assad.

On the other hand, there were those who praised the Obama administration's cautiousness – particularly as it followed an administration that had perhaps been too quick to engage in military action, and that had inaugurated a decade of 'massive foreign commitments and interventions, which proved enormously expensive in blood and treasure – and highly unpopular around the world'.[57] The foreign policy model Obama has attempted to emulate, according to Fareed Zakaria, was that of George H.W. Bush (not George W.), a president 'known as a foreign policy realist, whose watchwords were prudence, cost-effectiveness, diplomacy and restraint'.[58] The Obama doctrine was multilateral in nature and was one that sought to restore a balance between interests and capacity. As such, the administration actively backed the NATO action in support of Libyan anti-Gadafi rebels, but it allowed its European and Arab League allies to take the lead, absorb more of the risk, and foot more of the bill. It is no surprise, then, that the United States was being cautious over Syria, taking care not to contribute to a situation that would necessitate military involvement at a time of domestic economic difficulties, when it had just withdrawn its forces from Iraq and was in the process of drawing down in Afghanistan. The Libyan episode, especially following Gadafi's fall, loomed large over the situation in Syria; many wanted to replicate it, without realizing how different the situations were on the ground and in the international arena of diplomacy. As Blake Hounshell prudently noted in early August 2011:

> Thus far, the Obama administration has been rightly cautious. For one thing, it's not up to the United States whether al-Assad stays or goes – that's a choice only the Syrian people can make. And with no way to know whether a majority supports regime change, it would hardly be wise to declare al-Assad illegitimate and denounce dialogue with the government as folly without a critical mass of Syrians making it clear they felt the same. Second, the Syrian opposition is a bit of a mess right

> now. Years of repression inside the country and fragmentation outside of it has (understandably) made it hard for a motley crew of activists, professionals and ideologues from all over the world to band together around a common agenda. The State Department has been urging the opposition to choose official representatives and start laying out a serious agenda for a democratic transition so that the silent majority of Syrian who have sat out the protests begin to see it a viable alternative to al-Assad, but these things take time.[59]

Adopting a multilateral approach, the Obama administration needed the support of the European Union – and preferably that of the United Nations and the Arab League as well – to build up pressure effectively on the Assad regime. The hope was that either the combined pressure would convince Assad to genuinely reform (although this was considered extremely unlikely by this time), or that his supporters would see the writing on the wall and would peel away from supporting the regime, thus undermining Assad's support base and compelling him to step down. The EU had, throughout the summer, issued a series of escalating sanctions against Syria. In many ways, these followed the US example, although the EU had some catching-up to do, since American sanctions against the Syrian government and certain individuals in Syria (such as Rami Makhlouf) had been in place even prior to the uprising. European Union economic sanctions actually have more impact on Syria, since the EU countries interacted with Syria at the economic level much more than the United States did; indeed, a quarter of Syria's trade was with the EU.

What would really put pressure on Syria would be an EU oil embargo, as Germany, Italy, France and the Netherlands were the top consumers of Syrian oil. The EU formally announced the adoption on 2 September of Council Implementing Resolution 878/2011 to ban the importation of Syrian oil and all petroleum products. An already depressed Syrian economy was almost instantly debilitated that much more, and the Syrian government scrambled fast and hard to find new buyers – a difficult task, to say the least, as Syrian oil is very heavy and requires a specific type of refinery to process it into petrol and other petroleum-based products. Iran, of course, would pick up the slack with financial aid, but the long-standing desire of some Syrian officials to look east (to Iran, Russia, India and China) for markets (rather than west) was becoming a necessity now.

On 1 August, the Muslim world entered the holy month of Ramadan, when unrest traditionally escalates. Sure enough, the carnage in Syria increased: it was now on a daily basis rather than just on Fridays. With it – alongside all the potent images of death and destruction captured on mobile phone cameras and broadcast on television and the Internet – pressure grew on the Obama administration to cut ties completely with Assad, once and for all. The first day of the holy month was a particularly brutal one in Hama: as many as 120 people were killed. In a statement released by the White House, Obama said:

> I am appalled by the Syrian government's use of violence and brutality against its own people. Through his own actions, Bashar al-Assad is ensuring that he and his regime will be left in the past, and that the courageous Syrian people who have demonstrated in the streets will determine its future.

The US president went on to say that the United States would work 'with others around the world' in the coming days to 'isolate the Assad government and stand with the Syrian people'.[60] On 4 August, White House spokesman Jay Carney commented: 'Assad is on his way out . . . We all need to be thinking about the day after Assad, because Syria's 23 million citizens already are.'[61]

At long last, on 18 August, President Obama officially called on Assad to go:

> The future of Syria must be determined by its people, but President Bashar al-Assad is standing in their way. We have consistently said that President Assad must lead a democratic transition or get out of the way. He has not led. For the sake of the Syrian people, the time has come for President Assad to step aside.[62]

In a coordinated diplomatic onslaught, the leaders of Canada, France, Germany, the United Kingdom and the European Union did the same. In a joint statement, British Prime Minister David Cameron, French President Nicolas Sarkozy and German Chancellor Angela Merkel said:

> Our three countries believe that President Assad, who is resorting to brutal military force against his own people and who is responsible for the situation, has lost all legitimacy and can no longer claim to lead the country. We call on him to face the reality of the complete rejection of his regime by the Syrian people and to step aside in the best interests of Syria and the unity of its people.[63]

The action was accompanied by further US and EU sanctions against individuals and institutions in Syria.[64] The noose seemed to be tightening around Assad's neck.

The Syrian government-owned newspaper *Al-Thawra* condemned the US and EU statements, saying that such calls revealed the 'face of the conspiracy' targeting Syria and adding that it had been the strategic aim of Israel and the United States to sideline Syria in the region. The editorial stated that Syria rejected any kind of foreign intervention in its internal affairs: Damascus 'will never permit anyone' to interfere now.[65] The United States and the EU now began to work harder in the United Nations to tighten the noose even further, and (as had happened with Libya) perhaps even to get the Arab League to play a leading role. All this would allow Washington and its allies to consider a wider range of options, including some sort of military response. But all this would also mean having to get the Russians, Chinese and others to play along in the UN Security Council, encouraging the Arab League to assume a role to which it was unaccustomed. A tall order.

Al-Qaida

I almost did not include al-Qaida on the list of anti-Assad players. However, I finally decided to do so, even though (at the time of writing) it is only peripheral to the situation in Syria. That said, it probably deserves a mention because, after Osama bin Laden was killed by US forces in late May 2011, its new leader, Ayman al-Zawahiri, came out vociferously against Assad and in support of the protesters, and al-Qaida has established a presence in Syria – especially as the country has descended into civil war. Just think what al-Qaida was able to do in Iraq in the aftermath of the 2003 US-led invasion.

Al-Qaida has long been against what it considers to be the heretical Alawites, the secular nature of Baath rule and the Syrian regime's actions over the years against al-Qaida's fellow Sunnis in the Muslim Brotherhood. In July 2011, al-Zawahiri called Assad 'the leader of criminal gangs, the protector of traitors'.[66] On the other hand, he also called on the Syrian protestors not to side with the West:

> Oh free people of Syria and its *mujahedeen*, it is better for you not to ally yourself with the colonialist powers of the world and the new crusades. America, which had committed itself to Bashar for the length of his rule, announces today that it stands with you. After what it saw and the ground shook from the thunder of your rage and after it was devastated by the loss of its two biggest agents in Egypt and Tunisia. Today Washington seeks to put in the place of Assad who loyally protected the Zionist borders, another regime against your revolution and jihad with a government that follows America and cares for the interest of Israel.

While protestors scoffed at these pronouncements, saying that al-Qaida was simply trying to clumsily work its way into the picture, they feared that the government would use such statements to reinforce its narrative that armed terrorists and jihadists were behind the unrest and violence – and sure enough, it did. Observers on the ground in Syria pointed out that, while the majority of the protestors are from middle to lower classes in the rural areas (and thus are more traditional and conservative), they are not in any way, shape or form Islamist extremists. While al-Qaida did not seem to be gaining serious traction with the protest movement, there was a series of bombings of government facilities in late 2011 and early 2012 that had all the hallmarks of Islamist extremist suicide attacks. It was very al-Qaida-like. Some began to wonder if some Islamic State of Iraq (ISI) elements, who are affiliated to al-Qaida, were crossing into Syria and taking advantage of the uprising to graft their movement onto the existing situation. There is a genuine possibility of Islamist extremism increasing in Syria, and this is an issue that will be addressed later.

CHAPTER 8

All In

In retrospect, August 2011 seems to have been a turning point. Ramadan had revealed not only the tenaciousness of the opposition, but also the increasing lengths to which the regime would go to stay in power. Additionally, the international community was beginning to give up any faint hope it might have had regarding Bashar al-Assad's ability or willingness to implement substantive (rather than cosmetic) political reform in Syria and to enter into a serious national dialogue with the opposition. When, on 18 August, President Obama called on Assad to step aside, and when the European Union countries quickly followed suit, the die was cast. There seemed to be no turning back for any of the principal parties involved in the uprising.

Early on, the Syrian regime adopted a security solution to the crisis. Assad and his closest supporters decided to dig in and do whatever it took to stay in power, but without incurring the wrath of the world by doing something drastic, like using chemical weapons against the rebels, which would result in large-scale civilian casualties, or unleashing a repeat of Hama 1982. If it tried to do any such thing it would be caught on camera (via mobile phones) and that would shock the global community into action. Therefore, the regime engaged in a Machiavellian calibration of bloodletting – enough to do the job, but not enough to lose what international support remained. Too much blood was already on its hands, though. As early as June, respected human rights organizations were calling on the United Nations to refer regime figures to the International Criminal Court at The Hague. It was becoming increasingly clear that the regime was going to swim together or sink together: cracks and fissures at the top were not developing as the opposition and many in the West had hoped – and even expected. In any event, Bashar and others in the regime still believed they could wriggle out of the mess relatively intact. Enough important international players – Russia, China and Iran – were supporting their version of events and their prescription for resolving the situation, allowing them the necessary diplomatic cover and breathing space to settle the crisis.

The opposition became more desperate as the government crackdown intensified. As the situation on the ground deteriorated, the previously largely peaceful demonstrations increasingly became dotted with armed elements that sought to protect themselves and their families and to take the fight to the regime forces. Soon enough rebel militias formed, drawn in part from Syrian army defectors and operating as the 'Free Syrian Army'. Blood was now also on their hands, and they knew that they could not turn back. They realized that, even if there were some sort of compromise solution in which Bashar's inner circle and the security apparatus remained largely intact, their lives would still be in danger. The regime would not forget. Therefore, the regime had to fall. The protestors were ready to give up everything to ensure this outcome: their livelihoods and even their lives. All the while, the opposition political groups inside and outside Syria tried to form and present a unified front; this, of course, belied the deep divisions that existed and that hampered efforts to appeal to the silent majority and stalwart supporters of Assad to abandon a sinking ship. As 2011 drew to a close, there were calls for someone from the outside – the United States, the United Nations, the European Union, the Arab League, Turkey, almost anyone – to intervene militarily, at the very least on moral and humanitarian grounds.

Most of the international community had 'cut bait' with Assad by the end of August – or would do so by the end of the year. In Washington,

Paris and London there were even surreptitious attempts by envoys from countries still on good terms with Damascus to negotiate a peaceful solution that would result in Assad remaining in power. They were rebuffed. The unambiguous response was that Assad had to go. The ultimate objective was clear; the way to achieve that objective was not.

The key was to build up pressure on Damascus politically, diplomatically and economically through sanctions. The military option was not yet seriously being considered, as Syria was not Libya. But as the violence intensified, by February 2012 whispers could be heard in certain Western capitals of some sort of military response (similar to the NATO action in Libya). This cheered some, but frightened many more. Diplomatic pressure and isolation were not working. UN resolutions either did not pass or were merely symbolic. Even the Arab League, with Qatar and Saudi Arabia leading the way, uncharacteristically got involved directly, but again without success. Turkey came out more actively against Assad, launching sanctions of its own and more robustly supporting Syrian opposition groups operating out of its territory.

But most people underestimated the resilience of the regime. In summer and autumn 2011, there were numerous gung-ho headlines in leading international news outlets: 'Assad, Going Down',[1] 'The Last Stand of Bashar al-Assad?',[2] 'Plotting a post-Assad Road Map for Syria',[3] 'Beginning of the End for Assad?',[4] Tyrant Now a Pariah',[5] 'Syria Hits Point of No Return amid Broad Isolation',[6] and 'The Squeeze on Assad: The regime of Bashar Assad is tottering'.[7]

By the end of 2011, however, while many were still predicting the imminent fall of Assad, stories had started to appear on the durability of the regime: 'How Assad Stayed in Power – and How He'll Try to Keep It',[8] 'Syria Will Not Bow Down',[9] 'Assessing Assad: The Syrian leader isn't crazy, he's just doing whatever it takes to survive',[10] and 'Syria Is Used to the Slings and Arrows of Friends and Enemies'.[11] This was not going to be an easy nut to crack. All the while, with each passing day, the situation on the ground was deteriorating.

Political and military opposition

In late summer 2011, as the government crackdown intensified, the opposition faced some existential questions regarding direction and methodology. The main elements of the opposition inside and outside the country had, up to now, emphasized the peaceful nature of the protests. They advocated a peaceful resolution to the crisis, through dialogue and negotiation (assuming the removal of the Assad regime). But there were those in Syria who began to push for a more active, military approach to unseat Assad, as much out of self-defense as out of any perceived need to coordinate an armed rebellion. A bifurcated oppositional arc developed in August 2011: one political and diplomatic, the other armed resistance. They began separately and often found themselves working at cross purposes; but by the end of the year, there were concerted attempts to coordinate efforts and at least to *appear* to be on the same page. The Syrian National Council (SNC) became the clearing-house for political and diplomatic efforts by the opposition, while the Free Syrian Army acted similarly to galvanize military efforts to overthrow Assad on the ground.

Plans to set up the SNC were announced in Istanbul on 23 August (though that was about the limit of the agreement). The SNC was informally established in Turkey on 15 September. Officially, though, the SNC came into being on 2 October at a conference held in Istanbul; it was composed of a number of opposition groups, and had a charter and other accoutrements of organization.[12] The Council was modeled on the National Transitional Council in Libya, which had led the successful overthrow of the Gadafi regime. However, the SNC was, and continues to be, more of an umbrella organization of groups inside and outside Syria: it comprises a number of pre-existing Syrian opposition groups plus new groups that were formed during the uprising, and includes the Syrian Muslim Brotherhood, the Damascus Declaration, the Local Coordination Committees, the Kurdish Future Movement party, the Syrian National Current, the Assyrian Democratic Organization, and a host of smaller parties and independents. According to the SNC's official charter, its primary purpose is to oversee the implementation of a road map to democracy in Syria and to guide the transition from an authoritarian political system to a democratic, parliamentary one.

The avowed intention of the SNC's membership was to be as representative as possible (although it was accused of being anything but). It had a 230-member general assembly and a twenty-nine-member general secretariat, led by a seven-member executive committee, in which most of the decision-making took place (and which has been accused by critics, even within the SNC, of acting arbitrarily). The Council's first election was held in September, and longtime Syrian democracy activist Burhan Ghalioun was appointed its first chairman. He was formerly a professor of Oriental Studies and Political Sociology at Sorbonne University in Paris, where he lives. He was also a founding member of the Damascus Declaration in 2005. Although the chair position is supposed to rotate every three months, Ghalioun's tenure as chairman was extended well into 2012, in order to promote continuity in the organization at a critical time, as well as continued recognition in international circles. According to the SNC, 60 per cent of the membership resides in Syria and 40 per cent lives abroad. For security reasons, the names of many of the members in Syria have not been publicized.

The founding statement of the SNC was released on 2 October 2011 at a press conference held by Ghalioun. The charter was the most significant step to date in attempting to unify the fragmented opposition. In its statement, the SNC announced that it would function as the main representative of the Syrian 'Revolution', provide all necessary support to remove the Assad regime, and establish a civil state 'without discrimination on the basis of nationality, gender, or religious or political belief'. SNC participation would be open to all Syrians who were committed to a peaceful uprising, regardless of religion, gender or ethnicity. Ghalioun declared that the SNC rejected foreign intervention that would impinge on Syrian national sovereignty, but called on concerned international organizations to 'take responsibility for the people' and help to stop the violence against innocent civilians. A National Consensus Charter was also released that listed human rights, judicial independence, press freedom, democracy and political pluralism among its guiding principles.[13]

An important meeting of the SNC took place in the Tunisian capital in mid-December. In a series of meetings and workshops with international participation, organizational rules and procedures were established, and several specialist committees and executive offices were created to handle such things as foreign relations, media affairs, legal affairs, human rights, finance, and policy and planning. In essence, the conference produced a more unified political program that would make the SNC more appealing to an international audience and, perhaps more importantly, to people in Syria. SNC delegations traveled the globe trying to gain international acceptance as the true representative political organization of the Syrian 'revolution' – one that was ready to lead the transitional phase of a post-Assad Syria. They met the foreign ministers and representatives of Belgium, Great Britain, Bulgaria, Russia, Turkey, Saudi Arabia, Canada, the European Union, Egypt, the Arab League, Germany, Iraq, Norway, the Netherlands, Portugal, the Libyan National Transitional Council and the United States.

Many of these countries and organizations had come, by the end of the year, to officially recognize the SNC as the 'main interlocutor of the Syrian people', 'the legitimate interlocutor', 'the sole legitimate government in Syria', 'the official representative of the Syrian people', etc. By doing so, these countries and organizations seemed to have given up all hope of working with or achieving reconciliation with the Assad government. A particularly important meeting took place in early December in Geneva, where US Secretary of State Hillary Clinton publicly met an SNC delegation (US officials had had informal meetings with SNC representatives for months before). Clinton strongly encouraged the SNC – and all opposition groups – to work together and unite in their efforts. This was a clear sign that Washington wanted to establish a working relationship and dialogue with the Syrian opposition elements that would probably play a leading role in a post-Assad Syria (or at least with those that the United States and its allies wanted to play such a role). The Obama administration was being cautious, remembering how US support for the exiled Iraqi National Congress prior to the 2003 invasion of Iraq backfired after the removal of the Saddam Hussein regime. On 5 December, though, a few days after the meeting in Geneva, Clinton, by now back in Washington, declared the SNC to be the 'leading and legitimate representative of Syrians seeking a peaceful democratic transition', and committed the United States to helping the opposition toward a transition to democracy in Syria.[14]

At first the Syrian government paid little attention to the SNC, seeing it as a loose coalition of groups that would eventually implode. This was not entirely a bad assessment, as the SNC certainly did not give the impression at first of being a unified organization that was capable of mobilizing the opposition movement as a whole or of attracting international support. But as the SNC began to get its act together in early October and became the preferred option of most in the international community, the Syrian regime began to sit up and take notice. In October, once the SNC became 'official', Syrian Foreign Minister Walid al-Mouallem described it as an 'armed terrorist organization' and threatened to take 'strict measures' against any country that recognized the SNC, including withdrawal of protection for diplomatic missions in Damascus.[15] A member of the Syrian parliament, Khalid Abboud, was reported to have said that those who formed the SNC were 'deluding themselves' and that 'it's a dream that will never come true'.[16] One might ponder who was engaging in self-delusion. Nothing quite establishes the bona fides of an organization as firmly as when its competitors or enemies at the highest levels start ridiculing it. The SNC could no longer be ignored.

There was another opposition group, drawn mostly from people inside Syria, called the National Coordination Bureau for Democratic Change (NCB). The NCB had been formed in June and was led by Hassan Abd al-Azim. Unlike the SNC, it did not refuse to engage in dialogue with the regime. Moreover, it called for a gradual transition of power (not the immediate fall of the regime) and it eschewed outside military intervention. The SNC and the NCB have frequently been at odds with one another, and the NCB was not invited to join the SNC (nor would it have accepted).

NCB members are often accused of being willing dupes of the regime because they agree to meaningless dialogue with government officials, and their organization is even alleged to be an opposition group manufactured by the regime to present the illusion of national dialogue. *Quid pro quo*, after it was officially launched in October, the SNC was described by Haythem Mannaa, a prominent member of the NCB, as a 'Washington club', in essence bought and sold by the United States.[17] A number of members of the SNC had indeed over the years been funded by or been closely associated with the Bush and Obama administrations, particularly in the period following the Hariri assassination. The implication of this charge is that the SNC is almost traitorous and is in the pockets of Western governments and their allies in the Middle East, particularly Saudi Arabia, Qatar and Turkey. A member of yet another homegrown Syrian opposition group, the Popular Front for Change and Liberation (PFCL), has said that the SNC is 'non-patriotic ... has no roots inside Syria and is dependent on foreign powers to change the leadership and to come to Syria later aboard US tanks'.[18]

The NCB is a homegrown opposition organization, and that gives it an advantage over the largely exiled membership of the SNC. It is avowedly secularist and anti-imperialist. This is both a blessing and a curse: while it certainly attracts those in Syria – and there are many – who are inherently suspicious of associations with the outside, as well as those religious minorities and secular Sunnis who fear a Sunni-dominated, more religiously-based government, it also alienates the majority of Sunnis, who are religiously conservative, as well as those who find some of the NCB members' Baathist background distasteful. There are also those revolutionaries, particularly on the LCC and in the Free Syrian Army, who realize that, if they are going to successfully bring down the regime, they need greater diplomatic and military assistance from the international community than the NCB is in a position to provide. The NCB may also be deliberately placing itself squarely in the middle, so that, if the regime is forced to become more broad-based or if Assad steps down in some sort of negotiated settlement, it will appear as the most acceptable of the opposition entities and will be brought into the government as a legitimate opposition party. It appears that Russia and China, which are the countries most interested in a 'soft landing' engineered by diplomacy, favor the NCB and have held meetings with its leadership. On the other hand, the NCB's opposition to a military option may disqualify it from participating in a new post-Assad government if the regime is brought down by force; indeed, its members, whom critics regard as regime stooges, could be in serious danger.

The SNC and the NCB differ markedly on the issue of foreign intervention in Syria. Whereas, by early 2012, the former had certainly come to agitate vigorously for outside military intervention, the latter has remained dead set against any such thing. In any event, as Peter Harling comments, 'Syrians on the streets have made clear that they see the SNC's legitimacy as based on their ability to lobby for diplomatic pressure and see their mandate as stretching no further.'[19] NCB members say the SNC has been deliberately trying to marginalize it by questioning its legitimacy, because – whether by design or coincidence – its criticisms of the SNC and other Syrian exile opposition groups have been similar to those made by the Syrian regime (and thus lend credence to Assad's narrative of events).

The NCB also claims – as does the Syrian government – that the SNC is disproportionately made up of members of the Syrian Muslim Brotherhood and is not as representative as it makes itself out to be. The implication is that the SNC may actually be working towards the formation of a radical Sunni Muslim government, rather than a functioning democracy. While the Brotherhood does not have a majority in the Council as a whole, in the general secretariat or on the executive committee, its years of exile have made it by far the best-organized grouping, and there are fears that this will enable it to mobilize more effectively within the SNC and to shape its policies and positions. All these differences between the opposition organizations are exacerbated – and in some cases perhaps even caused – by personal antagonisms and power struggles that go back over many years and that have fatally weakened previous manifestations of opposition parties.

This is part of the problem of the Syrian opposition in general. It has been divided inside and outside the country, and each opposition group has vulnerabilities and weaknesses in the eyes of others that have prevented any single group from gaining the legitimacy and general acceptance necessary to offer a viable alternative to the regime. There is also a generation of personal antagonisms to overcome. Louay Hussein, a longtime, respected democracy activist in Syria (and head of another Syrian opposition group called Building the Syrian State), has raised other problems that have plagued the Syrian opposition. To his way of thinking, the media are guilty of focusing on the SNC and the NCB and of ignoring the role of other groups and individual opposition figures on the ground: 'Since the beginning of the uprising, different media outlets have created this picture at the behest of those who run or fund these outlets. There are thousands of opposition figures in the Syrian uprising who are not members of any political party or movement or any public gathering.'[20] Or as Rime Allaf, a political analyst at London's Chatham House, puts it: 'the power of the so-called street will have the last word,' not inorganic and opportunistic opposition groups.[21]

One of the inevitable progressions in any uprising or revolution is the question of whether or not to take up arms and when to turn a largely peaceful rebellion into an armed one. For many Syrians, as the government decision to wipe out the opposition became clear to them, taking up arms was simply a matter of self-defense. Others, however, began to believe in summer 2011 that the only thing that could dethrone Assad would be armed opposition. As one Local Coordination Committee member put it, 'After Libya, many people said it was a mistake to have a peaceful revolution and if they had done it like the Libyans they would be free by now.'

Nir Rosen is a widely-respected journalist, who has spent much time with members of the opposition at epicenters of the conflict. In my opinion, he has presented the most accurate and objective accounts of the situation on the ground. Here he captures the shift toward armed rebellion:

> As I spent more time in Syria, I could see a clear theme developing in the discourse of the opposition: A call for an organized armed response to the government crackdown, mainly from the opposition within Syria. Demonstrators had hoped the holy month of Ramadan would be the

> turning point in their revolution, but as it came to an end – six months into the Syrian uprising – many realized the regime was too powerful to be overthrown peacefully.[22]

The question of moving to an armed revolution was an important one. Any such move would reinforce the regime narrative that armed gangs and terrorists were generating the violence, and would provide the Syrian government's foreign backers – Russia and China – with the justification to continue their support of the regime, and perhaps even to provide military assistance. But many in the opposition felt their backs were up against the wall, and that the brutality of the government crackdown required them to take up arms.[23]

In addition, the vast majority of the opposition were Sunnis; certainly defectors from the Syrian army were almost exclusively Sunni, as deserters generally came from the Sunni-dominated rank and file. So again, this reinforced the regime narrative that it was the last line of defense against sectarian warfare. At the very least, this encouraged minority groups in Syria to maintain their wait-and-see posture; in some cases it prompted them to give the regime their outright support.

The Sunni coloring to the opposition also gave it the appearance of a more religious-extremist-based movement, thus creating fertile ground for fears of a possible *salafist* post-Assad government. According to those journalists embedded in the opposition, most of the rebels are conservative Sunnis, particularly in the rural areas where the uprising initially took root. But this is just symptomatic of the cultural and demographic make-up of Syria, i.e. it (along with most other Arab states) is religiously conservative and has become more so over the last decade or two.[24] This in no way makes the people Islamist extremists: they are simply more devout and are inspired by their religion; they are not blindly guided by it. We have seen this in Egypt, Tunisia and Libya following the Arab Spring removal of the regimes in those countries. This does not mean, of course, that there are no Islamist extremists in Syria. There are, and Syrian government support for *jihadists* making their way to Iraq in the aftermath of the US-led invasion may come back to haunt the regime, as some of these elements, familiar with the landscape and having established networks of contacts and safe zones, may have returned to Syria. The other side of the coin is that this opposition coloring feeds (yet again) into the regime's narrative that Islamist extremists are involved in the violence, and that it is the only buffer between a relatively secular society and a radical theocratic state.

Of those who have taken up arms, the best trained and most professional are army deserters; but they usually joined the ranks of the opposition without their weapons and as individuals, rather than as part of entire, well-equipped units.[25] There is really no organized armed resistance nationwide: it is more a case of local defense militias popping up organically in various towns, villages and city districts. There was the potential for an increase in armed opposition in autumn 2011, but in many cases it was just too difficult and/or too expensive for willing individuals to get their hands on scarce supplies of weapons and ammunition.

Towards the end of the summer, the Free Syrian Army (FSA) became a popular element of the opposition – perhaps the organized armed resistance that many had hoped for. Some saw this as the inevitable result of the Syrian regime's military crackdown. The first news of something known as the 'Free Syrian Army' came in June, when a Colonel Hussein Harmoush was captured by security forces and forced to recant on state-run television and to denounce the defectors.[26] By July, it was reported that Riad al-Asaad,[27] a colonel in the Syrian army who had defected, was now in command of the FSA, with some 7,000–10,000 troops by early autumn (he claimed 15,000 by November). The majority of these were inside Syria, but some were across the border in Turkey, Lebanon and Jordan. Certainly at first it appeared that FSA units preferred to operate near the border, so that they could easily evade government forces, if necessary. Proximity to the border also meant that they could be more easily resupplied. Asaad's overall operational headquarters (to the extent that there was any sort of overall operational command and control structure) were located in Antakya (Antioch), just over the border in the Hatay region of Turkey. In response, Syrian government forces laid minefields along the border to deter cross-border smuggling and military operations.

For the most part, there was not much coordination between those claiming to be part of the FSA; indeed, the armed resistance tended to be composed of local militias that claimed affiliation to the FSA simply in order to give the impression of being part of a whole. This created the illusion for the outside world of a more organized armed resistance than actually existed.

The goal of FSA units was to conduct guerilla warfare and hit-and-run raids against Syrian forces and symbols of state authority: they were obviously no match in pitched battles for the better supplied and more numerous Syrian troops, armed with heavier weapons. The heaviest weapons in the FSA arsenal were a few rocket-propelled grenade launchers, although improvised explosive devices (IEDs) and Molotov cocktails were also utilized. But the FSA was chronically short of weapons and ammunition, hence its appeals to sympathetic foreign powers for military support. As one FSA soldier commented:

> The more weapons we have the more progress we can make. We call on the international community, whether it's the EU, the Arab League, France or Germany, to provide us with weapons and ammunition. If we have a no-fly zone and a safe area for our base, the collapse of the regime's army will be swift. This is an army that serves a person and a family [Assad], not a country and its citizens.[28]

Establishing a no-fly zone and/or a safe haven, ideally along the border with Turkey, naturally became the constant refrain of the armed opposition. The hope was that, with a safe haven and no-fly zone in place, there would be a greater incentive for more troops to defect from the Syrian army – particularly whole units, with their heavy weapons, as they would not be deterred by fear of Syrian aircraft strafing them as they deserted. A safe haven would also make resupply easier (and more abundant) and would enable training by foreign sources (in much the same way as happened in Libya). The logistical and political difficulties of establishing a safe haven and a no-fly zone will be discussed in Chapter 9, but into 2012 the chatter surrounding these issues and their feasibility grew louder.

Ammunition became very expensive in Syria as the uprising gained momentum – reportedly around $4 a bullet on the black market in the Idlib area of northern Syria in February 2012. Armed opposition elements raided military depots for arms and ammunition, but it was not nearly enough to counter the superior forces of the regime. By early 2012, there were reports that the opposition was receiving arms and ammunition (or money for their purchase) from foreign countries, although not yet in any significant amounts. However, as the regime's crackdown intensified dramatically in February, especially in the city of Homs, and as the death toll increased, the horrific images of death and destruction prompted certain countries in the anti-Assad camp to stop ruling out the idea of some sort of military assistance. Leaks to the press indicated that military contingency plans were now being considered. If this developed into real assistance, the FSA (and indeed the armed resistance in general) would be given a huge boost – for better or worse.

By late 2011, the FSA approach had come to garner more support from ordinary Syrians opposed to the regime. Not only had the government authorized the security forces and the military to repress the revolt, but the so-called *shabbiha* ('ghost' – see above, Chapter 6) added to the ugliness of the crackdown. These were irregular units of civilian militia who fanatically supported the regime and reportedly were deliberately attempting to instill fear in the populace with their gruesome atrocities. Most of the *shabbiha* are (or are accused of being) Alawite: the designation was first applied in the 1980s to the largely Alawite armed gangs in northwestern Syria, in and around Latakia, who used to engage in various excesses, usually involving extortion and cross-border smuggling. Most of the Alawites in the *shabbiha* now, during the uprising, are poor and seem to be trying to earn some sort of salary; but they are also fighting for their own survival, out of fear that extremist Sunni elements would wipe them out if the Assad regime falls.[29] It appears that they are not entirely on the government payroll: it is reported that a number of prominent Syrian businessmen (both Alawite and Sunni) who, over the years, have utilized *shabbiha* to tighten their control of certain business activities, continue to pay the lion's share of *shabbiha* wages in order to protect their lucrative business privileges. Once again, this goes to show the almost incestuous connections among different sectors of Syrian society that have bought into regime maintenance.[30]

Of course, the *shabbiha* activities during the uprising served to intensify sectarian hostility – a by-product with which the regime was not entirely uncomfortable (as discussed above). But their nefarious activities were not always military-related: sometimes they were purely criminal in nature, leading to the emergence of street and neighborhood warlords in many cities. Indeed, as occurred in Iraq, the criminalization of elements on both sides of the conflict only added to the distress of ordinary Syrians, who were simply trying to survive the violence. As the days and weeks went by, the fear that the *shabbiha* generated swelled the opposition's call to arms. Popular support for the FSA increased, as the 25 November protests dubbed 'May the Free Syrian Army Protect Us' attest.

The FSA also claimed responsibility for an increasing number of attacks on symbols of the regime, such as an intelligence headquarters (on 16 November on the outskirts of Damascus), government installations and buildings; for ambushes against military convoys; and for assassinations of government officials and military officers. The FSA is not immune to charges of human rights violations and criminal activities: it often summarily executes Syrian army captives and alleged informants within its own ranks (some no doubt genuine spies, others less certainly so). All of this is the ugly by-product of a de facto civil war that is more inter-communal in nature and that is often fought in densely packed urban areas, rather than along traditional battle lines. In some of the most hotly contested cities, in late 2011 and early 2012, it was not uncommon to hear shots being exchanged between one building that was flying the government flag and another building – a matter of blocks away – that was sporting the opposition banner.

In an effort to present a more united front, representatives of the FSA and the SNC met in Turkey on 28 November 2011. The SNC persuaded the FSA to scale back its attacks, so as not to sully the image of the uprising as a primarily peaceful one, based on self-defense. An FSA spokesman explained that, under the agreement, its troops would not 'attack [Syrian military] units that are staying in their barracks' but would fight 'any unit that enters our cities and tries to kill our people'.[31] The SNC also announced that it would form a joint committee with the FSA to coordinate 'field mobilization, relief, media and political relations'.[32] The SNC was hopeful that the FSA would focus more on protecting the protestors and would allow the Council to maintain the public face of the opposition movement. This would also make the Syrian government forces appear the aggressors.

More importantly, as Nicholas Heras writes:

> As a full-spectrum movement, a Free Syrian Army–Syrian National Council coalition would be able to claim a political role as the major transition authority in a post-Assad Syria, with the added assurance to concerned foreign actors that it has the security organization to combat potential disorder and violence à la Iraq from the first day after the Al-Assad government.[33]

Despite all this, the agreement masked deep differences in terms of leadership, ideology and methodology. Those skeptical of the entente said it was all for show, and was aimed at the international audience, from which more assertive support was being sought.

The United Nations

The United Nations (UN) and the Arab League (AL) became significant players in the unfolding drama in Syria. The UN was accustomed to involving itself in such situations at the request of its member states; the AL was most definitely not (although its support for the NATO-led military backing of the Libyan rebels may have been a preview of things to come regarding Syria). Sometimes the two organizations ran on parallel tracks, and at other times they worked in tandem. But by early 2012, it appeared it was all for naught. The Syrian regime steadfastly resisted all international efforts to end the crackdown (and to remove it from power). In doing so, it drew on the backing of some important international actors (primarily Russia, China and Iran). The upshot was that events surrounding Syria soon came to resemble a multilayered cold war.

Very early on in the uprising, the alleged human rights violations by the Syrian government had put the regime smack in the center of the radar screen of international humanitarian organizations. As photographs and videos of the violence could spread almost instantaneously via the Internet, the human rights violations depicted could not be ignored – and nor was any extended investigation required to uncover them. Nor could the government conceal them (those days appear to be over for all authoritarian regimes). In early April, the UN Human Rights Council adopted a resolution condemning the government's use of lethal force against the protestors. It also established an independent investigation into the Syrian officials responsible for the actions, and from that point on the High Commissioner for Human Rights at the UN, Navi Pillay, took a visible and leading stand against the regime.

Human Rights Watch, a leading humanitarian watchdog organization, monitored the situation in Syria closely and, in analyzing the available data, interviewed a number of refugees and residents of Deraa. As mentioned above, in June 2011 it published a fifty-five-page report entitled *'We've Never Seen Such Horror': Crimes against humanity by Syrian security forces*, the first part of the title quoting a Syrian observer on the ground. The Middle East director of the organization, Sarah Leah Whitson, was quoted as saying: 'For more than two months now, Syrian security forces have been killing and torturing their own people with complete impunity. They need to stop – and if they don't, it is the [UN] Security Council's responsibility to make sure that the people responsible face justice.'[34] The organization also recommended that, if the Syrian regime did not desist, the Security Council should refer the situation to the International Criminal Court.

The international politics of the crisis in Syria, particularly the hesitancy of the international community to take rapid action (or, more to the point, their willingness to cut Assad some slack) lagged behind the attention to humanitarian issues. But as more and more countries retracted the leeway given to Assad and called on him to step aside, the UN became the natural repository for possible multilateral action, especially as this was the preferred approach of the Obama administration.

In early August, the UN Security Council (UNSC) unanimously passed a presidential statement condemning the Syrian government's crackdown and calling for an immediate end to the violence by all parties in Syria: 'The Security Council condemns the widespread violations of human rights and the use of force against civilians by the Syrian authorities.' It urged 'all sides to act with utmost restraint, and to refrain from reprisals, including attacks against state institutions. The Security Council reaffirms its strong commitment to the sovereignty, independence, and territorial integrity of Syria.' It further stressed that 'the only solution to the current crisis . . . is through an inclusive and Syrian-led political process.'[35]

The Lebanese representative on the Security Council dissociated her country from the statement, but did not block it. It was obviously carefully worded, in order to foster consensus in the Council, calling as it did on 'all sides' to end the violence, rather than solely focusing on the Syrian government. Not only was this intended to appease countries such as Russia and China, but it also, from the point of view of the West, was designed to exert pressure on Damascus without yet cutting Assad off entirely – something that would, in fact, occur a couple of weeks later. It was also a 'presidential statement' by the Security Council rather than a 'resolution', the latter usually being associated with some action. Earlier attempts to pass something with more bite had been shot down by Russia and/or China.

While many were pleased with the UNSC statement, taking it as an indication of the resolve of the international community against Syria, it was also just as much an indication of the divisions within the Security Council and provided a foretaste of how difficult any sort of resolute action by the UNSC would be. Certainly this was noticed in Damascus. Assad's decree the next day authorizing the creation of a multi-party system would seem, on the face of it, to have been in response to the presidential statement; however, the process of announcing these piecemeal reform efforts had been in motion for several months, and so it was probably a coincidence. Assad and his inner circle might have believed that the combination of the reforms announced and the seemingly rather tepid UN statement might turn the tide at home. If they thought this, they were wrong.

Rising international pressure did persuade the Syrian government to allow UN humanitarian teams to enter the country on 20 August to investigate areas such as Hama, Homs, Idlib and Latakia, which had seen some of the worst fighting. This came just days after a UN fact-finding mission found 'a pattern of human rights violations that constitutes widespread or systematic attacks against the civilian population, which may amount to crimes against humanity'.[36] At the same time, Assad was vehemently rejecting calls for him to step down, saying, 'What they say means nothing to us', while continuing to deny that the military had targeted peaceful protestors, despite widespread reports to the contrary. He would only admit that the 'security situation has turned into more of an armed situation', adding that 'security is important, but the solution is political'.[37] So, a typically mixed-message response from Assad.

The UN team's visit would be monitored and circumscribed to a considerable degree by government minders. The fact that, even with such restrictions, they would find firm evidence of human rights violations perhaps says something about the nature of the violence. This was not the first time the Assad regime had treated international inspectors in this way, and it would not be the last.[38]

In autumn 2011, as the violence continued unabated, the idea of a UN Security Council resolution aimed at the Syrian regime gathered momentum in Western circles. The problem (as is so often the case in the Security Council) was to make the language strong enough to give the resolution some real teeth, yet ambiguous enough to gain the support of those countries less inclined to adopt anything that was clearly anti-Assad. On 4 October, a Western-drafted UN Security Council resolution that condemned the violence in Syria and threatened more targeted sanctions (but did not include any mention of a transfer of power) if the regime did not cease its military actions against the protestors was finally put to the vote. Brazil, India and South Africa abstained, and Russia and China vetoed the resolution (a veto by one of the five permanent members of the

Security Council automatically kills a resolution in that forum). Moscow and Beijing had been saying that any resolution should be more even-handed in its opprobrium, and should hold the opposition as responsible as the regime for the violence. More importantly, having so recently felt duped by a similar UNSC resolution that opened the door to NATO military intervention in Libya (on which it abstained – see Chapter 7), Russia was that much more sensitive about supporting anything that might lead to Western-backed military action against another Russian (or former Soviet) client state, in this case one with which Moscow still enjoyed strong political, economic and military relations.

Mutual recriminations were hurled back and forth between Western capitals and Moscow (and even Beijing) in a way that was reminiscent of the superpower Cold War era. Active diplomacy over some sort of UN resolution continued for the remainder of 2011. However, the fact that in December, Russia held the rotating presidency of the Security Council considerably complicated matters, as the Russian representatives (at least according to their Western counterparts) manipulated their position to delay and thwart further attempts to table a resolution. Something of this sort would have to wait until early 2012.

The Arab League

The AL has frequently been called a dictators' club. As such, under normal circumstances, it would not have been expected to assume a leading role or to adopt a position against the Syrian government, as traditionally it has supported maintenance of the status quo. In addition, the fall of one dictator might have a domino effect, leading to the fall of many. Initial AL reaction to the increasing pressure on the Syrian government seemed to reinforce the notion that it would, at the very least, quietly support the Damascus regime. The Arab League chief, Nabil al-Arabi, said in mid-July that the United States had overstepped the mark by suggesting that Bashar al-Assad had lost his legitimacy to rule. After meeting the Syrian president, al-Arabi said Assad had assured him that 'Syria has entered a new era and is now moving on the road to genuine reform'. The AL head then declared that 'this issue is exclusively decided by the people'. Another AL official stated that Syria was a 'main factor of balance and stability in the region', a view with which al-Arabi agreed.[39] A *New York Times* editorial snorted: 'The Arab League is a disgrace.'[40]

However, the speed of the Arab Spring and certain geopolitical realities overwhelmed AL stasis. Two divides were forcing the AL's hand (or at least the hand of some of its member states).[41] First was the divide between Saudi Arabia, Qatar and their regional and international backers, in one corner, and Iran in the other: many have described this as the Sunni-Shiite divide in the region. As mentioned above, the more the Syrian crisis became a function of the Saudi-Iranian regional power game, the more the AL was used by Saudi Arabia and Qatar (which chaired the AL for most of 2011 and up until March 2012) as a way of bringing about the removal of Assad and thus severely damaging Tehran's regional influence. Taking a lead role in this regard was also important in terms of beating Turkey to the punch, so that Ankara would not be able to enhance its prestige in the Arab world (at Saudi Arabia's and Qatar's expense) by appearing to be the only regional power exerting pressure on Assad.

Second, there was (and is) a divide between the monarchies and the secular republics in the Arab world. The Arab Spring casualties have, to date, all been in the so-called secular republics (or dictatorships) of the Arab world; by early 2012 the leaders of Tunisia, Egypt, Libya and Yemen had all fallen (while the leader of Syria was stubbornly hanging on by his fingertips). The monarchies of the Arab world, by contrast, have (with the exception of Bahrain) been comparatively quiescent. There are various important reasons for this: some have to do with the oil-rich monarchies' ability to buy off discontent; some have to do with the greater historical legitimacy of most of the monarchical regimes; and some have to do with more prescient responses regarding reform initiatives, particularly by the non-oil-rich monarchies of Jordan and Morocco.[42] But once the Arab Spring became a contagion that spread throughout the Arab world, it was more prudent for the Arab monarchs to side with the protestors – if for no other reason than to appear to be on the 'right' side of history and therefore to diminish the chances of similar protests against their own regimes (which are, in many ways, just as authoritarian as those in Damascus, Tunis or Cairo). While it may have deflected domestic discontent for the time being, the monarchies' employment (if not exploitation) of liberal and humanitarian themes in support of the protestors in Syria may come back to haunt them, as the discourse of freedom and human rights becomes the norm. That may, in the end, be the most enduring aspect of the Arab Spring.[43]

It did not take long for the Arab League to start adopting a more assertive position vis-à-vis Syria, especially after mid-August 2011, when the United States, the EU and others began openly calling on Assad to step down. In late August, the AL publicly called on Damascus to exercise restraint and end the violence. In September, there was an AL initiative (which Nabil al-Arabi brought to Assad in Damascus) that detailed a plan to stop the violence and implement reforms. The plan called for an immediate halt to all violence against civilians, and proposed measures that would offer compensation to those who had been persecuted, arrested or injured by government forces. A general amnesty would be issued for all political prisoners arrested during the course of the uprising. The initiative also called for a 'declaration of principles' by Assad that would flesh out the various political reforms he had mentioned in his speeches since the beginning of the unrest. These included a shift to a multi-party system and a multi-candidate presidential election, to take place when Assad's current seven-year term ends in 2014. (Interestingly, Assad could run again for a third term, if nominated.) The AL plan outlined the parameters for a true national dialogue between the government and opposition forces, including the Local Coordination Committees, Islamists, democracy activists and others, under the rubric of 'no to violence, no to sectarianism, and no to foreign intervention'. Finally, the initiative called for fresh parliamentary elections, with the newly elected chamber mandated to develop a new constitution that was commensurate with a parliamentary democracy – first and foremost by eliminating Article 8 of the existing constitution, which designated the Baath party the 'leader of state and society', and which has long guaranteed single-party rule by the Baath.[44]

Most of the Syrian opposition accepted the plan, including the LCC (which up until then had been clear in their stated aim of getting rid of the regime). This showed that, despite all the bloodshed, a negotiated solution was still possible in August 2011, if only Assad had been willing and able. But the Syrian regime roundly rejected the plan, perceiving the hands of Saudi Arabia, Qatar and the United States behind it. Syrian officials claimed that the initiative was a 'clear violation' of the Arab League charter, because it 'meddles in the affairs of Syria'.[45]

Perhaps not surprisingly, the Syrian government then countered with its own initiative, unveiled at an AL meeting in Cairo. This called on all Arab states to lift their emergency laws and abolish all state security courts (as Syria had already announced it would do back in March/April). It also called for new constitutional frameworks throughout the region that would guarantee political pluralism and democracy, the rule of law and human rights. This was intended as a salvo at countries such as Saudi Arabia and Qatar, monarchical systems that would obviously reject such notions.

But now the AL had become directly involved in the Syrian crisis, and its plan (or variations thereof) would become the basis of discussion for a 'soft landing' via some sort of national dialogue and period of transition, combined with political reforms. In addition, Syria's rejection of the plan put the ball back in the AL court, and the relationship between the AL leadership and Damascus consequently became more antagonistic.

Arab League and Syrian officials would continue to meet to discuss plans to end the unrest. A pattern developed into October and November, whereby the Syrian government would tentatively accept AL mediation and initiatives, but would argue for a different set of terms that required still more negotiation. Deadlines for compliance were frequently shifted. Opposition figures at the time – and many others – decried the Syrian government's willingness to engage with the AL as nothing more than diversionary tactics, designed to create the impression that it was interested in a peaceful solution, while it continued the violent crackdown in the country. They pointed out that, while the AL and Syria dithered, the mass arrests, torture, disappearances, assassinations and brute military force continued.

A televised interview by Assad in October presented a totally different narrative (or threat). During the interview, he contended that Syria

> is the faultline, and if you play with the ground, you will cause an earthquake. Do you want to see another Afghanistan, or tens of Afghanistans? Any problem in Syria will burn the whole region. If the plan is to divide Syria, that is to divide the whole region.

He compared the unrest to the Islamist uprising back in the 1980s, again attempting to color the opposition as primarily led by radical Islamists: 'We have very few police, only army, who are trained to take on al-Qaida . . . Now we are only fighting terrorists.'[46]

By the end of October, the UN estimated that 3,000 Syrians had been killed since the start of the uprising. By mid-November, the figure was 3,500; and by the beginning of December the estimate had risen to 4,000. In late December, the Syrian state news agency claimed that over 2,000 of the country's security forces had been killed since the protests broke out.

As the government's crackdown continued, despite its eventual acceptance of the Arab League plan, the AL held an emergency meeting in Cairo on 11 November. At this meeting, eighteen of the league's twenty-two members voted to suspend Syria's membership: Lebanon and Yemen voted against the measure; Iraq abstained; and Syria was barred from voting. The AL also called for unspecified sanctions against the Assad regime and urged member states to withdraw their ambassadors. Qatari Prime Minister Shaykh Hamad bin Jassem al-Thani read out the league's decision. The Syrian representative to the AL claimed the decision was illegal and said it was 'a eulogy for Arab common action and a blatant announcement that its administration is subordinate to US-Western agendas'.[47] Of course, Syrians had long considered themselves to be the beating heart of Arabism, and so their country's suspension from the AL was, indeed, something of a blow. On the other hand, in the past Syria had not been shy about taking action that clearly went against the Arab consensus. In any event, Syrians' pride (even arrogance) about their central position in the Arab world and in Arab history would lead Syrian officials to express disdain for the AL decision: Damascus was still the only Arab country that stayed true to issues at the core of Arabism.

Many expected that the AL action against the Syrian regime would (as had happened over Libya) pave the way to a more concerted international response, especially a UN Security Council resolution. Keeping up the pressure, at an AL meeting of foreign ministers on 27 November nineteen member states voted to slap a raft of economic and trade sanctions on the Syrian regime (Iraq abstained and Lebanon voted against). These included a ban on any private or commercial flights from the league's member states into or out of Syria; the termination of dealings with Syria's Central Bank; the freezing of the assets of Syrian government officials; and a ban on high-profile Syrian officials from visiting other Arab nations. Syria's state-run television network said the move 'lacks legality' and 'the economic sanction against the rights of the Syrian people indicates a halt in trade and economic relations ... and targets the Syrian people'.[48]

By mid-December, with the AL threatening to take the Syrian issue to the UN Security Council, the Assad regime agreed to a proposal hammered out in Doha to send AL observers to Syria to monitor compliance with the regime's previous commitments to end the violence and release political prisoners. Damascus was under heavy Russian pressure to accede to the AL mission: the Russians wanted to prevent the issue from going straight to the UN, as that would again put Moscow in a very uncomfortable position.

The AL observers would accumulate data and evidence, with the aim of producing a definitive report on the situation in Syria. The details of this mission were discussed for almost seven weeks, with AL and Syrian officials arguing over the amount of access the observers would have to trouble spots, their remit and the size of the team. Again, the Syrian opposition and many in the West, while cautiously supporting the AL initiative as the least worst idea at the time, were left generally unimpressed. SNC leader, Burhan Ghalioun, responded by saying that 'The Syrian regime is playing games and wants to buy time. We are quite surprised that the Arab League is allowing this to take place.'[49] At the same time, Ghalioun took the opportunity to call on the international community to establish a buffer zone in Syria to protect civilians: 'This regime has proven time and time again that it is a regime built on lies and force. We need a safety zone to protect and prevent efforts by the regime to transform the crisis into a civil conflict.'[50]

There were several doubts raised about the AL mission. First and foremost, Lieutenant General Muhammad Ahmad al-Dabi, from Sudan, was named as the leader of the league delegation. He had been head of military intelligence under Sudanese President Omar Bashir when Bashir had been issued with a warrant for arrest by the International Criminal Court for genocide in the Darfur region of Sudan. Apparently, Dabi had barely escaped censure. So the Syrian opposition was quite cautious when he was appointed; their suspicions were confirmed when Dabi said he was 'reassured' after visiting war-torn Homs. On the other hand, the Syrian regime was also suspicious of Dabi because he had been Sudan's ambassador to Qatar in 1999–2004; it therefore thought he had been hand-picked – and was controlled – by the Qatari government (which, as we have seen, had taken the lead in the AL against Syria).[51]

The other issue was that the AL really had no experience in carrying out missions of this sort. The team members were wholly unprepared – particularly as they were working with a government that was quite experienced in controlling visiting delegations and limiting their access to only those things it wanted the observers to see (see above and note 38).

As Richard Gowan wrote at the time of the AL mission, the Kosovo Verification Mission that was deployed in 1998 under the auspices of the Organization for Security and Cooperation in Europe to protect Albanians in Kosovo had far greater resources available to it than the Arab League delegation, and had over 1,400 observers, compared to the AL's hundred or so (at most) in Syria.[52] In addition, the mission in Kosovo had had a NATO extraction force in neighboring Macedonia, ready to move at a moment's notice if the observers encountered any problems. Furthermore, they generally enjoyed far greater freedom of movement than did the AL observers. Yet even with all this going for the mission in Kosovo, it failed to curtail the violence and had to be withdrawn in 1999, when NATO decided to use air power to resolve the conflict. As Gowan indicates, though, while the AL observer mission may have failed in its objective (i.e. to ensure Syrian compliance with the AL mandate on the regime to halt its attacks on civilians), it did play an important role in highlighting the brutality of the Syrian regime and the suffering of innocent civilians in Syria, thereby magnifying the issue for all the world to see.[53] This might, in turn, enhance the prospects of UN action, or so it was thought at the time.

Just as the Kosovo Verification Mission eventually led to NATO military action in the Balkans, perhaps what was initially viewed as a failed AL mission might be seen by future historians as a necessary prelude to eventual military action in Syria. The UN put the death toll in Syria by mid-January 2012 at 5,000, although opposition groups claimed that over 6,000 Syrians had died since the outbreak of the uprising.

United Nations *and* Arab League

In the wake of its observer mission in Syria, the Arab League announced a new plan on 22 January 2012 that would see President Bashar al-Assad step down and hand over power to his vice president, following the formation of a national unity government. It called for the Syrian government to begin a dialogue with opposition groups within two weeks, and for a new government to be formed within two months.[54] It did not call for military intervention. The plan was unveiled at the AL headquarters in Cairo by the Qatari foreign minister, Hamad bin Jassem al-Thani. He also announced that the AL would take the plan to the UN, in order to build up international support. At this point, the UN and the AL began to work in concert, in order to introduce a new resolution in the Security Council that had more diplomatic weight behind it; hopefully that would persuade Russia and China to refrain from using their veto.

Of the AL plan, *Time* magazine said the following:

> The epithet that seemed to be perpetually attached to the Arab League was 'toothless'. On Sunday . . . however, the organization bared its fangs at Syria. In the absence of a detailed political road map from the Syrian opposition, the Arab League presented its own audacious plan[.][55]

Saudi Arabia started to emerge from behind the scenes and adopt a more forceful – and public – position against Syria. Riyadh had decided to withdraw its support for the observer mission – and the other states of the Gulf Cooperation Council followed suit – effectively ending it. Saudi Foreign Minister Saud al-Faisal said that 'all possible pressure' should be applied to the Syrian regime to cease its military repression, adding: 'We are calling on the international community to bear its responsibility, and that includes our brothers in Islamic states and our friends in Russia, China, Europe and the United States.'[56] The Qatari foreign minister even called for the dispatch of an Arab peacekeeping force to enter Syria. He likened such a military mission to the Arab Deterrent Force (ADF) that the Arab League had sent to Lebanon during its civil war in the mid-1970s. This is a comparison he probably wished he had not made, for the ADF was composed almost entirely of Syrian troops, most of which then stayed on in Lebanon for thirty years as the instrument of Syrian domination over its neighbor to the west.

Shaykh Hamad probably also wishes he had not likened the league's road map for political change in Syria to Yemen: there it took months of on–off negotiations and supposed agreements before Yemeni President Ali Abdullah Saleh finally agreed to step aside – and then many more months for him actually to leave, almost a year after the uprisings began in Yemen.

Lebanon, as expected, rejected the new AL plan, and Algeria abstained from the vote to take the initiative to the UN Security Council. The Syrian government obviously rejected the initiative. According to the news agency SANA, the plan was a violation of Syria's sovereignty and 'flagrant interference in its internal affairs'.[57]

According to Syrian Foreign Minister Walid al-Mouallem, his country needed 'a Syrian solution driven by Syrian interests'. He reiterated the claim of an international conspiracy against Syria, saying that some Arab states are 'implanting the stages of the plot against Syria, which they agreed upon abroad. We are perfectly aware of the dimension of the conspiracy and we will deal with it firmly . . . It is the duty of the Syrian government to deal seriously and firmly with armed elements'. He also noted that Russia would 'not agree on the foreign interference in Syria's internal affairs and this is a red line. During talks with Russian Deputy Foreign Minister Mikhail Bogdanov, I sensed that the Russian stance is solid and no one can question the Russian-Syrian relations, as they are deep-rooted'.[58]

While Syria continued to burn, the diplomatic drama moved back to the UN. On 27 January, Morocco introduced to the Security Council the Arab League plan for a political transition and unity government in Syria. There ensued vigorous discussion and posturing by the UN delegates. Displaying continued support for the Syrian government, the Russian envoy to the UN, Vitaly Churkin, said:

> The red lines include any indication of sanctions. The red lines included any sort of imposition of arms embargo, because we know how in real life, arms embargo means that you supply weapons to illegal groups but you cannot supply weapons to the government. We cannot accept that. Unfortunately the draft which we saw today did not ignore our red lines but also added some new elements which we find unacceptable as a matter of principle.[59]

To the envoy, that included the idea of imposing a political solution.

The Syrian representative to the UN, Bashar al-Jaafari, dismissed the proposed resolution and adopted a defiant tone:

> Some of these ambassadors who have been entrusted by the so-called international community to maintain peace and security in the world through their important role in the Security Council have chosen to

> undermine peace and security in the world – following their narrow strategic and geopolitical interests. They deal with us as if we are a former colony – that we should subjugate ourselves to their will. They are wrong and will be disappointed. Syria will not be Libya; Syria will not be Iraq; Syria will not be Somalia; Syria will not be a failing state.[60]

A few days later, he commented: 'That organization [Arab League] is not speaking on behalf of all Arabs right now. Without Syria, there is no Arab League.'[61] Iranian President Mahmud Ahmadinejad chimed in: he said that the efforts of regional governments that had never held elections (i.e. Saudi Arabia and Qatar) 'to prescribe freedom and elections' were 'the most sarcastic joke of history'.[62]

The advocates of the resolution tried hard to assuage Russian concerns, especially regarding any measure that could be perceived as a precursor to military action. A draft resolution stated that the Council 'is reaffirming its strong commitment to the sovereignty, independence, unity and territorial integrity of Syria, emphasising the need to resolve the current crisis in Syria peacefully, and stressing that nothing in this resolution compels states to resort to the use of force or the threat of force'.[63] Even so, Russia was in no mood to compromise on any resolution that would lead to the departure of Assad. Russian Foreign Minister Sergei Lavrov defended the Russian role, including its continuing arms shipments to Syria: 'We're arming the constitutional government, which we don't approve of what it is doing, using force against demonstrators, but we're not picking sides, we're implementing our commercial contractual obligations.' He warned that a resolution could lead to 'another Libya', which would, in his opinion, be disastrous.[64]

Russian diplomats tried to broker talks between the Syrian government and opposition elements, but the opposition would have none of it: it cited the continuing violence perpetrated by the regime and noted that the crackdown had persisted through numerous efforts to negotiate a peaceful solution. The Obama administration opined that countries needed to accept the reality that Assad had to go – in other words, stop supporting him. According to White House spokesman, Jay Carney, 'it is important to calculate into your considerations the fact that he will go'.[65]

Most, however, were just hoping that the threat of international opprobrium and isolation on this issue would be enough to turn Russia and China. As Jeffrey Laurenti, an astute observer of UN diplomacy, commented:

> The Western strategy of seeking to press Russia to acquiesce in a stronger Security Council demand on Damascus assumes that Russia does not wish to stand alone in vetoing action as the death toll mounts in Syria. But the United States itself has not hesitated to stand alone in vetoing council resolutions on Israeli settlements or fighting in Gaza when all fourteen other members were united. On Syria, the Russians count a third of the council in their corner . . . Perhaps revealingly, leaders of the Syrian opposition acknowledge they do not expect Assad would heed a Security Council demand to step down, regardless. It is this that feeds suspicions of council skeptics that . . . [it] is intended to give outsiders a legal pretext for coercive steps to achieve compliance.[66]

It was no surprise, then, that on 4 February the resolution failed to be passed in the Security Council, as Russia and China vetoed it. The other thirteen members of the Council voted for the measure. In the aftermath of the vote, the back-and-forth rhetoric between Russian and Chinese officials, on the one hand, and those who represented countries that supported the resolution, was heated – to say the least. The US ambassador to the UN, Susan Rice, said she was 'disgusted' at the veto by Russia and China. Referring specifically to Russia, she added: 'this intransigence is even more shameful when you consider that one of these members continues to deliver weapons to Assad'. She went on: 'Since these two members last vetoed a resolution on Syria, an estimated 3,000 more civilians have been killed.'[67] Hillary Clinton called the vetoes 'a travesty', saying the Security Council was now 'neutered'.[68] The French and British UN ambassadors declared that Russia and China had aligned themselves with a regime that is massacring its people.

The Russian ambassador to the UN, Vitaly Churkin, said the text 'did not adequately reflect the real state of affairs and sent an unbalanced signal'. He noted that Russia was continuing its diplomatic efforts on the ground to resolve the situation by sending its foreign minister to Damascus. The Chinese UN representative, Li Baodong, called on all parties in Syria to stop the violence and restore order. He said the UN resolution would only have served to 'complicate the issue', would have 'put undue emphasis on pressuring the Syrian government' and would 'prejudge the result of dialogue'.[69]

As for those in Syria fighting against the regime, they felt abandoned: one opposition figure called the uprising the 'orphan revolution'.[70] Another lamented: 'The UN isn't doing anything about it [the violence]. The Arab League isn't doing anything about it . . . While they're having their little discussion, people are sitting here and they're dying.'[71]

The consequences

The repercussions of the failure to pass the UN Security Council resolution were profound. Most parties were at a loss as to what to do next. A number of opinion pieces and editorials commented that, in the aftermath of the vote, there was no good solution. Even the worst (to many people) alternative – Assad staying in power – had to be considered, or else Syria would be consigned to a protracted, bloody civil war that could produce the dreaded regional doomsday scenario.[72] It seemed that, with the failure of UN and AL diplomacy, there was greater momentum for a more muscular response to the crisis in Syria. Senior politicians in Western capitals, such as Senators John McCain and Joseph Lieberman in the United States, openly called for military support for the Syrian opposition. Press leaks regarding contingency plans for military operations against the Syrian regime began to appear in Western newspapers, while Western government officials did their best to distance their countries from military intervention. An article in *Time* magazine in early March was entitled 'Who Will Save Syria?': it pitted an argument in favor of military intervention against one that argued against military action.[73]

The anti-Assad states attempted to regroup. About a week later, with Saudi Arabia leading the way, the Arab League transition plan was moved to the UN General Assembly, where it garnered 137 votes in favor to 22 against. However, this was more a sign of failure than of success, as General Assembly resolutions do not carry anywhere near the weight of a Security Council resolution. AL members then called for a joint peacekeeping force with the UN to intervene in Syria. Although they hoped to keep the pressure up on Assad, it was clear that their ability and readiness to act were lacking. The Syrian regime, obviously more confident about its position, said the new proposal reflected 'the state of hysteria affecting some Arab governments, especially Qatar and Saudi Arabia, after Qatar's failure to pass a UN resolution that allows foreign intervention in Syria'.[74]

On the ground in Syria, it seemed very clear that the regime believed the failure of the UN Security Council resolution (and thus the Arab League plan) gave it a green light to escalate the military pressure on the rebels, particularly in the city of Homs, where the opposition, backed by the Free Syrian Army, had established a virtual autonomous zone in the Baba Amr district of the city. After a siege lasting almost a month, in which hundreds of Homs residents, activists and rebel fighters were killed (and in which several Western journalists were also killed or wounded), the district fell to government forces on 1 March and FSA units fled the city, as the world watched on in horror. Syrian television surveyed the devastation, reporting that the residents of Homs were relieved that the Baba Amr area was rid of the 'terrorists', who had occupied schools and medical centers 'by force of arms'.[75] Buoyed by this success, government forces fanned out to focus their attention on other rebel strongholds in the country.

The failure at the UN Security Council also undermined the path of diplomacy championed by the Syrian National Council. As a result, the existing fissures within the SNC (and between it and other Syrian opposition groups) became more manifest. The diversity of the Syrian opposition groups and the lack of a unified hierarchical structure had always prevented the regime from focusing its wrath on a single entity; but now this apparent advantage turned sour on the opposition, as previously concealed cleavages opened up. In late February, around twenty prominent members of the SNC, including executive committee member Haythem al-Maleh, announced that they had broken away and formed a new opposition organization called the Syrian Patriotic Group (SPG). It was the aim of the new group to forge closer relations with rebels inside Syria, in support of a more militaristic approach to unseating the Assad regime. One of the leaders of this new group, Walid al-Bunni, reflecting original concerns about the composition of the SNC, said: 'We do not have Muslim Brotherhood members amongst us . . . and we object to [SNC chairman] Burhan Ghalioun's mild approach . . . where he neglected to mention the importance of arming the FSA.'[76] One Syrian businessman – a financial backer of the organization – blasted the SNC chairman: 'The Muslim brothers . . . have a toy name Ghalioun and they play inside as they wish.'[77] Another leading SPG member, Kamal al-Labwani, stated that the main objective was to get out of 'paralysis' mode; he said that 'the 20 members would remain as part of the SNC, but they will have a different mechanism of work.'[78] In a statement released by the SPG, the group explained its stance:

> Syria has experienced long and difficult months since the Syrian National Council was formed without it achieving satisfactory results or being able to activate its executive offices or adopt the demands of the rebels inside Syria. The previous mode of operation has been useless. We decided to form a patriotic action group to back the national effort to bring down the regime with all available resistance means including supporting the Free Syrian Army.[79]

Reflecting this turn toward a more militaristic approach, on 1 March the SNC announced the creation of a military bureau. According to a press statement, it would 'track the armed opposition groups, organize and unify their ranks under one central command, defining their defense missions while placing them under the political supervision of the SNC.'[80] A senior member of the SNC said 'an office on the ground inside Syria will coordinate providing weapons to the FSA, and that will be the only mechanism to supply weapons to the FSA.'[81] However, a senior figure in the FSA, Colonel Malik al-Kurdi, disputed this. He told CNN: 'We are surprised on the formation of the military consultation council without taking our opinion ... How could such a decision be taken by the SNC without informing Colonel Riad Al Asaad leading the military opposition.'[82] Not wanting any political interference in his organization's activities, Riad al-Asaad himself told the BBC that the FSA would not cooperate with the new SNC military bureau.[83] Despite past accords, the SNC and the FSA were still clearly not on the same page.

Under intense pressure from the regime crackdown at this time, the SNC seemed to be splintering over whether or not to assume a more militant posture. Labwani ended up resigning from the SNC because 'there is a lot of chaos in the group and not a lot of clarity over what they can accomplish right now. We have not gotten very far in working to arm the rebels.'[84] On the other side of the spectrum, Rasha Yousef also quit the SNC, but for very different reasons. She said that she could no longer 'be a partner in bloodshed ... their policy is taking the country to a civil war ... They are calling for international intervention and calling for arming the opposition without any plan or organizing which is very dangerous.'[85]

Others fondly harked back to the early days of the uprising, when it was based on peaceful protests, and wondered if the movement could return to this. As one activist commented, 'Instead of mourning, let's go to strikes. Instead of bearing arms, let's organize non-cooperation campaigns.' Another claimed: 'It's never too late for civil resistance and peaceful change. In the end the militarization will not end the violence. Meeting them with arms ... will only push them to use survival instincts.' But there was also recognition of the difficulty of doing this: 'With this level of repression it is becoming extremely difficult to convince people to participate in peaceful activities.'[86]

As Syrian dissident Hazem al-Nahar said in early 2012,

> Now we have the very situation I feared: a Babel of contradictory and competing voices that leaves everyone, regime loyalists and opponents alike, mistrustful and dismissive of the Syrian opposition ... The

> situation is just as the regime would have it: an opposition fractured and divided over issues that have no basis in reality.[87]

Aron Lund points out that this disunity is a major hurdle to any negotiated solution to the conflict for the following reasons:

1. Civilian politicians will be needed to fill the vacuum of power if the government suddenly falls.
2. A legitimate and cohesive opposition will be necessary to control the military factions and their commanders, thus preventing 'warlordism'.
3. If Bashar is removed in an internal coup and the regime remains largely intact, it will only want to bring opposition elements into government as a fig leaf of political pluralism; however, if the opposition is strong and united, it can use this opportunity to push for more reforms than it could otherwise.
4. If there is an internationally negotiated solution that keeps Bashar in power, the regime may be compelled to co-opt opposition elements in order to regain some lost legitimacy, thus once again offering an opportunity for a real, united opposition to press for political reforms.[88]

All of this is, of course, speculative (and perhaps unlikely); but unless the opposition becomes more cohesive and coordinated, the regime will more than likely survive in the near term.

Rubbing salt into the wounds of those opposition elements clamoring for more military assistance, Secretary of State Clinton, responding to pressure to start delivering more tangible US military aid to the opposition, said:

> What are we going to arm them with and against what? We're not going to bring tanks over the borders of Turkey, Lebanon and Jordan. We know al-Qaeda [leader, Ayman al-] Zawahiri is supporting the opposition in Syria. Are we supporting al-Qaeda in Syria? Hamas is now supporting the opposition. Are we supporting Hamas in Syria? If you're a military planner or if you're secretary of state and you're trying to

> figure out do you have the elements of an opposition that is actually viable, that we don't see. We see immense human suffering that is heartbreaking.[89]

She went on: 'sometimes, overturning brutal regimes takes time and cost lives. I wish it weren't so'.[90] State Department spokeswoman, Victoria Nuland, commented: 'We don't believe that it makes sense to contribute now to the further militarization of Syria. What we don't want to see is the spiral of violence increase.'[91] The chairman of the Joint Chiefs of Staff, General Martin Dempsey, said the United States needed to be cautious and obtain more information:

> There's indications that al-Qaeda is involved and that they're interested in supporting the opposition. There's a number of players, all of whom are trying to reinforce their particular side of this issue. And until we're a lot clearer about . . . who they are and what they are, I think it would be premature to talk about arming them.[92]

Meanwhile James Clapper, the Director of National Intelligence, in testimony to the Senate Armed Services Committee, pointed out that the FSA was made up of disparate groups and had no centralized command and control structure; he added that 'the opposition groups in many cases may not be aware they [al-Qaida operatives] are there'.[93] Finally, then-Senator John Kerry, the influential chairman of the Senate Foreign Relations Committee, echoing Clinton, said the SNC compared unfavorably with Libya's Transitional National Council, primarily because there was no real address for what is an amorphous and divided Syrian opposition: 'This is not Libya, where you had a base of operations in Benghazi, where you had people who were representing the entire opposition to Libya.'[94]

Indeed, as this collection of statements shows, there was a real concern in Washington that the Syrian rebellion could be hijacked by radical Islamists, especially al-Qaida elements crossing over from Iraq. The US ambassador to Syria, Robert Ford (who had by this time been withdrawn from Syria over security concerns), told the Senate Foreign Relations

Committee: 'We have cautioned the opposition that if they declare some kind of big jihad they will frighten many of the very fence-sitters still in places like Damascus.'[95] In essence, it would be feeding into the Syrian regime's narrative from the start of the uprising. Whether this is a legitimate fear is questionable, but a number of suicide bombings aimed at the regime in Syria did bear the hallmarks of al-Qaida, and the specter of what happened in Iraq looms large.

In early 2012, most people would agree that the Syrian opposition on the ground, while comprising mainly conservative Sunnis, is clearly not a *salafist* movement; but there is a tangible fear in Washington and elsewhere that deteriorating conditions could open the way to al-Qaida. A video released online on 11 February rather points up this fear. In it, al-Qaida leader Ayman al-Zawahiri calls Bashar al-Assad 'the butcher son of a butcher' and praises the Syrian people for waging a *jihad* against him.[96]

There is a general sense that the period of diplomacy – when some sort of 'soft landing' might have been engineered – has passed. In the wake of the failed UN and AL resolutions, in late February the United States organized a meeting in Tunis of what was called the 'Friends of Syria' – a group of over sixty countries – in an attempt to organize and coordinate actions that would end the violence, to formulate a political solution and to deliver aid (though not of the military kind) to the opposition.[97] This appeared to be an attempt to work outside the purview of the United Nations, but developing a coordinated response was difficult. Some countries in the Arab League called on the Arab states to cut diplomatic relations with Syria entirely, and Saudi Arabia and Qatar (and Kuwait) urged states to arm the rebels; indeed, there were numerous reports that Doha and Riyadh had already been funneling funds to the Syrian rebels to purchase weapons (if not indeed the arms themselves). The black market in arms entering Syria from Iraq and Lebanon has also been booming.

A regional proxy war in Syria between Saudi Arabia, Qatar and Turkey, on the one hand, and Iran and Lebanon (Hizbullah), on the other, was clearly gaining momentum. The opposition became more militarized, and with this the Syrian regime's military response intensified. At the international level, US Assistant Secretary of State Jeffrey Feltman testified before the Senate Foreign Relations Committee that the 'demise of the Assad regime is inevitable';[98] and on 6 February President Obama said that Assad's fall 'is not going to be a matter of if, it's going to be a matter of when.'[99] At the other end of the spectrum, Russian Prime Minister Vladimir Putin was saying at the same time: 'I very much hope the United States and other countries . . . do not try to set a military scenario in motion in Syria without sanction from the UN Security Council.'[100] Another Russian official (who had come from a meeting with the Syrian president) commented: 'Assad doesn't look like a person ready to leave, because . . . there is no reason for him to do that as he is being supported by broad layers of the population.'[101]

The regime itself went on to hold a referendum on 27 February on the long-promised new constitution: according to the Syrian authorities, it was approved by about 90 per cent of voters (although they admitted that, at 57.4 per cent, the turnout was lower than usual because of the unrest). The constitution was the centerpiece of Assad's reform program, as announced by him (in piecemeal fashion) since the beginning of the uprising, almost a year earlier. Of course, Western capitals and the Syrian opposition were very skeptical and, for the most part, dismissive. The State Department referred to it as 'absolutely cynical', and other critics called it 'too little, too late', 'meaningless', 'window dressing' or yet another delaying tactic.[102] Meanwhile Moscow applauded the process as a step forward for Syria.[103]

Actually, if Assad had been smarter – or more courageous – and had introduced this constitution in the early part of the uprising, it may have taken some of the wind out of the sails of the opposition. The new document, drawn up by a twenty-nine-member constitutional committee chosen by Assad, dropped the highly controversial Article 8 (which ensured Baath party rule). Other references to Baathism in the Syrian economy, educational system, army and society were also removed (such as the president's pledge to the Baathist trinity of 'unity, freedom and socialism'). It theoretically establishes a multi-party system that would see more than one candidate running for president; presidential elections being held every seven years (with a two-term maximum); and aspiring candidates having to gain at least 20 per cent of the vote of parliamentarians (so at least 50 votes out of 250). The formation of parties is subject to government approval: they cannot be based solely on religion, ethnicity or geography. Under the new system, the president still wields tremendous power, as the office retains the right to appoint and dismiss prime ministers, and to assume legislative powers when parliament is not in session. The president also enjoys a seven-year term – the longest of any parliamentary-based presidential system in the world – and immunity before a court of law (except in the case of treason against the state).

However, as Syria-based academic Sami Moubayed writes, there may be a silver lining:

> The new constitution will not solve the country's political, security and economic problems. It won't end the military operations, bring about cheaper heating fuel and, certainly, will not offer a life jacket for the Syrian regime. It does, however, lay the groundwork for a democratic platform that can be used to stage upcoming parliamentary elections – and possibly – early presidential ones as well, which can achieve all [the political reforms], including perhaps authoring a new constitution entirely, which would make this one an interim charter.[104]

As the next presidential election should be held in 2014, when his current term is up, Assad could theoretically continue as president for another sixteen years. I am sure that, if he survives, this is his intention.

Subsequent to the referendum, parliamentary elections were held on 7 May. This was the first test of the political pluralism promised by the regime and the new constitution. About 7,200 candidates were reportedly up for election (including 710 women) to 250 seats in parliament across fifteen electoral constituencies.[105] While Bashar praised the elections as a milestone in the promised reform, the opposition in Syria and opponents of the regime outside the country dismissed them as a sham – nothing but a hollow attempt by the regime to give the impression of political reform, when in fact pro-regime elements were poised to dominate the new parliament. The Syrian opposition boycotted the elections and turnout was reported to have been 51 per cent of eligible voters (though independent observers at some polling stations put the figure much lower). What is interesting is that voter turnout was supposedly almost exactly the same as in the last parliamentary elections, in 2007, which were held under much more stable conditions. It strains credulity that the turnout in 2012 could have been the same as in 2007. As a US State Department spokesperson commented, the election 'borders on ludicrous. It is not really possible to hold credible elections in a climate where basic human rights are being denied to the citizens and the government is continuing to carry out daily assaults on its own citizens'.[106] According to some reports, only one person who could actually be termed an opponent of the regime was elected. All others were either members of the Baath party or its allies.[107]

More than a year after the uprising began, the Syrian crisis had become an existential battle on several levels. With so much invested in it by an array of internal and external players, the march toward a protracted and bloody civil war seemed inevitable. Indeed, US officials in early March testified that they could not see any 'fracturing' in the Assad regime, and military desertions had been minimal. A Pentagon official said that 'the assumption is Assad will continue to persevere until he and other regime leaders are sufficiently suppressed. He's enjoying tactical survival. He can wait it out. He looks to be dug in'.[108] He added that the hope was that Assad would feel the 'strategic weight and pressure of outside critics'.[109] As one member of a Syrian opposition group commented following the government's retaking of Baba Amr in Homs: 'People saw that the revolution wasn't achieving its goals, and there's a lot of head-scratching now. The regime has used this to send a message to Qatar and the USA and others, saying: you can't topple me, so you'll have to deal with me. And that was always Plan B, as far as the USA is concerned.'[110]

An already ugly situation was to get uglier. By the end of May 2012, the UN estimated that 9,000–10,000 Syrians had died, that 30,000 refugees had fled to neighboring countries and that 200,000 people were internally displaced. The Local Coordination Committees' estimate was that over

11,000 had died (with 60,000 imprisoned and 20,000 missing). The Syrian government put the number of civilian deaths at about 2,500.

There would be more and more pressure on the United States from several quarters to engage militarily in the crisis at some level. It could lead from behind, as it did in Libya, where NATO's European members and the Arab League were out in front. It could put boots on the ground: direct military intervention alongside allied forces to establish safe havens and protective corridors from which opposition elements could engage government forces more effectively and where civilians could seek refuge. Or it could actively arm the Syrian opposition. But as Syria analyst Marc Lynch warned, 'nobody should be fooled into thinking that this is a panacea: arming the weaker side in a fully fledged, internationalised civil war is much more likely to produce a painful stalemate than a quick, decisive outcome'.[111] Or as Patrick Seale wrote, 'the arming of the opposition . . . seems not to have advanced the opposition's cause but to have given the regime the justification for crushing it'.[112]

CHAPTER 9

Whither Syria?

Putrid piles of garbage lie on streets because basic services have ceased operating. Running water and electricity are either unavailable – by design, as a form of collective punishment, or as a result of disruption – or else are available only sporadically. Storefronts are shuttered, battered and broken. The stores themselves are empty of both people and products, as either the retailers have deliberately removed the stock, storing it for a safer day, or else – more likely – the goods have been pilfered by vandals on one or either side of the conflict. The walls of buildings are pockmarked by shells and bullets. Many streets are deserted, littered with debris and marked with the occasional bloodstain. Security checkpoints are ubiquitous; on the highways into and out of cities and along the main arteries, security personnel check identification and search vehicles, while those that have been stopped pray that their names are not on government lists of people to be arrested. Truckloads of soldiers and security personnel drive to hotspots; indeed, sometimes they are the only vehicles on the road. As the violence has increased, thugs and criminal elements on both sides have begun to appear, extorting money and bullying innocent civilians in a whole new way that is separate from the ugliness of the uprising itself.[1]

Even the elite in Aleppo and Damascus are wary of leaving their safe areas. In the cities that have been hardest hit, people have retreated into sectarian quarters. Homes have been abandoned as families have fled. Other families want to leave but cannot, as they are afraid their homes will be ransacked. Those that can afford to do so contemplate leaving the country, but they cannot obtain visas (particularly as many embassies have closed) and trying to leave the country surreptitiously is too dangerous. Damascus International Airport is almost devoid of people and planes. Tourism has virtually ceased. Credit cards don't work. Trade and commerce have declined sharply. Factories have closed, and even those still operating do so at well below capacity. Workers are routinely laid off. An already high unemployment rate (prior to the uprising) has doubled. The Syrian pound has plummeted against the dollar (from SYP 47 to the dollar before the uprising to as much as SYP 100 a year later). Public sector salaries have been halved, in order to reduce government spending (and redirect it toward security). Food and fuel prices are significantly higher. The agricultural sector has been severely disrupted, and basic food items have already become scarce. Schools are closed.

It has reached the point where sometimes people are killed and nobody knows who is responsible. For example, on 19 February 2012 a Syrian attorney general was assassinated in the city of Idlib, one of the epicenters of the uprising. The government, of course, bemoaned the loss and accused the rebels of his murder (as opposition elements had increasingly taken to assassinating civilian and military officials). But the opposition in Idlib said he had been a sympathizer and had stayed in his official position to act as an informant. They claimed, therefore, that the Syrian security forces were responsible for the murder. The fact that the attorney general's funeral was reportedly attended by a number of opposition elements lends some credence to this assertion (assuming the reports are true).

This is what life has become in Syria, especially in a number of Syrian cities that have been directly hit by the uprising and the government's attempts to suppress it.[2] Syrians in central Damascus and Aleppo, which had long remained relatively unscathed by the uprisings, began to feel the pain more and more well into 2012, as violence spread from the suburbs towards the downtown areas.

It is an excruciatingly sad picture. Almost every Syrian knows someone who has been killed (by one side or the other), arrested, tortured or bullied during the uprising. I have traveled to Syria over twenty times since 1989, with some of those visits lasting for months. I have acquired a number of Syrian friends who are now faced off against one another. A couple of the foreign reporters and photographers killed while covering the uprising in Syria were friends of mine. Thus even those of us who are keen observers of Syria but are far away from the horridness on the ground have been touched by it. Syria is a country with huge potential, given the right circumstances. It is a crossroads of history and can boast unparalleled historical and archeological sites. The people are like people in other countries: they love their families and yearn for a better life, greater opportunities and a peaceful existence. One feels so helpless watching this country implode.

How did it come to this?

The conceptual gap

Early in Bashar al-Assad's presidency, he decreed that military-style uniform would no longer be worn by students in primary and secondary schools. At the time, Western media, officials and analysts dismissed and ridiculed the change as virtually worthless. It was emblematic, they said, of how little Assad was actually doing to reform his country. This added to the growing disappointment in what was supposed to be a different type of Syrian ruler. However, on closer inspection, there was more to this decree than met the eye. Wherever Assad could – and it should be borne in mind that this was a system that was almost immune to change and that Assad's authority at the time was less than it later became – he tried to redirect Syria's operational philosophy away from the symbols and trappings of martial indoctrination to a more normal educational environment that focused on developing useful skill sets. Ironically, this may have contributed to a new generation of youth who thought not of battle against real (or imagined) foes, but of securing a sociopolitical milieu more conducive to a better life. In any event, between the West and

Syria the 'conceptual gap' as to the utility and effectiveness of this decree was quite wide.

On one occasion, Assad lambasted the criticism he had received in the West on account of the perceived slow pace at which private banks were being set up in Syria – a measure he had announced soon after coming to power (see Chapter 1): it was considered small potatoes when only four private banks actually came into being in 2004. Assad, though, thought it was a transformational moment and a harbinger of things to come in terms of economic liberalization.

At another meeting, this one soon after the withdrawal of Syrian troops from Lebanon in April 2005 (see Chapter 2), he expressed anger that the West – and especially the United States – did not appreciate the 'enormous' concession he had made by agreeing to withdraw. The implication, of course, was that he could have made a lot more trouble had he wanted to, or could even have kept the Syrian forces ensconced in Lebanon. He felt he had received no credit for his supposed magnanimity.

These are but a few examples of the 'conceptual gap' between Syria and the West in general. When Assad spoke in his first speech to the nation on 30 March 2011 in reaction to the growing protests in his country, he said terrorists, conspirators and armed gangs were the primary reasons for the unrest (at the time of writing he still maintains this). Most of those outside Syria scoffed: he was blatantly diverting attention from the real socioeconomic and political problems that had brought the Arab Spring to Syria. But many Syrians – maybe even Assad himself – readily believe such claims. Their perception of the nature of threat is vastly different from ours, outside Syria. One might blame this on Syrian paranoia bred by imperialist conspiracies of the past, on the Arab-Israeli conflict or on regime brainwashing to justify the security state; but it is, in large measure, a function of living in a dangerous neighborhood, where real threats are indeed often just around the corner.

It is the conceptual and perceptual gap that lies at the root of the impasse between what the United States and much of the international community demand of the Syrian regime and what Assad is actually doing (or feels he should do) to end the violence against protestors and enact far-reaching reform. This could be seen in Assad's (now infamous) televised interview with ABC's Barbara Walters in Damascus, broadcast in early December 2011. After the interview, Assad was ridiculed in the Western press for saying some rather strange things. One State Department official concluded that the Syrian president appeared to be 'utterly disconnected with the reality that's going on in his country'. Commenting on Assad's response to one of Walters' questions, when he had said that he would be 'crazy' to order his forces to kill his own people, one analyst joked 'it's now clear that Assad meets his own definition of crazy'.[3] When asked by Walters 'Do you think that your forces cracked down too hard?', Assad replied: 'They are not my forces; they are military forces belong [*sic*] to the government . . . I don't own them. I am president. I don't own the country, so they are not my forces.'[4]

In the West, of course, Assad seemed totally 'out to lunch' or (possibly even worse) not in control. I do not think this is the case at all. I have heard Assad say something similar on numerous occasions. We must bear in mind that although his command of English is impressive, it is by no means perfect; he has difficulty in conveying the nuances of what he means in a medium that, in effect, is his third language.[5] What he most likely meant was that he is not all-powerful in Syria – and in this he is correct. He has to constantly manage competing interests and listen to powerful voices on different issues. Although he has a great deal of power – far more than anyone else in Syria – he often cannot act in an arbitrary manner. He has stated again and again over the years that Syria has viable institutions, ones that he had been in the process of reshaping and revitalizing. Assad never liked to portray himself as acting outside the framework of these institutions, even though he did so quite frequently; indeed, on one occasion he admitted his frustration that he had signed a thousand decrees, but only a few had been implemented, which had forced him to go outside the purview of government ministries to get things done. For whatever reason, it is important to him that it does not seem as if every aspect of Syria is under his watchful eye. I do not think this is to avoid responsibility: it is more a question of him trying to depict his country as a modern, working state that functions like others. He does not want to appear to be the king who inherited the throne.

I am also sure that, during the uprising, Assad would have pointed out that he has made extensive concessions and enacted dramatic reforms. He would again have complained that he is not receiving any recognition or credit for this; he would conclude, as he has done in the past, that the United States and the West 'have it in for him' – no matter what he does, it will not be enough. And I think he would sincerely believe this.

Assad is the product of an authoritarian system – one that is a paradigm of stagnation and control. The Syrian system is not geared to responding to people's demands: it controls people's demands. Nor is it geared to implementing dramatic reform: it is constructed to maintain the status quo and survive. At any other time, the reforms thus far announced – lifting the emergency law, providing for Kurdish citizenship, creating political parties, a new constitution, etc. – would be viewed as significant. Now, however, they are seen as self-serving, after-the-fact and inadequate. In any event, to reform more deeply and rapidly is anathema to the Syrian system, simply because it would spell the end of the regime itself. Rapid reform runs counter to the basic instincts of an authoritarian, neo-patriarchal system.

I got to know Bashar al-Assad fairly well. I do not see him as either eccentric or as a bloodthirsty killer, along the lines of Muammar Gadafi or Saddam Hussein. People I know who have met all three readily agree with this assessment. There are those, however, who differ (sometimes vehemently), viewing Bashar as a corrupt tyrant from the very beginning. Many of these people have never even been to Syria. Many of them have agendas that have been (or still are) assisted by this characterization. And almost none of them have ever met Assad or any other top Syrian official. They often base their position on the evidence of continued repression and repeatedly delayed reform. This is understandable. If they said that the Syrian system had been corrupt and repressive from the beginning of Assad's rule, then I would wholeheartedly agree.[6] If they said that he was bound eventually to succumb to this system, even if he was altruistic in the beginning, then they would be correct. But Bashar was different from the typical Middle Eastern dictator, and this led many people (including me) to hope for the best – and maybe even indulge in a little wishful thinking. That Bashar was perceived by most who met him as a relatively ordinary person, and that this ordinary person then sanctioned a brutal crackdown on the uprising in what seems to have been a very matter-of-fact manner says something about human behavior and about how even normal people can become corrupted under the pressure of power and delusion.[7] He learned soon enough that to succeed in the Syrian system one had to conform to it.

Somewhere along the road, however, Assad lost his way – the arrogance of authoritarianism. Either he convinced himself or he was convinced by sycophants that his well-being was synonymous with the well-being of the country, and that what he was doing – violently putting down protests and not meeting the demands for change – was both necessary and the correct response. A self-reinforcing alternate reality was orchestrated and constructed around him, and there was no way of testing it against what was real.[8] A friend of mine, Ayman Abd al-Nour, is a prominent voice on things Syrian. He went to college with Bashar in Syria and got to know him well as a friend. Ayman was forced into exile several years ago because of his criticisms of the regime that appeared on his blog, 'All4Syria'. On Assad he said the following: 'After he became president, when people showered him with compliments and inflated his ego, he became totally different – as if he was chosen by God to run Syria. He believed he was a prophet and started to build his own world.'[9] This is human nature in all walks of life, from kings and presidents to corporate CEOs.

While the rest of the world thinks Assad has been delusional (or at the very least has been trying to deflect attention from the real causes of the uprising) ever since his 30 March speech, when he blamed foreign conspiracies for the unrest in Syria, it is my contention that he and his inner circle really believe – more than most people can imagine – that there have indeed been foreign conspiracies from the very beginning. It is simply the very different way in which the Syrian leadership perceives the nature of threat, based on its own historical experiences. The Syrian leadership just has a different conceptual paradigm that frames the nature of internal and external threat to the country. From the Western point of view, it appears extremely paranoid; from the perspective of Damascus, it is prudent and based on historical circumstances. And the violence Assad has unleashed has helped to create a context in Syria whereby external forces are, in fact, involving themselves in the uprising more assertively; it has, then, to some extent become a self-fulfilling prophecy.

The Syrian government's crackdown is a push-button, convulsive reaction to domestic threat. It is not that Assad does not control the security forces, but this is the way Syria has worked under the Assads. They reach into their historical pocket and pull out what worked for them in the past; in this case what they found was much closer to Hama in 1982 than to anything else.[10] And to date, Bashar has not been willing to reduce the tremendous amount of leeway he has given the security forces to deal with threats, both domestic and foreign (the latter often seen as causing the former). In my view, this has empowered the thuggish security forces, which know only one way of dealing with threats. He believes it is an unfortunate necessity in a dangerous neighborhood. As I mentioned in Chapter 4, rather than adequately comprehending the new circumstances of the Arab Spring, Bashar simply went along with business as usual. In addition, the regimes of Hafiz and Bashar al-Assad have always refused to make concessions from a perceived position of weakness: they will only do so from a perceived position of strength. Cracking down hard on demonstrators while offering political reforms are two sides of the same coin. This is the Syrian way – under the Assads.

Thus, there was not much the Obama administration could do. The United States tried to squeeze blood from a stone: it pushed for dramatic political reform from a system that simply is not built for it, either mechanically, institutionally or intellectually. The regime seems to have the willpower, incentive and means to stick around for a while. Unless Assad somehow finally starts to 'think outside the box' (unlikely, given what I have just said) and assents to a transitional period of reform that ends up with him willingly stepping down, the regime's legitimacy has been so tarnished that it will eventually alienate those remaining bases of support that have kept him in power – or at least that is the hope of the opposition and most of the international community. Assad's removal perhaps will just be a matter of time (although it may take longer than many want). Unfortunately, it is unlikely to be a pretty sight. As Anne Applebaum wrote in an article on revolution and the former Soviet leader Mikhail Gorbachev, for there to be an orderly transition from dictatorship to democracy, two elements are crucial: 'an elite willing to hand over power, and an alternative elite organized enough to accept it'.[11] In Syria neither exists. Will it at some point? Probably not. Many in the opposition realized that the system could only be changed through revolution. There was no other option.

Despite support from countries such as Russia and Iran, Assad and his loyalists believe they are essentially on their own and must do things their own way, because ultimately they feel they have a better understanding of what is going on and of what it will take to succeed (i.e. stay in power). I believe they truly think they will work their way through this. The Syrian leadership views events over the long, not the short term. They trust that, if they can hang on by creating a favorable stalemate, they will outlast the protestors and outlast world attention. Eventually, in ten years or so, they think they will be able to work the country back into the good graces of the international community. The vagaries of the Middle East mean that there are usually such opportunities for rehabilitation: the Syrian leadership (it believes) has been through it all once already and survived, following the intense international pressure after the Hariri assassination. They may not fully appreciate the differences between the uprising that began in 2011 and the post-Hariri environment, but the latter reinforced an already existing nationalistic confidence – if not triumphalism – and an instinct for survival. Assad probably thinks the opposition inside and outside the country is largely smoke and mirrors in terms of its cohesiveness (and he would not altogether be wrong about this), and thus its ability to take the fight to the regime over the long term is (he believes) minimal.

Most of us watching from the outside, those making policy decisions in Washington, at the United Nations or in European capitals, are from a decidedly different world and have a conceptual paradigm that diverges markedly from that of the Syrian leadership. To think that we could all get on the same page and collectively find a peaceful way out of the mess was, in retrospect, more fantasy than reality. The *Weltanschauung* prisms are anchored in vastly different experiences, preconceptions, histories and ideologies, and they have a very hard time getting aligned with each other.

Scenarios

There are three basics ways in which the Syrian uprising could pan out: 1) Bashar al-Assad could fall from power; 2) Bashar al-Assad could stay in power; or 3) the crisis could turn into a protracted stalemate or civil war. Each of these scenarios contains a multitude of variations, one or more of which could already have occurred by the time this book is published.

Falling from power

This is, of course, the preferred option of the Syrian opposition and the bulk of the international community. The sooner Assad falls, the better. There are many different ways in which it could come about. The opposition could forcibly remove Assad and the regime from power (much as the Libyan rebels removed the Gadafi regime). Without outside help, however, this seems unlikely, given the current asymmetry of power between government forces and the opposition (as it is currently made up). Furthermore, as was noted above, the political, business and military core of the regime has remained pretty well intact, with relatively few defections. Indeed, US intelligence sources testified in March 2012 that they could see no sign of significant deterioration in support for Assad.[12] As one intelligence official stated, 'this leadership is going to fight very hard . . . Assad is very much in charge of how Syria is handling this'.[13]

While wholesale – and meaningful – defections could occur (especially if some notable figures in the regime jumped ship and thus caused the whole house of cards to collapse), that seems unlikely at this juncture. The 'core' sees itself in the same boat, and there are no life jackets; so either the boat stays afloat or it sinks with everyone in it. The current power structure must be maintained at all costs, or else the leaders will all be annihilated. In addition, the Syrian military's retaking of the Baba Amr district in Homs (and its subsequent fanning out to quell other rebel strongholds in March 2012) created the impression among loyalists – and perhaps among the silent majority – that the ship is in fact *not* sinking. As a result, the regime hardliners – those who have consistently advocated a security solution to the uprising – have been empowered. There is, therefore, very little chance in the foreseeable future that what is now a weakened and divided opposition could overcome Syrian government forces.

This calculus could change, however, if support for the opposition from the outside were to increase substantially (which would actually be a closer approximation to what happened in Libya). While military contingency plans for some form of intervention in Syria were drawn up in Western capitals in early 2012, and while more officials in those capitals are calling for a more robust international effort to assist the opposition, there appears to be little appetite in the West (or capability in the Arab world) actually to do anything. As President Obama stated on 7 March, 'For us to take military action unilaterally as some have suggested, or to think that somehow there is some simple solution, I think is a mistake'.[14]

As with the situation surrounding Iran, Obama does not want the United States to get so caught up in a frenzy of moral outrage over Syria that the result is precipitate military intervention that is more convulsive than well thought through. Few in the West – certainly in the United States – want to engage in actions that could escalate into another military operation in the Middle East, just when US troops have withdrawn from Iraq and are drawing down in Afghanistan. The economy is slowly recovering and does not need another jolt of war expenditure. And 2012 is a presidential election year: no sitting administration ever wants to initiate military intervention if it does not have to. (Particularly as the war drums appear to be beating even louder on whether to support an Israeli attack on Iran to damage its alleged capacity to develop nuclear weapons.)

Finally, the West must think about the aftermath of any military intervention to overthrow the Syrian regime. It is not a happy thought. The United States (and the West in general) does not want to be saddled with the responsibility and the huge cost of rebuilding a shattered Syria. The country has fewer resources with which to jump-start the process than its neighbor, Iraq – and we all know how expensive and lengthy the US commitment was there, following the removal of Saddam Hussein in 2003. The cost of helping Syria to recover, to say nothing of helping it to thrive, will be immense (in all likelihood even greater than the costs incurred in Iraq). The democracy that was supposed to appear in Iraq has yet to emerge; in Syria, the generally accepted prerequisites for democratic transition – the existence of civil society, an older median-aged population, functioning state institutions and the prospects for economic growth – are lacking at least as much. To cap it all, Libya can hardly be regarded yet as a success story of military intervention – there is still a long way to go there. In the end, many believe a Syrian solution to the crisis is preferable, even if that involves civil war; just so long as there are clear winners and losers, rather than a jumbled mix of rival militias and armies supported by external actors.

The main argument against military intervention, however, is that Syria is not Libya. The NATO and Arab League military support for the Libyan rebels is considered to have been successful, but any attempt to apply the same methodology to the Syrian situation is problematic. First of all, the Libyan National Transitional Council (NTC), while hardly a paragon of unity (as the post-Gadafi environment in Libya has demonstrated), was at least unified in purpose. As US officials have repeatedly emphasized when comparing the situation to that in Syria, the NTC at least had an address, a headquarters; the SNC, FSA and the myriad other Syrian opposition groups do not even have that. The NTC also had Benghazi under its control, i.e. territory (indeed a major port city), so the Libyan rebels could be resupplied more easily. In Libya there was something that resembled battle fronts, which facilitated resupply and targeting; in Syria, by contrast, the rebellion is spread out over the entire country and is being fought in densely populated cities, where it is almost impossible to figure out who is who. Nor should it be forgotten that, even with NATO and Arab League military support, it took over seven months to defeat Gadafi's forces.

Benghazi (and Tobruk) also acted as a safe haven for those fleeing from Gadafi's forces, and it provided organizational cover for the NTC to form and at least to give the outward appearance of a real opposition government that could take over once the regime was overthrown. All of this made local and international support for the Libyan rebellion that much easier: there seemed to be a reasonable chance of a stable post-Gadafi political system, since a rudimentary form of it was already identifiable. At the time of writing, this is not the case in Syria. There has been talk of creating a safe haven or *cordon sanitaire* of sorts, but the logistical difficulties and lack of diplomatic support mean that nothing has materialized. Indeed, the Syrian cities that have been most talked about as candidates for becoming 'Benghazis' – Homs and Hama – are completely landlocked and are located along the country's north–south axis.

In any case, as most military planners readily indicate, the establishment of any such haven would have to be accompanied by a no-fly zone, such as NATO imposed in Libya. But Syria's anti-aircraft defenses are significantly better than Libya's were. US intelligence officials have described Syria's air defense system as 'massive' and 'very dense'. It includes thousands of sophisticated, Russian-supplied surface-to-air missiles, anti-aircraft artillery and advanced radar with digital gear that is more difficult for US aircraft to jam.[15] Taking out Syria's air defense capability would be extremely difficult and dangerous, and would probably result in significant 'collateral damage', since many of the air defense missile batteries are located in or around densely populated cities. The related diplomacy could be complicated as well: Syria has tended not to use its air force to combat the rebels, whereas in Libya Gadafi boldly stated that he would indiscriminately bomb his country's rebels into submission. In fact, overall, the Syrian military is simply more stout and numerous than Libya's forces, and it would take much greater effort generally to defeat it. Doing so could also have unforeseen consequences: an unpredictable regime's last act could be to unleash an attack (using conventional or chemical weapons) on its neighbors, including Israel; and that would most likely ignite a regional conflagration.

Syria's topography and geography is different from Libya's (and from the military planning perspective is significantly more problematic). In Libya, most of the fighting occurred near the coast, where there are none of the mountains, valleys, hills and rivers that surround Syria's population centers and that would allow government forces to hide and escape aerial bombardment. Most of the areas targeted by NATO were within easy reach of its air bases in Italy, but it still took upwards of 21,000 missions over six months to establish and enforce the no-fly zone, to suppress Libya's much less daunting air defenses and to destroy the command and control centers.

As discussed in Chapter 7, as the uprising progressed, Syria's neighbors split into two camps: those who were friendly and those who were not so friendly. The friendly neighbors (Iraq and Lebanon) offer Syria some strategic depth and areas to pre-position supplies and troops out of the way of enemy air power. The not-so-friendly ones (Turkey and Jordan) could theoretically serve as forward bases for the establishment of a safe haven. But Turkey and Jordan would both have practical and political problems with this: both countries could be flooded with Syrian refugees. In addition, the appearance of foreign troops on Turkish or Jordanian soil could create difficulties for Ankara and Amman in terms of dealing with a potential domestic backlash. And for Turkey, the Kurdish issue is a complicating factor. Neither country would even consider any such thing without the preconditions of strong international consensus and a guarantee of success. At the time of writing, neither of these preconditions exists.

It was important, too, that the international community generally believed Muammar Gadafi to be at the very least eccentric (with most going much further and describing him as deranged). Bashar, on the other hand, is not generally regarded as such, and thus does not evoke the same disgust that Gadafi did. Even though the Libyan leader had improved his relationship with Washington during the Bush years, the aversion felt towards Gadafi perhaps made the decision to actively support his overthrow rather easier.

There is also the question of what the collapse of the Syrian regime would mean for Syria itself. Would it implode, especially with the relative dearth of institutions or civil society that could help pick up the pieces? There would be vendettas, open antagonisms and possibly all-out sectarian warfare, as in Iraq and Afghanistan. Would the implosion of Syria in fact lead to the doomsday scenario of regional instability and war?[16] Would the international community be committed to rebuilding the country if its military might had partly contributed to its devastation? With neither the United States nor Europe in the right political, diplomatic or economic mood, why undertake action that may precipitate something they desperately want to avoid?

Then again, perhaps the Saudis and the Qataris would pay the lion's share of rebuilding the country. But (as was pointed out earlier) Western governments are wary of what type of government Riyadh and Doha would countenance – it might well end up being Islamist. Concerns have already arisen regarding those two countries' roles in promoting Islamists in Libya, Tunisia, Egypt and elsewhere in the wake of the Arab Spring. On the other hand, as the uprising entered its second year, and as the opposition carved out small areas (usually city districts) under their control, municipal councils organized by the Local Coordination Committees did emerge to supply the necessary services and leadership that the government had provided before it was expelled. The Homs Revolutionary Council (HRC), for example, established a clandestine network of mobile hospitals, and built up an elected committee structure to handle security and armed operations, media relations, the planning and mounting of protests, and humanitarian and legal needs.[17] If this pattern is replicated, then perhaps, when the regime collapses, Syria will not disintegrate or descend into chaos to the extent that many predict.

Maybe most importantly, the rebellion in Syria began and escalated after the one in Libya – and after it had attracted outside military intervention. Perhaps if the Syrian uprising and the concomitant government crackdown had come before the Libyan revolt, the international community would have been able to assert itself in support of the Syrian opposition with fewer diplomatic complications. Without the previous UN Security Council vote on Libya, the Russians and Chinese would not have felt duped and perhaps would not repeatedly have used their Security Council vetoes to block measures against Syria. In addition, the Syrian uprising has lasted long enough for some serious post-Gadafi problems to surface in Libya: militias unwilling to disarm, intense tribal differences that undermine the ability of the transitional government to govern, humanitarian atrocities, lack of basic services, etc. As one Libyan expert has noted, 'The genie is out of the bottle and that means the armed groups are the dominant political players. The people making decisions are the ones with guns.'[18] We have learned time and again through history that arming the opposition improves its chances in the short term, but also militarizes and divides society in a way that is detrimental to its recovery. Should the fall of Assad occur via military means, it will be next to impossible to get the guns back afterwards.

The Syrian uprising has also lasted long enough for us to witness the rise of Islamist groups and parties in the aftermath of the revolutions in Tunisia, Egypt, Libya and Yemen. This has caused many in the West to ponder what might happen in Syria should the regime fall. I have no doubt that, well into 2012, there are those in Western capitals thinking in Machiavellian terms, in a way that they dared not think early on in the Arab Spring. They may be quietly hoping that Assad does indeed quell the Syrian rebellion – by means of a 'thousand cuts', rather than in a repeat of Hama in 1982: there would then be no moral imperative for the international community to act. There would thus be one less opportunity for Islamists to come to power in a strategic part of the Middle East, and, as there are already extensive sets of sanctions imposed on Syria, it would be much easier to continue to isolate and contain it without the diplomatic or popular pressure to engage in military action. Syria would then recede from the front pages of newspapers. However, massacres by government troops are exactly the kind of thing that could produce the moral outrage to fuel a more robust international response. One such incident is reported to have occurred in the town of Houla, outside Homs, in late May 2012. There over a hundred people were killed, including at least thirty children, in execution-style murders.[19]

A second way in which Assad could be removed is in an internal military coup. No doubt one of the objectives of the targeted sanctions and the other forms of diplomatic and economic pressure on the Syrian regime has been to generate enough dissatisfaction among core members of the government for them to start to see the Syrian president as a liability – both for the country and, more importantly, for their own personal futures. Officers in the military-security apparatus, and perhaps some civilian officials, would then enter into negotiations with the opposition, possibly brokered by the UN or the Arab League, in the hope of maintaining – or at least protecting – their positions, their status and their wealth, as well as in the hope of securing immunity from prosecution. This would be akin to what happened to Husni Mubarak in Egypt, in what was, to all intents and purposes, a military coup. There the Supreme Council of the Armed Forces (SCAF), a conglomerate of generals, assumed power after nudging Mubarak aside and has been working on the transition of Egypt into a working democracy – with mixed results.

Many analysts and commentators have been trying to read between the lines and to detect any sign in statements from Russian officials (particularly President Vladimir Putin) that Moscow may be willing to go down this route, thus protecting its long-term strategic and economic interests in Syria, but getting rid of the person who has placed the Kremlin in such an awkward diplomatic position. It was reported in early March 2012 that Putin had 'forcefully defended' Russia's position on Syria but had 'distanced himself somewhat' from Assad, 'refusing to answer' when the question came up of whether he would survive.[20]

That same month, Syrian commentator Sami Moubayed entitled one of his essays 'Will There Be a Kremlin U-turn on Syria?' He sees Putin positioning himself to act as the go-to person internationally in terms of resolving the situation in Syria, thus enhancing his country's image and 'position as a powerful and influential Middle East broker'.[21] Moubayed goes on: 'Moscow may like the Syrian regime, but it certainly likes Russian interests in the Middle East a whole lot more.'[22] He also notes that several statements by Russian officials seem to indicate less than unconditional and unlimited support for Assad. And, as Moubayed observes, the assistant secretary of state for Near East affairs, Jeffrey Feltman, in testimony before the Senate Foreign Relations Committee, was emollient towards Russia – a contrast to the ugly epithets hurled by US officials at Russia following Moscow's 4 February veto in the UN. Feltman even recognized Moscow's importance in resolving the matter, saying that Russia 'is a key element in how this goes forward' and that it had 'to be part of the solution in Syria'.[23] Finally, Moubayed notes that the 1980 Treaty of Friendship and Cooperation between Syria and the (then) Soviet Union does not include a clause governing mutual defense, and therefore Moscow is not committed to protecting Syria against foreign aggression.[24] A change of tack by the United States and the EU toward Russia (and perhaps even China) – one that sees Moscow as part of the solution rather than part of the problem, and that opens the way to working with the Kremlin rather than against it – could alter the diplomatic equation in a way that dramatically increases the pressure on Damascus.

It seems that the United States and its European allies are attempting to do just this: a diplomatic offensive was launched in late May and early June. US and European diplomats flooded Moscow in an attempt to persuade Putin to adopt the so-called 'Yemen option' (discussed below), which would remove Assad and his relatives but keep the ruling structure largely intact. A senior Obama official went to Moscow in early June for a meeting with Putin, leading a high-level Western diplomat to say: '[We] try to detach Assad from Russia and convince the Russians that Assad for cold, geopolitical reasons is a bad horse . . . that Assad is now a liability in the Russia–Syria strategic alliance.'[25] On the other hand, as former US Secretary of State Henry Kissinger warned in a *Washington Post* editorial on 1 June: 'If the objective is confined to deposing a specific ruler, a new civil war could follow in the resulting vacuum, as armed groups contest succession, and outside countries choose different sides.'[26]

This has always been the question in such patron-client relationships: when do you cut ties with a leader who has largely become discredited? The United States faced this dilemma with the shah of Iran in the late 1970s. For a variety of reasons, Washington stayed with the shah for too long, thus getting caught up in the anti-shah wake of the 1979 Iranian Revolution and preventing it from developing any sort of positive relationship with the subsequent Islamic Republic of Iran (not that establishing good relations with the ayatollahs was likely).[27]

Certainly, similar debates and discussions will have gone on in the Kremlin regarding the fate of Bashar al-Assad. This would not be a first for Moscow: one only has to look at Afghanistan in the 1970s, especially in the year or so prior to the Soviet invasion of December 1979, to realize that Russia (or the Soviet Union) was not shy about removing leaders who pursued policies inimical to its interests. On the other hand, the ultimate failure of such action in Afghanistan – an invasion and a decade-long quagmire that accelerated the end of the Soviet Union – may make the Kremlin more hesitant to try anything like that again. But (at the time of writing) Moscow seems firmly committed to the Assad regime. Since Vladimir Putin (who has taken a more hardline position on Syria than his predecessor) regained the Russian presidency in February, this is unlikely to change in the near term, unless the Syrian regime starts to lose its grip on power, and there were some signs by July that the opposition had gained some ground, with the regime comumensurately more on the defensive. Indeed, Moscow's willingness to advocate more assertively for a negotiated solution that leads to Assad stepping down might be one of the first indications that the Syrian regime is in serious trouble. As Russian expert Mark Katz noted, '[the Russians] won't switch until Assad is on the run.'[28]

Moreover, playing the nationalist card, Putin pinned responsibility for the demonstrations against him in Russia during the presidential campaign (reminiscent of the Arab Spring) squarely on the United States, equating US backing for the Syrian opposition with its tacit support for Russian protestors.[29] He was showing that he was standing up to the United States in Syria – unlike his predecessor President Medvedev vis-à-vis Libya – as part of Russia's resurgence against US dominance.

The leadership in Moscow is also wary of how the Islamists who have gained power in a number of Arab states in the wake of the Arab Spring could affect the dominant (and restless) Muslim populations in Russia's North Caucasus, Dagestan, Chechnya, Northern Ossetia and Ingushetia.[30] They would not want anything similar to happen in Syria if the Assad regime should fall.

With all this in mind, Moscow's support for the status quo in Syria is likely to remain, particularly as it clearly senses that the West is strong on rhetoric regarding the Syrian crisis, but light on military action. Nevertheless, if the international pressure continues to mount on Russia – especially if it comes in the wake of such atrocities as that committed in Houla (discussed above) – that could change. President Obama apparently pressed Prime Minister Medvedev on this issue, advocating the 'Yemen option' for Assad, during a G8 meeting at Camp David, Maryland, in May 2012. According to reports, Medvedev was fairly receptive to the idea. That said, as we know, President Putin will call the shots on this issue, and he is much less inclined to go down this route.[31]

There remains one question, however: if there is a realistic chance of a military coup against Assad from within the core ruling circle, could Russia be involved? Bashar had over a decade in which to insert loyalists – many of them family and longtime Assad supporters – into the crucial positions of power in the government and in the military-security apparatus. He apparently did a good job. As of May 2012 there have been no defections by senior members of the regime, and the core units of the military and the security forces, mostly composed of fellow Alawites, have remained loyal.[32] It is all very well to hope for an internal coup (or even to try to generate one from the outside). But one never knows if (or when) a disgruntled member of the inner circle may feel moved to put a bullet in Assad's head for some reason. And could a lone assassin or suicide bomber even get to the Syrian president? Dictators (almost by definition) have a security apparatus that is well honed to prevent coups, and the Assads built a huge, crisscrossing intelligence matrix that would be very difficult to penetrate. The United States hoped for years after the 1991 Gulf War that someone in Saddam Hussein's inner circle would move against the Iraqi president and remove him from power, finishing the job started with the liberation of Kuwait. As we all know, however, he remained in power until he was forcibly removed by a US-led armed invasion in 2003.

The extensive patronage system that the Assads constructed has also co-opted many different parts of Syrian society into regime maintenance. Not only fear, but also co-optation through a system of rewards has kept the political and business elite vested in the system that has enriched them. They do not want to have to renegotiate their privileged status with a new leadership and/or within a new system. The desire for this continuity after the death of Hafiz al-Assad is what helped his son come to power in the first place. And despite everything that has happened to date, Bashar has retained a not insignificant level of support – if not popularity – according to informal observations in Syria and certain polls taken in the country. While a good bit of this support may be due to the fact that people view the continuance of the regime in power as the lesser of two evils, it is nonetheless important. On-the-ground observers have put Bashar's support at about 20–30 per cent of the Syrian population – a figure arrived at by adding up the Alawite and Christian sects in the country (plus some other groups traditionally identified as supporters).

More interesting on the surface, however, was a poll conducted in Syria in December 2011 by YouGovSiraj, a Dubai-based arm of a British polling company sponsored by *The Doha Debates* television program. The fact that this poll was conducted by a group based in a country that has taken the lead in the Arab world against Assad perhaps lent it greater credence. The survey found that 55 per cent of Syrians wanted Assad to stay in power. The results were widely reported in the Western media as a sign that perhaps overall Syrian sentiment may have been misrepresented.[33] It also found that half of those who wanted him to stay in power also believed that he must implement free elections in the near future. There is certainly a great deal of skepticism regarding the poll, particularly over the size of the sample: one report found that only ninety-eight Syrians (rather than 1,000, which is the sample size usually required for such polls to be declared representative) had been interviewed, and they had been contacted via the Internet, which may again have skewed the results.[34] What is clear, however, is that enough of the Syrian population supports the Syrian president staying in power to encourage him, his inner circle and the silent majority to actually *believe* that he should remain in office. But perceptions can change quickly if the regime encounters more problems militarily and/or economically.

A third way in which Assad could be removed from power is through some negotiated solution, perhaps again with Moscow and/or the United Nations and Arab League playing key roles. Presumably this would be a version of what happened in Yemen, although, given the level of violence in Syria, the time frame for the president to actually accept his departure and get out of town would have to be considerably shorter than in Yemen (where it took the president almost a year finally to go). During late 2011, when opposition military pressure seemed to be building, the diplomatic isolation of Damascus was increasing and Syrian opposition groups seemed to be getting their act together, there were rumors that Assad had sent messages via third parties to Western capitals exploring just such a 'soft landing'. In this event, Assad – and anyone else who went with him – would no doubt demand immunity from prosecution inside or outside Syria and would then agree to go into exile somewhere – probably Russia, especially if Moscow played an instrumental role in getting the Syrian president to step down. Under this scenario, Assad would then hand over power to some sort of transitional government that would include some less tainted members of the current regime, as well as representative elements of the opposition (if, as pointed out above, there is a representative opposition with which to negotiate). This was the basis of the Arab League plan that went to the UN Security Council in early February and that failed to pass.

This option could be revived, depending upon circumstances on the ground and the temperament of the international community. In fact, in one form or another, it is probably always going to be on the table. Unfortunately, what usually happens is that, when a dictator finally agrees to a soft landing, his position may have deteriorated so badly that the offer is no longer available. In any event, I do not see Bashar al-Assad, under current conditions, voluntarily leaving office any time soon. To date he has been utterly defiant. He has consistently maintained that the violence is due to armed gangs and terrorists supported by the external enemies of Syria, thus absolving himself of responsibility. He reiterated this yet again at a meeting with former UN Secretary General Kofi Annan, who, in his new capacity as a UN special envoy, met Assad in Damascus in March 2012 to advocate a diplomatic resolution to the crisis that would bring both sides of the conflict together in some sort of dialogue, following a mutual ceasefire. As reported by SANA, Assad stated that 'the Syrian people, who have in the past managed to crush foreign plots . . . have again proven their capacity to defend the nation and to build a new Syria through their determination to pursue reforms along with the fight against foreign-backed terrorism'.[35]

Annan generated support for his plan (which came to be known simply as the 'Annan Plan') from the UN, the Arab League and, most importantly, Russia, which could most effectively apply pressure on the Syrian regime.[36] No doubt the fact that the plan seemed even-handed in terms of who was expected to cease fire (and the fact that it allowed Assad to stay in power) was important in gaining Moscow's acquiescence. In an unusual display of cooperation on the crisis in Syria, the UN Security Council then unanimously supported the plan in a presidential statement of 21 March.[37] On 14 April, following Syria's agreement to the plan, the Security Council unanimously approved a resolution (UNSC 2042) to allow UN observers into Syria to monitor what was (even then) a very shaky ceasefire, with dozens of reports of Syrian government forces continuing military operations. By mid-June, most of the observers had been withdrawn on account of the continuing violence and the dangerous conditions.

Right from the beginning, however, most officials in the Syrian opposition and in the international community were highly skeptical of the plan, given the Syrian regime's track record: as we have seen, the regime had agreed to variations of such plans during the previous year, only to dither over the terms and then to implement them only patchily, which ultimately led to the failure of the plans altogether. The Syrian government was again in this case accused of only agreeing to the plan to buy time and appease the Russians, and of implementing only some aspects of the plan, while using any excuse to scuttle it. The limited chances for the plan's success came to light almost immediately, when the Syrian government demanded that the rebels lay down their weapons before implementation – the opposition said this would be akin to committing suicide. Syrian officials also reiterated that they would continue to defend Syrian citizens against armed gangs and terrorist violence. All the while, it was presumed, the regime would continue the crackdown wherever and whenever it could. This is exactly what happened.

The government and the opposition blamed each other for ceasefire violations. Russia and the West engaged in the same old finger-pointing exercise, with Moscow falling back on its default position of defending the Syrian regime. Russia's UN ambassador, Vitaly Churkin, stated in defense of his country's position:

> As a matter of principle, we believe that the UN Security Council is not about regime change. And when we saw some of the resolutions, which included sanctions, we knew that those were resolutions which were heading in the direction of regime change by force, which would, in turn, lead only to much more bloodshed in Syria.[38]

The BBC's Jim Muir summarized the almost impossible task of the UN observer force, officially called the UN Supervision Mission in Syria (UNSMIS): 'Normally it is a case of monitoring respect of a formal truce involving states, not trying to ensure compliance with a work-in-progress peace plan in a situation which in some ways resembles civil war. In other words, the observers are being expected to help create the peace they are supposed to be monitoring.'[39]

It is also important to understand that the Syrian leadership is tremendously suspicious of any agreements brokered by the UN, the West or the Arab League. While the Syrian opposition, their Arab supporters and the West see Assad as untrustworthy and prevaricating, the Syrian leadership sees years of what it regards as inaccurate and prejudicial coverage of Syria in the media, in academia and by governments. It does not trust the West or its regional allies. The efforts by these same organizations and states are regarded by Damascus as pernicious attempts to buy time through diplomacy for the Syrian opposition to regroup and re-arm. Syrian officials believe that these diplomatic efforts are a set-up, and that they are undertaken in the sure and certain knowledge that the Syrian government will ultimately be obliged to reject the agreements; this then opens the door to more robust action, as the West can say that diplomatic efforts have been exhausted. Perhaps this is why the regime goes along with such agreements for a time, before ultimately ignoring them. Assad and his inner circle no doubt feel that, if they do not keep up unremitting pressure on the rebels, the latter will have time to strengthen their positions and possibly establish safe havens, from which they can be supported from the outside. A Friends of Syria meeting in Turkey, held while Annan was carrying out his diplomacy, was, in my opinion, imprudent and ill-planned: it most certainly raised doubts in Damascus about the legitimacy of the Annan plan, while the United States, its allies and the Syrian opposition were agreeing at the very same time to measures that would stiffen the resistance.[40]

At this Friends of Syria meeting, the Gulf Arab states, led by Saudi Arabia and Qatar and supported by the United States and Turkey, promised substantial financial assistance in support of a more militant line.

Since the SNC and FSA are the recipients of most of this assistance, other independent militias and opposition groups may 'follow the money' and submit to SNC leadership, which, having adopted the more hardline FSA approach, may again become relevant to the street demonstrators who are doing most of the fighting and dying.[41]

Since the NCB did not attend this Friends of Syria meeting, it is clear that important divisions remain in the Syrian opposition. This became even more apparent when Burhan Ghalioun, the head of the SNC, abruptly announced on 17 May that he was stepping down. He did so in response to an outcry against his reappointment for another three-month term (the position is supposed to be a rotating one, but his tenure had been repeatedly extended). The Local Coordination Committees threatened to pull out of the SNC, saying that the 'deteriorating situation in the SNC is an impetus for us to take actions, which could begin with a freeze [of its membership in the SNC] and end with a withdrawal if errors are not solved and demands for reform go unmet'. The LCC statement further said that the 'errors' consisted of 'a total absence of consensus between the SNC's vision and that of the revolutionaries [i.e. the LCC members], a marginalization of most LCC representatives, and a monopolization of decision-making by influential members of the executive committee'.[42] The fact that Ghalioun stepped down in the face of this threat certainly displayed the power of the LCC (i.e. those on the ground in Syria). This also indicated that the various opposition elements were still not at all on the same page.

Assad also knows that, even with a soft landing, heads will have to roll; and even if his head is not among them, they will include the heads of those close to him – maybe even family members, such as his brother, Maher al-Assad – and several of those in the Makhlouf clan. If Bashar was unwilling to 'fire' his brother even under intense Turkish pressure (as discussed in Chapter 7) – and by this refusal risked losing one of Syria's most important friends internationally – then he is probably not going to feed him to the wolves. Family and tribal ties mean that he is unlikely to agree to this type of resolution, if for no other reason than that, if he does so without securing protection for those in his inner circle with blood on their hands, he might literally find a loaded gun to his head. At this point, however, there is so much blood on these people's hands that it may be difficult to grant them any sort of immunity (although, if the alternative is more bloodshed and instability, it might happen).

If my reading of Bashar is correct – that over the years he has developed a tremendously heightened sense of his own self-importance and believes in the delusions fostered by Syrian authoritarianism – then I doubt very much whether he is even considering any course of action but to stay in power and see the business through to the end. During the Arab Spring, many people wondered why Ben Ali, Mubarak and Gadafi did not just leave power when they could, go into exile and live a life of luxury with the billions they had stashed away in foreign banks. This question is also asked about Bashar al-Assad. But these dictators do not see or get it: they live in their own worlds, worlds shaped and contoured by the undying praise of a cowed or brainwashed population and the propaganda of sycophants. They believe in the cult that they themselves have created. They have drunk the Kool-Aid and injected the opium of power. Time and again, the old adage that 'absolute power corrupts absolutely' has proven correct. Bashar may very well leave power – and may have done so by the time this book is printed – but he will not go voluntarily, unless there is absolutely, positively no other option.

Staying in power

This is obviously the preferred option of Bashar and his supporters. By this I do not mean staying in power over the short term and then falling (or being removed) from power by one of the methods described above. I mean remaining in office for the long term, far beyond the estimates of most prognosticators during the uprising. The resilience of this regime has already impressed (and at the same time confounded) those who believed it was on the brink of collapse on numerous occasions. Almost every analyst (including me) thought Assad's days were numbered, especially as we witnessed the rapidity of the fall from power of other dictators in the Arab world and as we witnessed the staying power of the rebellion. I did, however, always indicate that Syria was a harder nut than other Arab Spring countries, and that the regime could stay in power for months, if not years.

Many of us also thought that Syria would be one of the last to be hit by the Arab Spring – or that the spring might pass it by altogether. The very factors that led us to say this are the same factors that have contributed to the regime's staying power: the cohesiveness of the military-security apparatus, the general Syrian fear of chaos and instability, Bashar's relative popularity, the fractured opposition, the survival instincts of the regime (including its willingness to brutally repress any dissent) and its endurance against previous attempts to isolate it internationally. As Robert Fisk entitled one of his essays published in early 2012, 'Syria is Used to the Slings and Arrows of Friends and Enemies'.[43]

As I write this, the notion of Assad remaining in power for the long term is not as far-fetched as it was in the summer and autumn of 2011, when most of the international community, led by the United States, publicly stated that Bashar must step down. At that heady time – when Gadafi was killed by his own people in October; when a more robust Arab League position against Assad emerged shortly thereafter; and when the Syrian opposition apparently jelled, with the formation of the Syrian National Council – it seemed Assad's eviction or death could not be far behind.

A year after the uprising began, however, people were starting to wonder if Assad would fall from power in the foreseeable future. The strategic position of the regime could turn around at any moment, but after Syrian troops drove the FSA out of Homs and Idlib in March, intelligence estimates started to reassess the staying power of the Syrian regime. In this scenario, the regime simply outlasts the opposition, wearing it down over months or even years. As I stated earlier, in terms of its survival the Syrian leadership thinks in this long-term way. The most loyal forces of the regime, though they dwarf the opposition forces in size and capability, are still not large enough to overwhelm the rebels in one fell swoop. Right from the start of the uprising, government forces adopted a 'whack-a-mole' approach, and they will no doubt continue with this until a critical mass is reached and the opposition is reduced to low-level conflict in small doses. The regime can live with that; it feels it has no choice. Of course, from the regime's perspective, this has a better chance of happening if there is no foreign military intervention along the lines of Libya; therefore, it has no doubt worked out that it cannot engage in wholesale massacre of the 1982 Hama variety or use chemical weapons, either of which might compel the international community to intervene militarily on humanitarian and moral grounds.

So long as the morale of the military and security forces is maintained, this continued pressure on the opposition and any progress made in gaining the upper hand over them will keep the so-called silent majority silent. The regime will continue to have on its side the key constituencies in the country that have kept it in power to date. It will also keep Russia, China, Iran and others solidly on the side of Damascus in the diplomatic arena and in terms of providing much-needed military and economic assistance – and political support in international forums. This, combined with the actual implementation of the reforms promised by Assad (including the constitution passed in the February 2012 referendum and the May parliamentary elections), could pare off enough of a weary populace for the regime to muddle through.

Even the illusion of more freedom and democracy might be enough to attract all but the most die-hard of rebels to accept another Faustian bargain with the regime. Thomas Hobbes it was who argued that polities are born of a trade-off: elites and the citizenry, when under threat, willingly trade their political and civil liberties for guarantees of stability.[44] As Ed Husain points out, 'Iraqi refugees are ubiquitous in Syria, and they recount how post-Saddam Iraq went horribly wrong'.[45] Or, as Sharmine Narwani commented: 'If Assad delivers a new constitution and national elections, it may be all the space he needs to confound his critics . . . People may yearn not so much for bread, but for the ability to walk to the market to buy it.'[46] In essence, enough Syrians who are currently opposed to Assad – especially those who sought political reform at the beginning of the uprising, rather than the ouster of the Syrian president – might be drawn back into supporting the regime because they are more fearful of an all-out civil war that would likely destroy the country and would, because of Syria's sectarian composition, be a bloodbath. The regime would have brought to reality the very narrative it helped create in order to justify its rule. This narrative hopes to convince most Syrians that the regime should continue in power; but it could just as easily unleash forces that spiral out of the regime's control and lead to its downfall.

Assad could also suddenly agree to a negotiated solution along the lines of the original Arab League proposal (the one that could keep him in power for another sixteen years) or some variation of the Annan Plan. But he would probably only do so if he were convinced that he could not defeat the rebel forces. This is probably why he has kept the lines of communication open with Arab League, UN and other envoys – just in case. With an agreement, the regime probably hopes it would split the opposition, with only the die-hard rebels deciding to continue the fight. No doubt there would still be conflict in Syria, but the regime could deal with it – especially if the alternative was not to accept a negotiated solution and be driven from power. By weakening the opposition, the regime would probably then think it could eliminate the remaining pockets of resistance over time – and Syria would also be off the radar screen of the international community.

If the regime does stay in power, in the absence of a negotiated solution it will be tough-going economically, especially as the sanctions imposed on it would no doubt remain in force. Its foreign reserves have been depleted and its oil output cut drastically. There were even reports in April 2012 that Damascus was trying to sell off its gold reserves to raise revenue.[47] But its economy is used to sanctions, and over the years it has found ways to survive, and at times even to prosper. Importantly (as a previous chapter indicates), maintaining trade and commercial access to its neighbors Iraq and Lebanon (as well as further afield in Russia, Iran, India, China, South Africa, Brazil, Venezuela, Cuba, etc.) will allow the country to limp along. If it is able to recreate markets for its crude oil – in addition to finding oil and gas companies willing and technologically able to engage in exploration for more oil and gas – it might even end up having some impressive GDP rates down the road. And if the regime manages to stay in power with little to no internal turmoil, most of the Arab League states that have opposed Damascus will kiss and make up with it, thus allowing Syria the opportunity to re-establish important political and economic relationships.

There will most likely be events in the Middle East (especially in the Arab-Israeli arena) that will afford Damascus opportunities to ingratiate itself once again with the Arab community. For instance, the Iran–Iraq War in the 1980s allowed Egypt to reintegrate itself into the Arab world after it was almost totally isolated – in fact, kicked out of the Arab League, much as Syria's membership was suspended in autumn 2011 – for signing a peace treaty with Israel in 1979. The longer the war went on and the more vulnerable Iraq became, the deeper Egypt was drawn back into the fold to buffer the Arab side against Persian Iran. The end of the superpower Cold War in the late 1980s also caused monumental shifts in the Middle East, dramatically altering the balance of power and compelling many Arab countries, including Syria, to adopt policies that were, in many cases, the polar opposite of what they had adhered to previously.

Bashar al-Assad and his cohorts are well aware of this history; they know that, if they can only hold on long enough, the chances are that something will happen to allow their country to come in once again from the cold. If this means being the North Korea of the Middle East for a decade or so, then so be it. The scars on the country will be deep, however. It will never be status quo ante: there has been too much violence, abuse and bloodletting. Society has become too radicalized. For many, the House of Assad has already fallen, regardless of whether or not the regime survives. The hope that people once pinned on Bashar has dissipated, and I suspect this is the case even among many of his supporters, who have backed the regime only because the alternative could be even worse. He will be isolated and discredited, limping towards an uncertain future. If he can hold on.

Protracted stalemate or civil war

This has in essence become a reality, especially as the assets and advantages of each group continue to offset the other, i.e. there is no single advantage big enough to enable either side to win (or lose) in the near future. As stated above, even though the Syrian government is militarily dominant, it appears unable to deliver a hammer blow to the opposition. This will continue to be the case, especially if the rebel forces adopt more in the way of guerilla warfare tactics, rather than try to do too much too soon by attempting to hold cities against superior government forces (as happened in Homs and Idlib). Even though the regime's military fortunes against the opposition are at times in the ascendant it will still need to tough it out. This grinding approach, however, will allow opposition forces the opportunity and time to regroup and to escape across the porous borders of the country to safety in neighboring states (Turkey, Jordan, Lebanon and Iraq). If the opposition starts to receive more substantial military support than it has so far, then the clear military advantage that the regime currently enjoys will be leveled. The very fact that the Syrian military is concentrating so much on suppressing the opposition prevents it from adequately policing its borders (never an easy task at the best of times). Even if the carnage in Syria does not rise to a level that would draw more direct military assistance from NATO or the like, there will be countries, groups and individuals that will continue to support the resistance directly and indirectly with (at the very least) funds to buy weapons, ammunition, supplies, medicine, etc. In addition, the nihilistic approach taken toward the 'other' by important groups on both sides of the equation will ensure that a certain level of violence continues well into the future.

We have talked about the resilience of the regime; but we must also recognize the resilience of the opposition in the face of a long and withering crackdown by government forces. The opposition mostly comprises ordinary Syrians who, inspired by the Arab Spring elsewhere, decided to shake off the decades-long yoke of repression and fight for a fair and free society. They are often deprived of basic services, food, water and medicine, yet they have endured and continued to battle against the odds. The fact that, as I write, they are still going out every day to confront the government more than shows that many of them are in this for the long haul. Most are involved too deeply now ever to accept that the Assad regime could stay in power. They could never live without fear of retribution by an empowered government, should it emerge as the victor. As one Syrian activist lamented: 'If we had known it would reach this point, we probably wouldn't have dared oppose the regime. But we did it, and now we can't stop, because if we do, they will kill us all.'[48]

Should there be a protracted stalemate or civil war, the country will die a slow death, with some areas under government control and others held by the rebels. Any sort of sustained economic growth and development would be next to impossible. There would most likely be a mass exodus of Syrians – a reversal of the flood of Iraqi refugees into Syria during the height of the instability following the 2003 US-led invasion; only in this case, the refugees would go to Turkey, Lebanon and Jordan as well, straining the capacities of those governments to deal with them and (particularly in Lebanon) potentially exacerbating already tense local politics in a way that would simply transfer the Syrian unrest to another location. The brain drain of Syrian talent would take at least a generation to replace.

The longer the conflict goes on, the more external powers, particularly at the regional level, will support certain factions of the opposition, sometimes even against each other. Syria will become even more of a proxy battleground between regional powers, akin to the sectarian-based civil war in Lebanon in the 1970s and 1980s. The longer the conflict continues, the more radically Islamist it may become, as jihadists are quite adept at taking advantage of chaos and instability. Most observers believe that the threat of an al-Qaida-type organization gaining control of the rebellion has been blown out of all proportion, particularly in Western circles, which are perhaps using it as a convenient rationale not to arm the opposition. It is interesting that the likelihood of radical Muslim extremists being in the Syrian opposition could be a smokescreen to rationalize *not* sanctioning military action, whereas during the Bush years, following 9/11, it was often used as a smokescreen *for* military intervention. The rebels are, indeed, mostly conservative Sunni Muslims; but that does not make them *salafis*. As is described in Chapter 8, this simply reflects trends throughout the Muslim Middle East over the past decade. The rebels are, in part, supported by the Syrian Muslim Brotherhood and similar groups in the Gulf Arab states, but these are not (yet) a dominant element within the opposition. The Syrian Muslim Brotherhood has the largest membership of all the Syrian opposition groups, but the years of repression in Syria mean that its members are mostly in exile, and so are thin on the ground in Syria. Furthermore, over the years it has shifted alliances and has had a variety of partners that span the political and social spectrum; the upshot is that a number of Syrians simply do not trust it.[49]

In any event, most of the rebels are not fighting for the imposition of an Islamic republic; indeed, most want a more democratic, still secular polity – if anything, more along the lines of Turkey than Iran. As Nir Rosen pointed out from his discussions with a wide array of Syrian rebels, when facing the possibility of death they became more religious (but not necessarily more radical).[50] But the suicide bombings in Damascus and the use of IEDs in other parts of the country raised the profile of Islamist extremists, some of whom may be fighters who gained experience in Iraq or Afghanistan.[51] Although this conveniently fits the narrative of the regime, the narrative could become a self-fulfilling prophecy, especially if the Saudis and Qataris, on the one hand, and the Iranians and Hizbullah, on the other, start supporting different groups in Syria, based on religious affiliation. The al-Qaida type jihadists hate the Alawites and have longed for an opportunity to get rid of them. Many of them, as Rosen comments,

> are an experienced bunch who would support suicide bombings against security forces working for a regime they could describe as infidel . . . As the crackdown increases, as the local oppositions' sense of abandonment by the outside world increases, and the voices calling for jihad get louder, there will likely be more radicalization.[52]

In other words, Syria could very well become a failed state locked in a prolonged, bloody civil war with a strong extremist Islamist element, on the border of Israel, at the epicenter of several fault lines in the Middle East. This is not a pretty picture.

Final thoughts

Towards the end of *The New Lion of Damascus: Bashar al-Asad and modern Syria* (2005), I wrote: 'Bashar cannot become a modern reincarnation of his father. If he does, he would indeed become the new lion of Damascus, but this is exactly what Syria does not need.' I also posed the following questions: 'Will the shell of the dictatorship molded by his father, the repressive and controlling institutions of the state, transform Bashar into a reluctant dictator? Or will Bashar, the president of Syria, eliminate the institutional basis of Syrian dictatorship . . .?'[53]

From my meetings with Assad and other Syrian officials in the course of researching that book, I came away with a sense of hope that perhaps he could initiate a period of real reform in Syria. Of course, I was not alone. Many inside and outside Syria were energized in a positive way by the new young president. In retrospect, I do not necessarily think that the feeling of hope was misplaced or that somehow we were all led astray. I do believe that, at first, Bashar was genuinely interested in serious reform. But he soon realized what he could and could not do – not unlike US presidents who, on coming to office, soon find that they are unable to implement the sweeping changes typically promised during their campaigns. There are established interests and established ways of doing things that stifle attempts at change. In Syria, politics is more of a life-and-death game. Soon enough, Bashar found that all he could do at first was to make some cosmetic changes and engage in reform in areas such as education, which did not threaten the cozy socioeconomic and political positions of the establishment.

Hafiz al-Assad did his job well. He constructed an airtight but stultifying array of family, tribal and sectarian-based patronage relationships that produced loyalty and stability, but little else. As Peter Harling writes:

> For the regime, its supporters and its allies, Syria's is an immature, if not disease-ridden society. They posit – with evidence both real and invented, and generally blown out of proportion – that Syrian society shows

> sectarian, fundamentalist, violent and seditious proclivities that can be contained only by a ruthless power structure.[54]

Ultimately, Bashar and his cohorts could not trust anyone else in Syria. He had little faith that anything other than his presidency could lead the way forward. The Assad regimes were simply not geared to implementing change in anything close to an expedient or dramatic fashion, which is exactly what was needed at the beginning of the uprising. Bashar's initial strategic vision for an internationally respected and integrated Syria became consumed by a Syrian paradigm of political survival. He was either unwilling or powerless to stop what in Syria is a reflexive response to perceived threat. He retrenched and retreated into a typically Syrian authoritarian mode of survival, an Alawite fortress to protect the sect's chokehold on power. In the end, when the pressure was greatest, Assad was not the enlightened, Western-educated ophthalmologist. As stated in Chapter 1, he returned to his roots as a child of the Arab-Israeli conflict, the superpower Cold War and Hafiz al-Assad: those are the influences that appear to have shaped the nature of his response more than anything else. In one of the rare interviews Bashar al-Assad has allowed during the uprising – this one on Russian state television in May 2012 – he made his position clear. In a swipe (if not a warning) aimed at Saudi Arabia and Qatar, Assad said: 'for the leaders of these countries, it's becoming clear that this is not "spring" but chaos. If you sow chaos in Syria you may be infected by it yourself, and they understand this perfectly well.'[55] He also stated, in reference to the 2012 passage of the new constitution and the parliamentary elections, that 'the political course will not free us from terror'. In other words, only repression and military force will – and so the violence will continue.

Twenty-five years ago, US President Ronald Reagan gave a stirring speech in Berlin on the cusp of the end of the Cold War. At the Brandenburg Gate near the Berlin Wall, long the symbol of the Iron Curtain that had been drawn across Europe by communism, President Reagan beseeched the leader of the Soviet Union, Mikhail Gorbachev, to 'tear down this wall'. Not that Gorbachev needed any prodding: he had already realized the inevitability of the collapse of the Soviet system. But with international encouragement and tangible support, Gorbachev engaged in the process of *glasnost* and *perestroika*, an opening up and restructuring of the Soviet Union. He was one of those singular leaders who first recognized and then seized the moment, and his legacy in engendering transformational change is safe and secure in the history books, even though the change he wrought eventually meant his own fall from power, as he was swept away in the democratic processes he launched.[56]

Not unlike Gorbachev, Assad desperately needed to break out of the stifling, anachronistic box of Syrian politics-as-usual and to embrace a transformational role in his country. No one denies the difficulty of this, especially given the powerful resistance to any significant change to the status quo that he faces. But he was not up to the task. He was shortsighted and became deluded. He failed miserably. All along, the ability of the Syrian regime to meet the demands of the protestors and the international community was slender. If the protests miraculously stopped today, the reforms announced so far would, without the internal and external pressure that generated them in the first place, most likely be diluted to insignificance or revoked altogether. After all, Assad has not inspired confidence in terms of his ability (or even his willingness) to actually implement reform beyond its mere promulgation. Some of this is his fault; some is the fault of the inert Syrian system. Many of us hoped that Assad would change the system. What seems to have happened is that the system has changed him.

It wasn't supposed to be this way. But it was inevitable . . .

Epilogue

In December 2012 I met one of the leading military commanders of the Syrian opposition as part of a wide-ranging research project in which I am involved.[1] He drove up from Syria to meet us in a town in southern Turkey along the Syrian border. He was a pediatrician before the uprising and was exceedingly well-read. Among the issues we raised with him, one concerned the fear in the West that if the Syrian regime of Bashar al-Assad fell from power, there might very well be a bloodbath of revenge against the Alawites in Syria. In response to this question and in his own way trying to allay this fear, he matter-of-factly commented that two days earlier he had personally executed a Sunni member of the Syrian government's armed forces. In effect, he was saying that to him it did not matter what his foe's sectarian identity was, only that he was the enemy and as such should be resisted, opposed, and even killed when necessary. He had been treating young children before the conflict began, saving lives. Now he is a respected military commander who obviously has to be prepared to take away lives.

On a rather harrowing visit to Damascus in February 2013, I met with some Syrian government officials as part of the aforementioned research project. One of the people with whom I met was a high-level official whom I had known for many years. This person was bemoaning the fact that even a short trip to visit the family outside of Damascus was out of the question.

It appears that this official had been targeted for assassination by the opposition, thus severely curtailing freedom of movement, even to visit with family.

These are but two among thousands, if not millions, of examples of how life in Syria has been unalterably changed for individual Syrians due to a conflict that is now about two-and-a-half years old, with very little to indicate as of this writing that it will soon abate, much less end. Since the hardcover edition of this book was published in the summer of 2012 the death toll and dislocation in and destruction of Syria has multiplied many times over. The last estimated death toll figure I entered in that book was as of June 2012 and numbered around 11,000. Today, in May of 2013, the estimated number of deaths is officially 80,000, but most well-placed observers say it is probably well over 100,000. Over 1.5 million Syrian refugees have fled the country for a variety of reasons, mostly to get out of the way of the fighting, and/or their towns, villages, and homes have been damaged or destroyed. The vast majority of these refugees have found temporary and often squalid sanctuary in Turkey, Lebanon, and Jordan. There are also an estimated 4 million internally displaced Syrians, roaming around the country homeless or squatting in makeshift quarters living day-to-day. Altogether this is approximately one quarter of the Syrian population whose lives have forever been changed. In addition, countless Syrians are missing, many imprisoned or otherwise unaccounted for. This is not even to speak of the many Syrians who have died but do not register on any casualty list because they perished not through any direct effects of the war but indirectly, due to not receiving their needed medicines, or to not getting to a hospital – because the hospital had been destroyed or had been emptied of doctors, nurses and equipment – that otherwise would have saved them from life-threatening illness. Many have also died due to malnutrition or other maladies caused by the conflict environment.

I wrote in the hardcover edition (summer 2012) that the likely future of Syria certainly did not paint a pretty picture. What an understatement that was in retrospect.

The stalemated conflict

There was a spasm of hope in late June 2012 when the foreign ministers of a number of countries that are involved in and/or affected by the Syrian conflict, as well as representatives of the United Nations, Arab League, and the European Union (together known as the 'Action Group'), met in Geneva, Switzerland to carve out what became known as the Geneva Communiqué.[2] In essence, this document stated that the Action Group was working 'urgently and intensively to bring about an end to the violence and human rights abuses and the launch of a Syrian-led political process leading to a transition that meets the legitimate aspirations of the Syrian people and enables them independently and democratically to determine their own future'. It also mapped out some basic principles regarding a period of transition from conflict/civil war to a more stable, inclusive Syrian polity. The idea of some sort of transition in the broadest sense is widely accepted among the Syrian opposition and even within the Syrian regime, although the nature of this transition on each side of the conflict differs dramatically. Although the plan of action outlined in the text of the document links the way forward to what was already at the time the failed six-point plan of Kofi Annan (discussed in Chapter 9), the collective effort was promising. Perhaps the document may even ultimately serve as the paradigm upon which an eventual political settlement will be based. But there are a number of flaws that for a year kept it within the confines of diplomatic circles and academic conferences rather than acting as a catalyst for a political settlement.

First of all, as the roster of participants indicates, there are actually no Syrians involved in the Action Group. While the dynamics of the conflict made this understandable at the time, it presents an immediate complication in that the 'solution' appears to be generated externally by the usual suspects of great powers rather than by Syrians themselves, which contradicts the whole premise of a Syrian-led process outlined in the text of the document. Next, one of the most important countries involved in the conflict, Iran, is nowhere to be found. This underscores one of the major problems that has plagued a political settlement all along, i.e. the major Western powers, especially the United States, as well as regional powers such as Saudi Arabia and Qatar, seem to be able to dictate who can and cannot participate. No legitimate and sustainable political settlement, in my opinion, can be arranged without Iran, which is probably the country that has the most influence on Damascus and, of course, can rein in Hizbullah, which has placed itself so openly on the side of the Syrian regime, including, reportedly, sending its fighters in no small numbers into Syria. But there is considerable doubt as to whether or not Washington (or Riyadh or Doha, for that matter) would consent to Iranian participation, as one of the main premises underlying the West's policy is to eliminate Iranian influence in Syria, therefore reducing Hizbullah's capabilities in Lebanon. However, there were ambiguous comments from some Obama administration officials in mid-May which indicated that the United States may bend on this matter. Certainly the Russians were pressing for it, and in the end, if a process gets under way, it might look much closer to what Moscow had envisioned all along for a political settlement bringing the Syrian conflict to a close.

Additionally, who determines what the actual 'aspirations' of the Syrian people are? Once again this smacks of something being imposed from the outside with little (or misplaced) consideration given to what the people of Syria actually want. For that matter, the religious and ethnic mosaic that is Syria, one that has been exacerbated and stressed to (or perhaps beyond) breaking point by the conflict, makes it immensely difficult for Syrians themselves to develop a consensus on this. Certainly the jihadists have different aspirations – i.e. an Islamic state of some kind – than do other Syrians, who want a political system and society that is more secular. And which Syrians will lead this process? At the time of the publication of the Communiqué the opposition was divided on many different levels. The fracturing had become acute. Despite numerous attempts led mostly by the West and its regional allies to form a cohesive and representative opposition body, as of this writing it is still very much divided; indeed, with the influx of more jihadists into Syria accompanied by the corresponding rise of jihadist militia groups, such as the al-Qaida-affiliated Jabhat al-Nusra, the divide between various opposition groups has in many ways widened over the past year. In the first half of 2013 there were reports of violence between various Syrian opposition groups. For instance, there was a pitched battle in Raqqa, the only Syrian city totally controlled by the Syrian opposition, between elements of Jabhat al-Nusra and the Farouq

Brigades. It is not clear why the two groups were fighting. It could have been ideological, territorial, or simply something that began as a personal dispute; however, this sort of thing does not bode well for the future development of a more unified Syrian military command. No doubt regime officials view such incidents as working in their favor, reinforcing the notion that the opposition is hopelessly divided. Trying to construct legitimate opposition representation at any international conference, whether it is in Geneva or elsewhere, is thus a very tall task. Emblematic of the problem is a statement by noted Syrian observer Frederic C. Hof: 'Some in the opposition see the prospect of an international conference as an opportunity for personal advancement at the expense of rivals. The Geneva initiative may well be the secretary of state's [John Kerry's] diplomatic version of football's desperate, last second, Hail Mary pass, rather than an integral part of a broader US strategy.'[3]

The most celebrated, if unsuccessful, attempt to form a viable Syrian opposition organization occurred on 11 November 2012 when the formation of the National Coalition for Syrian Revolutionary and Opposition Forces (otherwise simply known as the Syrian Coalition) was announced in Doha, Qatar. It was supposed to be an improvement over the Syrian National Council (SNC) based in Turkey, which has not particularly distinguished itself. As the name suggests, it is a coalition of Syrian opposition groups, the unwieldy official name of the organization itself suggesting the difficulty of capturing elements from across the Syrian opposition spectrum. A widely respected former imam of the famed Umayyad mosque in Damascus, Moaz al-Khatib, was named the president of the Coalition, with longtime democracy activist Riyad Seif appointed vice president along with Suheir Atassi, a well-known secular feminist in Syria from a historically prominent Syrian family. A council of sixty-three members was chosen as its primary governing body, with twenty-two of these seats going to the SNC; critics complained that a number of the other seats went to those who were formerly members of the SNC. Thus, one of the biggest criticisms of the Coalition within the opposition itself was that it was a glorified re-creation of the SNC, this time more under Qatari than Turkish sponsorship.

In fact, the support for the Coalition among those Syrian opposition groups actually inside Syria fighting and dying, was usually only lip-service at best – and only because the Coalition has been viewed as a viable conduit for receiving desperately needed financial and military aid from outside. Otherwise, as expressed to this author by numerous Syrian opposition leaders inside Syria, there was at the very least suspicion and at the most open disdain of the Coalition. It was seen as being a puppet in the hands of foreigners, made up mostly of exiles who had not lived in Syria for years and who were, in the eyes of many, enjoying the comforts of five-star hotels and the diplomatic cocktail circuit while they were suffering the daily hardships and dangers of war. There were some who held the SNC and Coalition in such utter contempt that they refused to even refer to them by their names; one opposition figure derisively referred to them as the 'old thing' and the 'new thing'.

Although receiving recognition from most of the countries supporting the Syrian opposition as the sole legitimate representative of Syria (or the Syrian people), and even going so far as to officially occupy in March 2013 the Syrian government's seat at the Arab League, the Coalition has experienced its fair share of difficulties and internal divisions; indeed, Moaz al-Khatib threatened to resign in March, and then, bemoaning the lack of support from the international community, officially did resign in April 2013.[4] George Sabra, a Syrian Christian who had become a vice president of the Coalition, assumed the position of interim president. On 19 March, at a meeting in Istanbul, pushed by the Friends of Syria, members of the Coalition elected Ghassan Hitto, who hailed from Texas, as prime minister of an interim Syrian government. He then engaged in a process that amounted to appointing a temporary government with what are essentially cabinet positions, with a minister of defense reportedly drawn from the ranks of the Free Syrian Army (FSA). All of this was quite confusing to the outside observer, and most did not have a clue as to who Hitto was nor could fathom if he had any experience or credibility for the job other than being known as a good manager – which the Coalition needs; but it also needs credible leadership. One suspects that al-Khatib's resignation was as much due to his disgust with the Coalition's internal machinations as with his expressed dissatisfaction with the international community – or a combination of both, since they appeared to be intimately linked. As one leading member of the Coalition told our research group with considerable lament, 'there are too many hands in the pot'. Nevertheless, to date the Coalition has continued to be the primary interlocutor of the Syrian opposition, at least with the international community. As one top Western official told me, 'we know it is quite flawed, but it is the best we've got at the moment'.

On the military front, the United States and its allies birthed in Antalya, Turkey, in December 2012, the Supreme Military Council led by General Salim Idris, a general in Syria's army who defected to the opposition in July 2012. The council is composed of thirty members who are opposition military commanders fighting inside Syria; Idris was chosen officially as chief of staff of the Council. Its purpose is to inject a much-needed unified command and control structure that can coordinate activities among the disparate militias that make up the Syrian opposition forces. Islamic extremist militias such as Jabhat al-Nusra and Ahrar al-Sham were not invited to the conference in Antalya and are not included on the Council. Despite much fanfare and some limited success, the Council to date has not been able to establish an effective command and control apparatus, perhaps because some of the most successful armed Syrian opposition groups, such as Jabhat al-Nusra, have been excluded. In addition, the militias still operate largely independently, and they only cooperate with others, including the Supreme Military Council, when they feel like it. The fact that the opposition forces are better known by their individual militia names, such as Ahrar al-Sham, Tawhid Brigade, Farouq Brigade, Jabhat al-Nusra, Suqoor al-Sham, etc. suggests the continuing problems of establishing a legitimate overarching military hierarchy.

As the carnage and destruction reached new heights (or, rather, lows) in Syria during the remainder of 2012 and well into 2013, and the international community (the West in particular) were reluctant to intervene more assertively on the side of the Syrian opposition, calls for some sort of negotiated political settlement to the conflict began to find their way into the overall discussion of Syria – usually fruitless dialogues that most often concluded with something to the effect of, 'there are no good answers' or 'we are looking for only the least worst option'. Even so, some opposition figures admitted that it was a strategic mistake to declare from the very beginning that Assad had to go before any negotiations could begin. As it became clear that Assad wasn't going anywhere anytime soon (indeed, he became more defiant) it placed the opposition – at least those who were willing to consider the option – in a negotiating conundrum.[5] The volatility of the question came to light when Moaz al-Khatib of the Syrian Coalition announced in February 2013 that if the Syrian government met certain conditions beforehand (ones, by the way, the Syrian government was never going to accept at that point), he would be willing to negotiate with it. Immediately Khatib came under intense criticism from inside and outside the Coalition, most disavowing any connection to his initiative. The Coalition produced a muddled compromise of sorts to prevent the appearance of total dishevelment, but the issue of the disposition of the Syrian president remained a very sensitive one.

For those in the Syrian opposition and more so in the international community that have recognized that a political settlement sooner rather than later is the only way to save Syria from total disintegration, the question of Bashar al-Assad (and his family members and military-security cronies) is a vexing one. Everyone who supports a political settlement understands that such an outcome would entail a transition period. Even Assad has spelled out such a transition, particularly in a speech he gave in January 2013 – one, however, that obviously has him continuing in power until a presidential election in 2014 when his current seven-year term expires. This is an election he fully intends to win, and he probably will if he lasts that long.[6] Those in the opposition and in the international community as a whole see a transition where at the very least Assad vacates his position either before, during, and most certainly by the end of a specified period of time encompassing the transition. Of course, there are still a great many in the opposition both inside and outside Syria who will not consider this option at all. Assad must go . . . that is the beginning and end of the discussion. As many on both sides believe they can still win, though what constitutes 'winning' frequently shifts, there is little incentive to come to the negotiating table under anything less than unconditional terms tilted decisively in their respective favors. In a meeting with a UN diplomat in early 2013, it became apparent that Bashar al-Assad's definition of winning had evolved; indeed, several Syrian officials had indicated that government forces were not going to be able to secure control of the entire country in the near future. Assad flipped on its head Henry Kissinger's axiom uttered during the Vietnam War – that insurgencies win by not losing and governments lose by not winning – by telling the UN diplomat with whom he met that his *government* would win by not losing. This clearly suggests that the bar defining his notion of success has been lowered to that of holding onto power, maintaining control of some if not all of the major cities, thus consigning to the opposition large swaths of the country, while hoping that at some point in the future simply surviving will turn into an opportunity to regain control of the country.

Another consideration is the Syrian economy and the ability of the Syrian regime economically to stay afloat. No one really knows how much money the regime has left. One former high-level regime insider who is now living outside of Syria told me that the inability of the Syrian government to pay public sector salaries will spell the end of the Assad regime, i.e. the 2–3 million Syrians dependent upon government salaries will abandon the regime if they can no longer be paid. This is something to monitor. Perhaps the regime's halting willingness to even consider negotiations is due the fact that it sees a monetary horizon drawing closer and closer. This former Syrian official also informed me that when the Syrian government hailed a $1 billion line of credit for manufactured goods obtained from Iran earlier in the year, in actuality Damascus had gone to Tehran for a $5 billion loan; the Iranians had had to turn them down because of their own economic problems caused by US-led international economic sanctions. Clearly the Syrian government has been receiving copious amounts of aid from both Iran and Russia and perhaps a few other countries with which it has good relations, including some of the BRICS members. But it is not an open-ended pipeline; there appear to be limits. There is also a vibrant black market, front companies set up abroad, and smuggling operations and open trade across remaining friendly borders, such as with Lebanon; indeed, when I was driven to Damascus from the Lebanese border this past February, there was a very long line of trucks transporting goods back and forth between the two countries. So, economic activity in Syria hasn't ceased completely, and authoritarian regimes are fairly adept at hoarding and then extracting rent. Furthermore, in areas outside of the oil industry, Syria was not really integrated into the international economy or subject to the political pressures of the IMF or World Bank or Western economies in general, so unlike in Egypt and Tunisia, both dependent on Western financial aid, tourism and trade, there have been very few economic levers the West have been able to employ directly against the Syrian regime.

To intervene or not to intervene?

This question has plagued the international community since the beginning of the Syrian uprising. And most of the chatter surrounding this question has focused on what the United States decides to do (or not do), for no one will take the lead in terms of asserting themselves much beyond humanitarian, financial, and tactical and training assistance to the Syrian opposition unless the Obama administration leads the way (even if it is from behind, as in the case of Libya). Certainly there has been a great deal of frustration, even anger, in the Syrian opposition and with those in the United States and in Western government circles who have long argued for a more robust US response to counter the Syrian government's escalation in military tactics against the opposition, from employing troops and tanks at first, then air force helicopter gunships and jet fighters, to SCUD missiles, and possibly even the use of chemical weapons – and the associated rising death toll and collateral damage.

But the Obama administration has remained very reluctant to go significantly beyond that which it was already doing in terms of humanitarian relief and the provision of some training and tactical equipment, especially computers and communication devices. It was prepared to continue to allow countries such as Turkey, Qatar, and Saudi Arabia to establish pipelines of financial assistance and military hardware to be delivered to the opposition fighters. The European Union had been categorically opposed to providing lethal assistance to the opposition much less direct military involvement, although France and Great Britain have succeeded in getting the EU to bend on this issue and have even threatened to go it alone if necessary, although they will not budge until the United States does.

Since 2012 was a presidential election year, there was very little chance that, short of some dramatic event in Syria that would compel the United States to act, the Obama administration was going to do anything but stay the course. The Obama administration is as poll-driven as any other recent US administration, and it could readily see that the American people had absolutely no desire to intervene in yet another Middle East war when the United States had so recently pulled out of Iraq and was drawing down in Afghanistan. Furthermore, with a sluggish recovery to the 2008 global financial crisis, Americans felt strongly that the United States, as Obama himself stated, should focus on nation-building at home rather than abroad. In addition, all of the reasons given in Chapter 9 as to why the US diplomatic and military response vis-à-vis Libya would be difficult if not impossible to replicate in Syria were still operative. Indeed, the problems that had arisen in the countries that had experienced the Arab Spring, not least of which was Libya, made the Obama administration that much more reticent to engage in something that might generate even more instability in the Middle East.[7] Despite the urging of a number of congresspersons in Washington and even some powerful voices within the administration, such as Secretary of State Hillary Clinton and CIA director David Petraeus, throughout much of 2012 the president himself and his close advisors in the White House seemed to be dictating foreign policy on this issue. And what Obama determined at the time was that arming a largely unknown and divided Syrian opposition with lethal weapons, and/or adding US military action to the mix (as with the establishment of a no-fly zone) were fraught with all sorts of potential negative consequences, most particularly creating a slippery slope of military intervention that would lead to direct US military involvement and Washington 'owning' the results of its policies in Syria. It would be similar to what had happened in Iraq following the US-led invasion of that country in 2003 at the significant cost of lives and treasure without measurably improving the situation in the country itself or the already sullied image of the United States in the region. Comparing prospective military intervention in Syria with what happened in Iraq, Fareed Zakaria wrote the following:

> In fact, we have seen atrocities much worse than those in Syria very recently, in Iraq under U.S. occupation only a few years ago. From 2003 to 2012, despite there being as many as 180,000 American and allied troops in Iraq, somewhere between 150,000 and 300,000 Iraqi civilians died and about 1.5 million fled the country. Jihadi groups flourished in Iraq, and al-Qaeda had a huge presence there. The U.S. was about as actively engaged in Iraq as possible, and yet more terrible things happened there than in Syria . . . All the features of Syria's civil war that are supposedly the result of U.S. nonintervention also appeared in Iraq despite America's massive intervention there.[8]

The call for US action became acute in April–May 2013 when allegations surfaced that the Syrian regime had used chemical weapons, specifically Sarin nerve gas against opposition forces in March in Aleppo. President Obama said early on in the Syrian conflict that the Syrian government's use of chemical weapons against its own people would cross a 'red line', and more recently the president stated that it would be a 'game-changer'. While not stipulating exactly what the United States would do if chemical weapons were proven to have been used, most believe that it was the tripwire for US military involvement, at the very least providing the pretext to deliver lethal aid to the opposition.

The Syrian government has vehemently denied using chemical weapons that in the first place it says it does not possess, and even if it did have them, it would never use them against its own people. Syrian officials, in turn, accuse the 'terrorists', its catch-all term for the opposition, of using chemical weapons or at the very least staging their use in order to create the crossing of the infamous red line so that the United States would be forced to respond militarily.

Could the Syrian regime's accusation be correct? Of course it could. In fact, a UN official, Carla Del Ponte, after interviewing outside of Syria doctors and victims involved in the purported chemical weapons attack, in a statement released on 6 May determined that there are 'strong suspicions' that elements of the Syrian opposition used the sarin gas.[9] The UN was quick to point out the next day that no conclusions on the issue had been reached. Could those pointing fingers at the Syrian government be wrong? Of course. Could it turn out that chemical weapons were in fact not used and that what was thought to be chemical weapons is something else entirely?[10] Absolutely. This is why the Obama administration was so careful about the whole situation. While acknowledging the intelligence from several sources that there was a strong likelihood of chemical weapons use, President Obama stated clearly: 'What we now have is evidence that chemical weapons have been used inside of Syria, but we don't know how they were used, when they were used, who used them; we don't have a chain of custody that establishes what exactly happened. And when I am making decisions about America's national security and the potential for taking additional action in response to chemical weapon use, I've got to make sure I've got the facts.' Echoing the controversy over what happened regarding Iraq before the US-led invasion in 2003, largely based upon what turned out to be the incorrect, if not false, intelligence that Iraq possessed weapons of mass destruction, the president further noted that, 'if we end up rushing to judgment without hard, effective evidence, then we can find ourselves in the position where we can't mobilize the international community to support what we do.'[11]

As of this writing, the Obama administration has not yet decided on what, if any, action to take, although the Pentagon has been authorized to prepare a menu of options ranging from airstrikes and commando raids to the establishment of a no-fly zone over all or parts of Syria.[12] Given that a UN official added considerable doubt as to the presumed culpability of the Syrian regime, the Obama administration may be somewhat relieved if the pressure to act recedes. Many believe that if Obama does choose to respond to this or some other incident, it will be in order to maintain US credibility when employing such threats and drawing red lines elsewhere – with North Korea and Iran in mind – as much as to accomplish anything tangible in Syria. As such, it is anticipated that if the United States increases its military involvement, it will be at some half-way point, such as providing lethal military aid directly to the opposition, although this in and of itself would probably not dramatically change the battlefield dynamics in Syria in the near term. Obama essentially ruled out boots on the ground when he stated on 4 May 2013 while on a visit to Costa Rica that, 'As a general rule I don't rule things out as commander-in-chief because circumstances may change. Having said that, I do not foresee a scenario in which [American] boots on the ground in Syria . . . would be good for America or be good for Syria'.[13] He further stated that other leaders in the region said that 'they agree with that assessment'.[14]

The United States must be very careful about this, however, and not react in a convulsive manner. Perhaps the mistake was drawing a red line in the first place, much as saying early on that Assad must step down has complicated steps toward initiating a negotiated political settlement. Can the United States militarily remove the Assad regime? Of course it can. Given the appropriate commitment of forces there are not many regimes in the world the United States cannot overthrow. Although removing the Syrian regime would be a tougher nut to crack than was the case in Libya or Afghanistan, and perhaps even Iraq, particularly as Syria has a sophisticated and mobile air defense system updated in recent years by the Russians, the question is not whether we can or cannot but what would happen in the aftermath. Would such action multiply rather than reduce the problems that already exist in the area? In other words, we do not want to see a repeat of what happened in Iraq. Even the Syrian opposition is unanimous in not wanting another Iraq, which is why many do not want US boots on the ground or fighter jets in the air. No one in the opposition wants to be seen as riding in on US tanks, as did the Iraqi National Congress during the 2003 invasion, subsequently being delegitimized in Iraq for having been too closely associated with the United States. Indeed, a number of Syrian opposition leaders simply want the United States to use its leadership to coordinate the delivery of financial and military aid in a much more efficient and systematic fashion than has been the case to date, where assistance has been sporadic, uncoordinated, and subject to the political agendas of outside powers, particularly those of Turkey, Qatar, and Saudi Arabia.

And what might the Russians, Iranians, or Hizbullah do in response? They may very well step up their level of support to Assad and company, thus leading to an even more dangerous escalation of the conflict. From the point of view of Washington, it could damage its attempts to form a consensus backed by Moscow regarding the curtailment of Iran's purported attempts to weaponize its uranium enrichment process toward developing a nuclear weapons capability. China could be less helpful reining in an unpredictable North Korea if it sees the United States getting bogged down in yet another Middle East theater. The number of al-Qaida-linked jihadists in Syria has already been growing, although they are still a minority of the fighters. This would change if the United States suddenly enters the front lines in Syria even if they are supposedly on the same side, as jihadists from all over the world would begin to flock to Syria to not only help defeat a *kafir* (unbelievers) regime, but also to take on the United States, as happened in Iraq. The Afghanistan experience is instructive in this regard. The United States supported Afghans fighting against the Soviet occupation in the 1980s. America was ostensibly on the same side, but it was not truly allied with the Afghan *mujahedeen*, as the United States was seen by them as much the enemy as the Soviet Union, but the one had to be confronted first before the other. Many of these elements would go on to form the backbone of the Taliban and al-Qaida, which, as we know all too well, came back to haunt America with 9/11.

President Obama does not want to take the risk of indirectly aiding jihadist elements in Syria because sophisticated weaponry finds its way to them in the confusing labyrinth that is the Syrian opposition landscape – and then is used in a spectacular fashion against American interests, property, and/or people. Many accuse the Obama administration of contributing to the growing jihadist problem in Syria by not engaging more assertively earlier in the conflict, thus allowing it to fester and opening the door for jihadists. The jihadists themselves, especially those from outside of Syria, are not particularly well liked by other Syrians, whether secular or *salafist*, but whether they are liked or not many see them as possessing much-needed military experience, effective tactics, and better weapons to more capably take on Syrian government forces.[15] In addition, Jabhat al-Nusra, with its steady supply of funding from a variety of Islamist sources abroad, its control of (and therefore revenues derived from) some oil sites in eastern Syria, and its effective organizational structure, has been able to provide a modicum of stability, justice, order, and services in towns and cities where it is present, which is eagerly welcomed by local populations grasping for any semblance of normality. This has long been the calling card for Islamist groups, such as the Muslim Brotherhood in Egypt or Hizbullah in south Lebanon, i.e. establishing a level of acceptance by filling the vacuum of services and aid left by governments. Neither are they viewed as corrupt, at a time when the criminalized element in Syria is on the rise, with a number of militia groups seen by locals as rapacious thieves and robbers rather than revolutionaries. This is an unfortunate by-product of almost any civil war: individuals and groups become invested in and empowered by the conflict environment, and they have little interest in seeing it end any time soon. Finally, it seems as though Jabhat al-Nusra and likeminded groups in Syria have learned from the mistakes made by al-Qaida in Iraq after the US invasion in 2003. There, al-Qaida tried to impose its ideology on the local Iraqi population, if necessary by force, thereby alienating many indigenous Sunnis to such an extent that they decided to cooperate with US forces and the Iraqi government against al-Qaida in Iraq. It remains to be seen, therefore, whether or not Jabhat al-Nusra can establish a deep and lasting presence in Syria.

But this is a moot point now, as the reality is that jihadist groups are in Syria, and although they are certainly in the minority, they have acquired influence out of proportion to their numbers, so much so that the Syrian government began something of a public relations campaign recently to convince Western powers that it is on the same side in the global war against terrorism, and, therefore, the West should cease any kind of support for the Syrian opposition. In an interview with Syrian state television on 17 April 2013, Bashar al-Assad said that 'the West has paid heavily for funding al-Qaida in its early stages [in Afghanistan in the 1980s]. Today it is doing the same in Syria, Libya and other places, and will pay a heavy price in the heart of Europe and the United States'.[16]

The question of al-Qaida-linked jihadists in Syria became a more pointed one when al-Qaida's affiliate in Iraq announced in April 2013 that it had merged with Jabhat al-Nusra to form the Islamic State of Iraq and the Levant. The announcement came from the al-Qaida in Iraq leader, Shaykh Abu Bakr al-Baghdadi. This was on top of the US State Department's December 2012 designation of Jabhat al-Nusra as a terrorist organization for its suspected ties to al-Qaida. It was a questionable move on the part of the United States. Of course, it can be seen as an attempt to help shape the Syrian opposition and separate out elements and groups that are clearly inimical to US interests and thus ineligible for any US aid. Many in the Syrian opposition, especially the more secular elements, however, saw the move as constraining their ability to counter the appeal of Jabhat al-Nusra and the like because to do so would appear that they were doing America's bidding. For Jabhat al-Nusra, on the other hand, the designation was something of a badge of honor, one that could be used to recruit more followers from inside and outside of Syria. But Jabhat al-Nusra has to be careful. Syrians are very possessive of their land, even if a nationwide Syrian identity has not entirely taken root.[17] As such, there is a great deal of suspicion regarding groups such as Jabhat al-Nusra, whose loyalties to external organizations have been questioned. As Leila Hilal of the New America Foundation said regarding the merger, it may 'confirm the suspicions of much of the Syrian public that al-Nusra is not fighting for a free Syria, but for the establishment of an ultra-fundamentalist state'.[18] Wary of creating this impression, the acknowledged head of Jabhat al-Nusra, Abu Muhammad al-Jawlani, was a bit fuzzy on the announcement. He stated that he was not consulted about the merger, instead announcing his pledge of allegiance to al-Qaida's leader, Ayman al-Zawahiri.[19] Al-Qaida would dearly love to establish a strong presence in a country on the border with Israel. The fact that the chosen name of the Jabhat al-Nusra leader, al-Jawlani (or 'the Golan' in Arabic), refers to the Golan Heights occupied by Israel, may be an attempt to situate his group into what traditionally has been every Syrian's first and foremost national goal: the return of the Golan.[20] Nevertheless, the positioning and continued growth of Jabhat al-Nusra and other like-minded jihadist groups in Syria have become part and parcel of the dynamics of the Syrian conflict.

A complicated conflict

Iraq showed the chaos that can occur when an authoritarian system is precipitously removed and the leadership structure decapitated. No one wants to see this happen in Syria, except, perhaps, al-Qaida and its affiliates because they can best fish in troubled waters – or in failed states. But there are no easy answers. Indeed, as one top Western official told me, 'what we don't want is a failed state. We will even take a failing state at this point, as long as it doesn't develop into a failed state'. What began as the hope of the Arab Spring spreading to Syria in a way that would sweep aside another long-entrenched authoritarian Middle East regime and replace it with a pluralistic, democratic system, has long been forgotten. Yet to date not much effort has been made toward establishing a process that might lead to a political settlement. In retrospect, it turns out that most of the Syrian opposition and its supporters in the West and in the Middle East grossly underestimated the staying power of the Syrian regime. As a result, for well over a year into the conflict, most academic and diplomatic conferences and meetings that dealt with the political and/or diplomatic side of the equation and were sponsored by countries supporting the Syrian opposition almost exclusively focused on the day after Assad, i.e. after the fall of the regime. As a result, many of these countries and organizations (including the UN) took it for granted that Assad would fall and tried to prepare the ground for what was thought to have been the inevitable. Unfortunately, when by the end of 2012 the realization did materialize that a political settlement or some sort of process that would lead to one was the optimal outcome, the situation had become much more complex, more ensconced in regional and international politics. By essentially adopting the day-after-Assad paradigm, these countries and organizations had largely discredited themselves as impartial brokers, particularly in the eyes of Damascus.

The three scenarios outlined in the hardcover edition are still operative, although some of the details have changed with time.[21] I stated then (summer 2012) that a stalemated civil war was the most likely outcome. This is still the case, unless something appears that creates a decided imbalance between the government and opposition forces. The only thing in the foreseeable future that might cause this imbalance is more robust US-led military assistance to the opposition, which, if it occurs, seems as though it would be fairly limited. It is clear to me that under current circumstances no one in the West is particularly interested in direct military intervention, even of the kind that occurred in Libya. In fact, some countries that went further than everyone else in the early stages of the conflict in calling on Assad to leave power and supporting the opposition, such as Turkey, have been looking at ways to dial down their commitment in line with the rest of the international community. Ankara has had to deal with the emerging refugee crisis as well as the complications generated by its forward position on Syria for its overall regional policies, as it is being seen as one of the lead Sunni players (along with Saudi Arabia and Qatar) in a sectarian-based regional conflict with the Shiites (Syria, Iran, Iraq and Hizbullah). Indeed, Hizbullah leader Hassan Nasrallah's comments in early May in strong support of the Syrian regime tend to paint the conflict ever more so in stark sectarian terms. The UN Commission of Inquiry warned in December 2012 that the civil war had become 'overtly sectarian', and the report it produced stated that the increasingly sectarian nature of the conflict is a motivator for proxy groups fighting in Syria.[22] There has also been considerable consternation within Turkey for getting itself so deeply enmeshed in a conflict that appears to have no tidy exit horizon.[23] As one can see, the intended and unintended tentacles of the Syrian conflict have crept across borders with the potential of causing instability far and wide in the region – which, quite frankly, is exactly what the Syrian regime would want everyone to believe: that if it crashes and burns, so will the rest of the Middle East.

Since the beginning of the Syrian uprising, many in the international community simply wanted it to go away, or at the very least be contained so that attentions could be directed elsewhere. The Obama administration has wanted to implement a strategic pivot toward East Asia, where China's rising power demanded more US foreign policy focus. At the same time the United States was drawing down in Iraq and Afghanistan while seeming to disengage from the Israeli-Palestinian situation, especially as the turbulence of the Arab Spring appeared to put any and all Arab-Israeli initiatives on hold. In addition, new domestic energy sources heralded by fracking could result in less dependence on Middle East oil at a time when, as mentioned previously, the administration and the American public demand more attention be spent at home on economic recovery.

But Obama may have to reluctantly turn his attentions back to the Middle East if the situation in Syria continues to unravel and/or spread across its borders, with the resulting increase in congressional and international pressure to intervene in a more direct manner. Some have suggested that the replacement of Hillary Clinton with John Kerry as secretary of state as Obama began his second term in office in 2013 may contribute to a turn towards the Middle East revolving around Syria. Kerry, as noted in Chapter 3, developed a keen interest in Syria when he was chairman of the Senate Foreign Relations Committee and after visiting and having frequent contact with Bashar al-Assad.[24] This certainly has the potential of becoming an albatross for Obama that hinders his ability to pursue what he really wants in his final four years in office. The Middle East has long been a burial ground for the foreign policy ambitions of presidential administrations. This is usually the result of an administration, especially in its relatively unfettered second term, deciding to actively invest itself in the Middle East, typically some aspect of the Arab-Israeli problem – yet failing miserably. It would be a cruel irony if this happens to an administration that to date has actively tried to avoid any further investment of political capital in the region.

Is this a conflict that must simply play itself out, whatever that means, while the rest of the region and the international community hopes and prays that it remains somewhat contained? Perhaps. It is difficult at times to know the truth of what is going on in Syria. As one leading European official told me, 'there are two wars, one is the real fighting on the ground;

the other is the information war'. The latter complicates the former, as there has been a tremendous amount of disinformation generated on both sides of the conflict. The Syrian government for its part has stayed afloat in the real war, but it has been losing the information war. This is not a real surprise as the Assad regimes have traditionally played this game abysmally, and Bashar and his cohorts undermine their own ability to play the game with their comments and actions as well as their own inability to understand the conceptual paradigm of the West. In addition, Syrian opposition groups based in the West, composed of many ex-pat Syrians who have lived there for years and are therefore well-accustomed to its media culture and public sentiments, have enjoyed a distinct advantage on this battlefront.

Oh, the good old days when foreign policy was more Machiavellian and the world was more Manichaean – a world in which authoritarian leaders ruled their countries with an iron fist without the complications of civil wars and the domestic instability characteristic of the process of building a democracy. It is emblematic of the confusion surrounding any sort of resolution of the conflict that some noted commentators have actually advocated a reversal, directing US support away from the opposition and toward that of the Assad regime for the sake of stability in the region, and ensuring that such a strategic outpost does not fall in the hands of Islamic extremists.[25] This is very unlikely to happen, but my impression is that individuals, groups, organizations, and countries are flailing about desperately searching for an answer that will end the conflict in the near term. Would it not be ironic if what the Arab Spring produced in the immediate sense was another round of authoritarianism before the final triumph of democracy? This is what happened in nineteenth- and twentieth-century Europe. It may be what happens in the Middle East.

It is difficult to see any resolution of the conflict without the Syrian opposition becoming a more potent and cohesive force. At the very minimum there should be an overall restructuring that creates a critical mass of the opposition, especially internal elements perhaps acting in concert with some external Syrian opposition leaders, in order to present a more consolidated and coordinated position. Easier said than done, but this would help on both the military and diplomatic fronts. The former is rather obvious, but the latter is also necessary in terms of a potential political settlement because one will not even be considered by the Syrian regime until there is an identifiable and representative negotiating partner on the opposition's side. Although it can be seen as somewhat self-serving, the regime is correct when it states that there is no one in the opposition with whom to negotiate; they are either seen as unrepresentative of a large enough portion of the (especially internal) opposition to make a difference, or subservient to countries that it views as the enemy. The continued fragmentation of the opposition is a serious problem. Even the FSA is more a brand name adhered to in various circumstances by different groups of opposition fighters rather than a fully integrated military command and control structure.[26] The more the opposition is seen as a self-interested rabble, the more the silent majority of Syrians will stay on the sidelines, supporting the government in essence by not supporting the opposition.

When the battle for Aleppo commenced in autumn 2012, it seemed the Syrian conflict rose to yet another level. Even though sections of Aleppo are still held by government forces, with the unfortunate destruction of large and historic districts of this ancient city, it signaled to Damascus that the opposition had the determination and wherewithal to take cities, including large swaths of northwest Syria along the Turkish border. The Syrian government responded with more attacks from the sky via helicopter gunships, fighter jets, and Scud missiles. Atrocities committed by both sides increased. Many Syrians just see themselves as bearing witness to the destruction of their country without taking sides. Many have simply left.

Most of the flaws in the Geneva Communiqué can be addressed in one way or another, but it will need a sustained and inclusive negotiating position that must be associated with the Syrian government's intent to truly participate (rather than using it as a stalling tactic) and the Syrian opposition coalescing into a viable representative body, which, in my opinion, must be top-heavy with Syrian leaders from inside Syria rather than the other way around, the latter painfully being the case to date. There was a hopeful sign at a joint news conference following a meeting on 8 May between US Secretary of State John Kerry and Russian Foreign Minister

Sergei Lavrov in which both committed their respective countries to implement the Geneva Communiqué by convening 'as soon as is practicable, possibly and hopefully by the end of the month' an international conference. Although the Russians are not particularly wedded to Bashar al-Assad, they still fear that his precipitous fall would lead to chaos and the growth of Islamic extremism, which to President Putin may be the greatest fear, something Moscow continues to deal with inside its own borders. Kerry told reporters that, 'it's impossible for me . . . to understand how Syria could be governed in the future by a man who has committed the things we know have taken place . . . but I'm not going to decide that in the end. Because the Geneva Communiqué says that the transitional government has to be chosen by mutual consent by the parties . . . the current regime and the opposition'.[27] UN Special Envoy on Syria, Lakhdar Brahimi, who assumed this post when Kofi Annan resigned in August 2012, called the remarks 'the first hopeful news concerning that unhappy country in a very long time'.[28] Brahimi correctly went on to point out, however, that this is only one step and that there is still much work to be done. Even if an international conference is convened, there are still the problems regarding the composition of the Syrian opposition as well as the fact that Bashar al-Assad, concluding that this initiative will lead to his ouster one way or another, may simply decline to participate, or agree to attend at some level but not abide by any results emanating from this process. Nevertheless, it is a sliver of hope, which is all we seem to have at the moment.

I have had friends on both sides who have died or had their lives irreparably – and disastrously – changed as a result of the conflict. There does not seem to be a resolution to the conflict on the immediate horizon, and it may be years before it truly ends and then a generation before Syria truly recovers. In October 2012 I wrote an essay for Al-Monitor media website entitled, 'The Lebanonization of Syria'. In it, as the title suggests, I advance the notion that the situation in Syria could resemble that of neighboring Lebanon in the 1970s and 1980s. Lebanon, similarly divided across sectarian lines, practically disintegrated amid sectarian conflict exacerbated by regional and international interference, culminating in the

1982 Israeli invasion. Subsequently, Lebanon has suffered decades of instability and factionalization, characterized by a weak central government subject to the vicissitudes of powerful sectarian based actors often supported by a variety of outside powers. I posited at the time that Syria could be headed in this direction. This would be potentially calamitous, especially as unlike Lebanon, the Syrian case probably would probably not be contained and would most likely spill across the borders in all directions, potentially resulting in a region-wide conflict. Since that time, with the continuing deterioration of the situation in Syria, I have been told by a number of people in the opposition, in the Syrian government, and top officials in foreign capitals, that the correct analogy should now be Somalia, i.e. the total breakdown of government control replaced by hundreds of warlords with their private militias, with the reconstitution of the country all but impossible. Even the political settlement in 1989 (the al-Ta'if Accords) that brought an end to Lebanon's civil war by reapportioning political power in the Lebanese government, did not come into being until after fifteen years of death and destruction. It had to reach a point where enough people believed that things could not possibly get worse, thus finally galvanizing the relevant political actors to compromise. Hopefully it does not take Syrians this long to come to this realization.

So much is lost in a conflict like this, even beyond lives and treasure. There appears to have been a significant opportunity missed due to the uprising and, more particularly, the regime's response to it. The decision of the Assad regime to respond violently to the protests in Deraa and elsewhere brought to a close a very quiet and potentially productive US effort to create a foundation for Syrian-Israeli peace. According to a former Obama administration official, very significant progress had been made in narrowing differences between the parties over the course of several months' discussions between US mediators and each of the parties singly. Recall that in 2008 there were very serious Syrian-Israeli negotiations mediated by Turkey that most believe came close to being successfully concluded, only to be derailed by the Israeli war in Gaza (Israel's Operation Cast Lead) in December 2008 and into January 2009. No doubt the 2011 effort picked up on progress made back in 2008. By the middle of March 2011, however, precisely when peaceful protests were beginning, the contours of a prospective Syrian-Israeli agreement were taking shape, even though neither side had made irrevocable commitments to each other or to the United States. This very promising US diplomatic initiative came to a halt as it became clear that the use of violence to counter the protests would be a permanent feature of the regime's policy. Clearly the regime thought it could stamp out the protests quickly and then resume the negotiations, but the protests neither stopped nor even diminished – and neither did the regime crackdown. The Obama administration, according to this official, concluded in the spring of 2011 that a regime reacting in this manner lacked the requisite legitimacy to be able to represent Syria in a diplomatic undertaking of such significance, and so the peace effort was abandoned. The return of the Golan Heights had been Assad's foremost policy objective bar none, but his hubris in cracking down on the protestors has probably now forever denied him this ultimate achievement. He should have known better. Someone who was so attuned to the new technology, so aware of (indeed, to a certain degree promoted) the benefits of high tech in understanding and integrating into the global social media revolution – the self-described computer nerd – ultimately failed to comprehend the effects of that with which his name was so associated.

Of course, Syria will never be the same. It will not be reconstituted as it once was, even if the regime of Bashar al-Assad survives and is able to maintain control of most, if not all, of the major cities. The Syrian president, I think, realizes the need for significant political reform. He and his ruling apparatus will attempt to do so while keeping as much power – and the socioeconomic positions that go with it – as possible. However, in a very poignant and emotional meeting I had in late 2012, one of the Syrian opposition leaders said the following regarding his experience in what he refers to as the Syrian revolution: 'I have heard my own voice for the first time.' In other words, all his life, he had no voice. It was whatever the ruling regime said it would be. So, even suffering under the tremendous hardships of war, he preferred it, with his own voice, to that of authoritarian stability. Ordinary Syrians have been empowered to expect more freedom and opportunity. Even if there is some sort of political settlement, whether or not it leads to Assad's exit sooner or later, this will have to be taken into account. Hopefully the collective desire held by almost all concerned to not let Syria disintegrate into another Iraq, Lebanon, or Somalia will generate the necessary political and diplomatic will to produce a political settlement in the near term. This is unlikely, but so was the Arab Spring itself, and even more so its extension into Syria.

Notes

1 The Hope

1. After the death of his elder brother Basil in 1994, there were pictures and banners all over the country of Hafiz, Basil and Bashar, along with the respective inscriptions, 'The Leader', 'The Example' and 'The Hope'. Many were taken down after Bashar came to power, but one could still find a number of them lingering around the country for years afterward.
2. For this and other excerpts from Bashar's 2000 inaugural speech see: www.al-bab.com/arab/countries/syria/bashar00a.htm
3. Charles Issawi, *The Economic History of the Middle East 1800–1914*, University of Chicago Press, Chicago, 1966, p. 505.
4. Steven Heydemann, 'The political logic of economic rationality: selective liberalization in Syria' in Henri Barkey (ed.), *The Politics of Economic Reform in the Middle East*, St Martin's Press, New York, 1992, pp. 11–39.
5. Volker Perthes, *The Political Economy of Syria under Asad*, I.B. Tauris, London, 1995, p. 254.
6. ibid.
7. Ghassan Salame, *Al-Mujtama wa al-Dawla fi al-Mashriq al-Arabi* [*Society and State in the Arab East*], Beirut, 1987, p. 206.
8. Patrick Seale, *Asad: The struggle for the Middle East*, University of California Press, Berkeley, 1988, p. 456.
9. David W. Lesch, *The New Lion of Damascus: Bashar al-Asad and modern Syria*, Yale University Press, London, 2005, p. 92; for a more extended discussion of the Damascus Spring and subsequent events, see pp. 81–97.
10. Congressional Research Service, 'Syria: US relations and bilateral issues', *Issue Brief for Congress*, 15 November 2002, p. 9.
11. United States Senate, Republican Policy Committee, 'Holding Syria accountable for its actions', 23 October 2003, available at: http://rpc.senate.gov/public/_files/fr102303.pdf
12. Jim Garamone, 'Syria–US relationship facing major deterioration', American Foreign Press Service, 27 September 2004.
13. Quoted in Lesch, *The New Lion of Damascus*, p. 117.

14. 'US sees Syria "facilitating" insurgents', *Washington Times*, 20 April 2004, available at: www.washingtontimes.com/news/2004/apr/20/20040420-115628-7182r/?page=all
15. An article, commenting on the Syrian-Iraqi border situation, stated that: 'Western diplomats characterize insurgents who pass through here as a contributing but not essential factor to the resistance in Iraq. They also dismiss accusations about serious weaponry flowing across or Iraq's deposed Baathist leadership huddling here.' The article quotes a senior Western diplomat as saying, 'I don't see the insurgency being masterminded from Syria.' Neil MacFarquhar, 'At tense Syria–Iraq border, American forces are battling insurgents every day', *New York Times*, 26 October 2004, available at: www.nytimes.com/2004/10/26/international/middleeast/26syria.html
16. Between 2003 and 2007, Iraqi-Syrian trade, even during the war in Iraq, amounted to approximately $100–200 million, and in 2007 the two countries managed to do more than $800 million in trade, which surpassed pre-war levels. Steven Simon, *Won't You Be My Neighbor: Syria, Iraq and the changing strategic context in the Middle East*, United States Institute of Peace Working Paper, March 2009, available at: www.usip.org/files/resources/april2009.PDF
17. This and subsequent quotes regarding the SAA can be found in 'US policy toward Syria and HR 4483, the Syria Accountability Act', Hearing before the subcommittee on the Middle East and South Asia of the Committee on International Relations, 107th Congress, Second Session on HR 4483, 18 September 2002.

2 Surviving

1. For more on the Sabawi episode, see David W. Lesch, *The New Lion of Damascus: Bashar al-Asad and modern Syria*, Yale University Press, London, 2005, pp. 193–5.
2. James Risen and David E. Sanger, 'Border clashes as US pressures Syria over Iraq', *New York Times*, 15 October 2005, available at: http://query.nytimes.com/gst/fullpage.html?res=9D0DE3D9143FF936A25753C1A9639C8B63&pagewanted=all
3. ibid. Some officials likened Syria to Cambodia in the Vietnam War, as a sanctuary for fighters, money and supplies that ended up in Iraq. The implication in this comparison was whether or not to bomb Syria, as the United States had bombed purported sanctuaries in Cambodia.
4. ibid.
5. As quoted in International Crisis Group, *Engaging Syria? US Constraints and Opportunities*, Middle East Report No. 83, 11 February 2009.
6. 'Syria's relations with Iraq', United States Institute of Peace Briefing, April 2007.
7. 'Iraqi official says Syria supporting insurgents', ABC News Blogs, 11 May 2007, available at: http://blogs.abcnews.com/theblotter/2007/05/iraqi_official_.html
8. Phil Sands, 'Syria stops insurgents on the Iraq border', *The National*, 2 November 2008, available at: www.thenational.ae/news/world/middle-east/syria-stops-insurgents-on-iraq-border
9. It must also be noted that this combined with deteriorating security conditions on the Iraqi side of the border after a heightened display of security around the Iraqi elections in early 2009. This became especially important as US troops began their redeployment from Iraqi cities in June 2009. One report in May 2009 noted that: 'Iraqi border interdiction efforts have been hindered by a chronic shortage of fuel, which keeps border police grounded for weeks at a time, and by corruption within their ranks, US military officials in Iraq said.' A senior US military official stated that 'Iraqi vigilance in general has decreased since the elections', and that al-Qaida in Iraq has 'been able to rebuild the network' (Karen DeYoung, 'Terrorist traffic via Syria again inching up', *Washington Post*, 11 May 2009). It is also important to realize that Iraqi capabilities increased when the price per barrel of oil was high, and therefore more money was

available for border security, and they decreased as the price per barrel of oil fell precipitately in the late summer and early autumn of 2008.

10. See an especially positive interview that Bashar gave: Ian Black, 'Assad urges US to rebuild diplomatic road to Damascus', *Guardian*, 17 February 2009, available at: www.guardian.co.uk/world/2009/feb/17/assad-interview-syria-obama
11. I experienced this at first hand. By 2008 it was much harder for me to see President Bashar, as his schedule was filling up with visiting foreign dignitaries and with his own trips abroad. Between 2004 and 2008, I essentially only had to compete with Hassan Nasrallah and Mahmoud Ahmadinejad for his time.

3 Syria is Different

1. The announcement of the indictments finally came on 17 August 2011.
2. Susan Spano, 'Syria a bright star in the Middle East', *Los Angeles Times*, 26 December 2010, available at: http://articles.latimes.com/2010/dec/26/travel/la-tr-syria-20101226
3. Nicolai Ouroussoff, 'Preserving heritage, and the fabric of life, in Syria', *New York Times*, 27 December 2010, available at: www.nytimes.com/2010/12/27/arts/design/27preserve.html
4. The CSID is a pro-democracy organization, headquartered in Washington, DC, that has supported the Arab Spring movements in general and the downfall of the dictators in Tunisia, Egypt and Libya. It must be said, however, that this particular email was sponsored by the Syrian-American Congress, long an anti-Assad group based in, and often supported by, the United States. The CSID email was sent from its office in Tunis, Tunisia, not un-coincidentally just after the Syrian National Council, the lead Syrian opposition group outside Syria, held a conference earlier in December there to coordinate anti-Assad activities and plan for the future.
5. Barak Ravid, 'US lawmaker, Syria's Assad working to renew peace talks with Israel', *Haaretz*, 24 February 2011.
6. Vogue.com, 19 March 2011. *Vogue* has since removed the story from its website.
7. Ashley Fantz, 'Will Asma al-Assad take a stand or stand by her man?', CNN.com, 26 December 2011, available at: http://edition.cnn.com/2011/12/25/world/meast/asma-al-assad-profile/index.html
8. Jay Solomon and Bill Spindle, 'Syria strongman: time for reform', *Wall Street Journal*, 31 January 2011, available at: http://online.wsj.com/article/SB10001424052748704832704576114340735033236.html
9. Sami Moubayed, 'Lesson from Egypt: West is not best', *Forward Magazine*, 48 (February 2011), p. 4, available at: www.forwardsyria.com/story/394/Lesson%20from%20Egypt:%20West%20is%20not%20Best
10. ibid.
11. Dr Bouthaina Shaaban, 'The real evils plaguing the region', *Forward Magazine*, 48 (February 2011), p. 16, available at: www.forwardsyria.com/story/395/The%20real%20evils%20plaguing%20the%20region
12. Philip S. Khoury, 'Islamic revivalism and the crisis of the secular state in the Arab world: an historical approach', in Ibrahim Ibrahim (ed.), *Arab Resources: The transformation of a society*, Contemporary Center for Arab Studies, Washington, DC, 1983.
13. For an excellent historical analysis of the long-term socioeconomic, geographic and demographic causal factors of the 2010–11 Tunisian uprising, going back more than a century, see Julia Clancy-Smith, 'From Sidi Bou Zid to Sidi Bou Sa'id: a *longue durée* approach to the Tunisian revolutions', in Mark L. Haas and David W. Lesch (eds), *The Arab Spring: Change and resistance in the Middle East*, Westview Press, Boulder, CO, forthcoming (November 2012). For a shorter historical analysis of all the pertinent uprisings in the Arab world in late 2010 and into 2011, see James Gelvin, *The Arab Uprisings: What everyone needs to know*, Oxford University Press, Oxford, 2012.

14. Even as late as 15 March, an anti-regime rally demanding reforms – held in Damascus and organized by an opposition group based in London called the Syrian Revolution against Bashar al-Assad – attracted only some 200–300 protestors. Gelvin, *The Arab Uprisings*.

4 No, It's Not

1. James Gelvin, 'The Arab World at the intersection of the national and transnational', in Mark L. Haas and David W. Lesch (eds), *The Arab Spring: Change and resistance in the Middle East*, Westview Press, Boulder, CO, forthcoming (November 2012).
2. Joshua Landis, 'Deraa: the government takes off its gloves: 15 killed', *Syria Comment*, 23 March 2011, available at: www.joshualandis.com/blog/?p=8692&cp=all
3. David W. Lesch, *The New Lion of Damascus: Bashar al-Asad and modern Syria*, Yale University Press, London, 2005, p. 222.
4. ibid., p. 208.
5. Author's interview with Bashar al-Assad, 27 May 2004, Damascus, Syria.
6. 'Syria reduces oil production due to western sanctions: minister', xinhuanet.com, 3 November 2011, available at: http://news.xinhuanet.com/english2010/indepth/2011-11/03/c_131226504.htm
7. Quoted in Dr Nimrod Raphaeli, 'New Syria report charts steady economic reform as country primes itself for key regional role', MEMRI Economic Blog, 22 July 2010, available at: http://memrieconomicblog.org/bin/content.cgi?article=332
8. 'Syria attracted USD 1.5 billion in FDI in 2009', SEBC, 12 July 2010, available at: www.sebcsyria.com/web2008/art.php?art_id=1802&ViewMode=Print
9. 'Syria reduces oil production due to western sanctions: minister', xinhuanet.com.
10. 'Corruption Perceptions Index 2010', Transparency International, available at: www.transparency.org. By comparison, the top three on the Middle East and North Africa list are Qatar, United Arab Emirates and Israel. The top three on the global list are, in a tie for first place, Denmark, New Zealand and Singapore. The United States comes in at twenty-two on the list.
11. Ed Blanche, 'Arab Spring and the Mukhabarat Moment', *Middle East Magazine*, 427 (November 2011), p. 33.
12. Bassem Mroue and Elizabeth A. Kennedy, '120 dead after 2 days of unrest in Syria', *Huffington Post*, 23 April 2011, available at: www.huffingtonpost.com/huff-wires/20110423/ml-syria/
13. Mark L. Haas, 'Turkey and the Arab Spring: Ideological promotion in a revolutionary era', in Haas and Lesch (eds), *The Arab Spring*. As Haas points out, examples of this clustering can be found in Europe in 1848 and the 'color' revolutions in Eastern Europe in the 2000s.
14. ibid.

5 The Regime Responds

1. Liz Sly, 'A year into uprising, Syrian protestors say they won't give up', *Washington Post*, 14 March 2012, available at: www.washingtonpost.com/world/as-violence-in-syria-escalates-a-year-into-uprising-protesters-say-they-wont-give-up/2012/03/14/gIQAGeA2BS_story.html
2. 'Syria unrest: government pledges political reforms', BBC News, 25 March 2011, available at: www.bbc.co.uk/news/world-middle-east-12853634
3. David W. Lesch, *The New Lion of Damascus: Bashar al-Asad and modern Syria*, Yale University Press, London, 2005, pp. 89–90.
4. ibid., p. 89.

5. David W. Lesch, 'Bashar's defining moment', unpublished essay. This essay became the basis for an op-ed piece: 'The Syrian president I know', *New York Times*, 29 March 2011, available at: www.nytimes.com/2011/03/30/opinion/30lesch.html
6. Indeed, on a number of occasions very high-level Syrian officials actually asked me to raise with Bashar various proposals or ideas that they had. They were afraid to do so personally because they had much to lose if it was something Bashar did not like. One Syrian official told me that Bashar had told him that he listened to and respected my views. Since I did not have an agenda or anything tangible to lose (such as my position), I often expressed these to him in an unreserved manner.
7. David W. Lesch, 'Ahead of the curve', *Syria Comment*, 26 March 2011, available at: www.joshualandis.com/blog/?p=8785
8. This and other translations from his 30 March 2011 speech are taken from www.al-bab.com/arab/docs/syria/bashar_assad_speech_110330.htm
9. Also possibly a swipe at Saudi Arabia, with which the Syrian regime has had a mercurial relationship, mostly antagonistic, since the assassination of Rafiq Hariri, to whom the Saudi family was very close. Saudi Arabia also sponsors the second most popular Arab satellite news station, Al-Arabiyya. Syria has accused Saudi Arabia (with some justification) of funding Sunni Muslim extremist *salafist* groups in Syria, especially when the Saudi-Syrian relationship soured over the situation in Lebanon.
10. This is also a reference to the persistent pressure on Syria from the Bush administration following the US-led invasion of Iraq in 2003 and what was termed by US opponents in the region the 'American project'. It was seen as an attempt by the Bush administration to promote the growth of democracy, but one that hid the real, more sinister goals of a US-Israeli plan to dominate the region.
11. All English quotes from this speech come from: www.al-bab.com/arab/docs/syria/bashar_assad_speech_110416.htm
12. When talking about improvements in agriculture, he also pointed out the importance of targeting the 'eastern region', which happens to be where most of the Kurds live.

6 Opposition Mounts

1. Alan George, *Syria: Neither bread nor freedom*, Zed Books, London, 2003, p. 40.
2. ibid., p. 44.
3. ibid., p. 49.
4. For a very good essay on the development of the different 'generations' of Syrian opposition to the Assads, see Aron Lund, 'Weakening regime, weaker opposition', *Near East Quarterly*, IV (May 2011), available at: www.neareastquarterly.com/index.php/2011/06/15/weakening-regime-weaker-opposition/. As Lund explains, many of the signatories to the Damascus Declaration began their efforts to bring about democratic reform with the formation in 1979 of the National Democratic Gathering (NDG), an amalgam of secular, leftist – and illegal – political parties, including the dominant group, the Democratic Arab Socialist Union (formed in 1973), and the Arab Socialist Movement, the Syrian Democratic People's Party, the Workers' Revolutionary Party, the Democratic Baath Arab Socialist Party, and, joining the NGD in 2006, the Communist Action Party. The influence of the NGD, however, steadily declined after the late 1980s, as differences arose between the various parties. This decline was exacerbated by the fact that other opposition movements emerged, particularly those of an Islamist or liberal bent.
5. Phil Sands, 'Syrian opposition group collapses', *The National*, 22 April 2009, available at: http://209.157.64.200/focus/f-news/2237809/posts
6. 'Syria: "A kingdom of silence"', Al-Jazeera, 9 February 2011, available at: www.aljazeera.com/indepth/features/2011/02/201129103121562395.html

7. ibid. Ribal al-Assad is the son of Bashar's uncle, Rifaat al-Assad, who commanded the elite defense brigades under Hafiz al-Assad, and who led the armed forces against Hama in 1982. Rifaat has been in exile since 1983 after he failed to remove his ill brother from power amid the crisis in Lebanon at the time. Both father and son have been leading anti-Bashar al-Assad players ever since he came to power. In fact, some Syrian officials feared that, after Hafiz died, Rifaat might try to seize the opportunity to return to Syria and take over instead of Bashar.
8. Quoted in 'Protests ripple across Syria; at least 7 dead', CNN.com, available at: http://articles.cnn.com/2011-04-01/world/syria.protests_1_witnesses-demonstrators-protests?_s=PM;WORLD
9. This one actually came from numerous reports posted by CNN.com.
10. 'Syria says 19 police killed in southern city', *Guardian*, 8 April 2011, available at: www.guardian.co.uk/world/feedarticle/9587493
11. For an on-the-ground observation of the relative quiescence in Damascus, see 'Life in Syria's capital remains barely touched by rebellion', *New York Times*, 5 September 2011, available at: www.nytimes.com/2011/09/06/world/middleeast/06damascus.html?pagewanted=all
12. 'Syria crackdown on dissent harsher with troop, tanks', *Arizona Daily Star*, 26 April 2011, available at: http://azstarnet.com/news/article_3a963d62-cefd-5fe0-a081-d5911fe77e46.html
13. Bassem Mroue and Elizabeth A. Kennedy, '120 dead after 2 days of unrest in Syria', *Huffington Post*, 23 April 2011, available at: www.huffingtonpost.com/huff-wires/20110423/ml-syria/
14. ibid.
15. For a text of the entire statement, see www.facebook.com/note.php?note_id=184086641639119&comments
16. Peter Harling, 'Crunch-time for the Syrian regime', *Foreign Policy*, 29 April 2011, available at: http://mideast.foreignpolicy.com/posts/2011/04/29/crunch_time_for_the_syrian_regime
17. Anthony Shadid, 'Syrian elite to fight protests to "the end"', *New York Times*, 11 May 2011, available at: www.nytimes.com/2011/05/11/world/middleeast/11makhlouf.html?-pagewanted=all. Anthony, rest in peace, my friend.
18. ibid.
19. Anthony Shadid, 'Reviled tycoon, Assad's cousin, resigns in Syria', *New York Times*, 17 June 2011, available at: www.nytimes.com/2011/06/17/world/middleeast/17syria.html
20. ibid.
21. Anthony Shadid, 'Violent clashes as thousands protest in cities across Syria', *New York Times*, 18 June 2011, available at: www.nytimes.com/2011/06/18/world/middleeast/18syria.html
22. Katherine Zoepf and Anthony Shadid, 'Syrian leader's brother seen as enforcer of crackdown', *New York Times*, 7 June 2011, available at: www.nytimes.com/2011/06/08/world/middleeast/08syria.html?pagewanted=all
23. Quoted in Aron Lund, 'Divided they stand: an overview of Syria's political opposition factions', Olof Palme International Center, Foundation for European Progressive Studies, Uppsala, Sweden, May 2012, p. 15.
24. Quoted in 'Syria: "A kingdom of silence"', Al-Jazeera.
25. Nir Rosen, 'Assad's Alawites: An entrenched community', Al-Jazeera, 12 October 2011, http://english.aljazeera.net/indepth/features/2011/10/20111011154631737692.html
26. Peter Harling, 'Syria's phase of radicalisation', International Crisis Group Policy Briefing No. 33, 10 April 2012, p. 4.
27. ibid.
28. ibid., p. 5.

29. Aryn Baker, 'Deepening divide', *Time*, 13 June 2011, available at: http://www.time.com/time/magazine/article/0,9171,2075377,00.html
30. Syrian human rights groups claimed that the defections were real and expected, given that soldiers have, according to Wissam Tarif, head of the Syrian human rights group Insan, little more than 'bread, potatoes and ghee to eat' and 'earn only about $10 a month'. According to him: 'There's a campaign in the military telling them that we have Salafis and militias all over Syria. When they arrive to these areas, they realize what they are facing is civilians, and of course, they start talking to each other.' Syrian ambassador to the United States, Imad Moustapha, countered the reports of the defections, saying: 'The guys who are trying to market this story are trying to insist that the army is suppressing peaceful demonstrators. The fact is, the army is engaging in fierce battles with armed criminal terrorists who have committed atrocities in Jisr al-Shughur yesterday.' See Zoepf and Shadid, 'Syrian leader's brother seen as enforcer of crackdown'.
31. Many people at the time referred to safe zones as 'Benghazis', from the safe zone that the Libyan opposition had established as it faced off against Muammar al-Gadafi's government forces.
32. Anthony Shadid, 'Syria proclaims it now has upper hand over uprising', *New York Times*, 9 May 2011, available at: www.nytimes.com/2011/05/10/world/middleeast/10syria.html?pagewanted=all
33. ibid.
34. ibid.
35. The report can be accessed at www.hrw.org/en/reports/2011/06/01/we-ve-never-seen-such-horror
36. Lauren Williams, 'Syrian businessmen back opposition conference', *Guardian*, 30 May 2011, available at: www.guardian.co.uk/world/2011/may/30/syrian-businessmen-back-opposition-conference
37. See ibid.
38. 'Syria's opposition dismisses amnesty gesture', Al-Jazeera, 1 June 2011, available at: http://english.aljazeera.net/news/middleeast/2011/06/20116153830904339.html
39. Anthony Shadid, 'Coalition of factions from the streets fuels a new opposition in Syria', *New York Times*, 30 June 2011, available at: www.nytimes.com/2011/07/01/world/middleeast/01syria.html?pagewanted=all
40. This and subsequent quotes taken from the official translation of the speech, available at: www.al-bab.com/arab/docs/syria/bashar_assad_speech_110620.htm
41. For more details on the proposed party law, see Sami Moubayed, 'The road to Syrian democracy', *Huffington Post*, 23 June 2011, available at: www.huffingtonpost.com/sami-moubayed/the-road-to-syrian-democr_b_882100.html
42. 'Activists at Syrian "national dialogue" call for end to violence', CNN.com, 10 July 2011, available at: http://articles.cnn.com/2011-07-10/world/syria.unrest_1_syrian-people-syrian-activists-president-bashar?_s=PM;WORLD
43. ibid.
44. ibid.
45. Daila Haidar and Muhammad Atef Fares, 'Time to talk?', *Syria Today*, June 2011, available at: www.syria-today.com/index.php/politics/15210-time-to-talk?
46. Shadid, 'Coalition of factions from the streets fuels a new opposition in Syria'.
47. The life-altering effect of social media is a global phenomenon, not just restricted to the Middle East. The following is a quote from a report by the FBI: 'Social media has emerged to be the first instance of communication about a crisis, trumping traditional first responders that included police, firefighters, EMT [emergency medical technicians], and journalists.' AP Report, 'US targets social media to track trouble', *San Antonio Express-News*, 13 February 2012, p. A4.

48. My thanks to my research assistant, Krystal Rountree, a student of mine at Trinity University, who has been of inestimable help to me, a technologically-challenged professor, in understanding the technical aspects and role of social media networks.
49. 'Ziadeh: Syrian revolution is the revolution of YouTube', *Ya Libnan*, 21 July 2011.
50. Nicholas Blanford, 'On Facebook and Twitter, spreading revolution in Syria', *Christian Science Monitor*, 8 April 2011, available at: www.csmonitor.com/World/Middle-East/2011/0408/On-Facebook-and-Twitter-spreading-revolution-in-Syria
51. Sari Horwitz, 'Syria using American software to censor Internet, experts say', *Washington Post*, 22 October 2011, available at: www.washingtonpost.com/world/national-security/syria-using-american-software-to-censor-internet-experts-say/2011/10/22/gIQA5mPr7L_story.html
52. Ronald Deibert, *Access Controlled: The shaping of power, rights, and rule in cyberspace*, MIT Press, Cambridge, MA, 2010.
53. Ziad Haidar, 'Navigating the red lines', *Syria Today*, April 2009, available at: www.syria-today.com/index.php/april-2009/278-ziad-haidar/744-navigating-the-red-lines
54. Obaida Hamad, 'Blocking things out', *Syria Today*, February 2008, available at: www.syria-today.com/index.php/february-2008/425-focus/3805-blocking-things-out
55. Robert F. Worth, 'Web tastes freedom inside Syria, and it's bitter', *New York Times*, 29 September 2010, available at: www.nytimes.com/2010/09/30/world/middleeast/30syria.html
56. Sharmine Narwani, 'Veteran US diplomat questions Syria storyline', *Al-Akhbar*, 10 February 2012, available at: http://english.al-akhbar.com/print/4002
57. Quoted in Sharmine Narwani, 'Stratfor challenges narratives on Syria', *Huffington Post*, 19 December 2011, available at: www.huffingtonpost.com/sharmine-narwani/stratfor-challenges-narra_b_1158710.html
58. This was thrown into further relief in an essay by David Kenner: 'Middle East coverage full of lies', *Foreign Policy*, 27 April 2012. In it he detailed stories on Middle East events in some more notable Western media outlets that proved to be blatantly false or highly questionable, including some about Syria. Available at: http://blog.foreignpolicy.com/posts/2012/04/27/middle_east_coverage_is_full_of_lies
59. Gregg Keizer, 'Syrian hackers retaliate, deface Anonymous social network', *Computer World*, 8 August 2011. On further attempts by the government in this cyberwar, especially its efforts to plant viruses in opposition sites, see Ben Brumfield, 'Computer spyware is newest weapon in Syrian conflict', CNN.com, 17 February 2012, available at: www.cnn.com/2012/02/17/tech/web/computer-virus-syria/index.html?hpt=hp_t2
60. Jay Newton-Small, 'A war on two fronts', *Time*, 25 June 2012, p. 48.
61. Baker, 'Deepening divide'.

7 The International Response

1. Liz Sly, '"Doomsday scenario" if Syria fails', *Washington Post*, 1 May 2011, available (in several parts) at: www.washingtonpost.com/world/unrest-in-syria-threatens-regional-stability/2011/05/01AF3OQtUF_story.html
2. ibid.
3. ibid.
4. ibid.
5. ibid.
6. On this, see Sami Moubayed, 'The Turkish-Iranian struggle for Syria', *Mideast Views*, 10 March 2012, available at: http://mideastviews.com/print.php?art=567
7. Geneive Abdo, 'How Iran keeps Assad in power in Syria', *Foreign Affairs*, 25 August 2011, available at: www.foreignaffairs.com/print/68150?page=show
8. ibid.
9. ibid.

10. 'Q&A: Nir Rosen on Syria's armed opposition', Al-Jazeera, 13 February 2012, available at: www.aljazeera.com/indepth/features/2012/02/201221315020166516.html
11. Abdo, 'How Iran keeps Assad in power in Syria'.
12. Daniel Treisman, 'Why Russia protects Syria's Assad', CNN.com, 2 February 2012, available at: http://edition.cnn.com/2012/02/02/opinion/treisman-russia-syria/index.html
13. Dmitri Trenin, 'Why Russia supports Assad', *New York Times*, 9 February 2012, available at: www.nytimes.com/2012/02/10/opinion/why-russia-supports-assad.html?_r=2&partner=rss&emc=rss
14. Although Dmitri Trenin wrote that the importance of Tartous is exaggerated, since it is primarily a naval resupply facility rather than a full-fledged naval base. See ibid.
15. Holly Yan, 'Why China, Russia won't condemn Syrian regime', CNN.com, 5 February 2012, available at: http://edition.cnn.com/2012/02/05/world/meast/syria-china-russia-relations/index.html?hpt=htm
16. ibid.
17. For a good analysis of this by a top Russian academic and political advisor, see Georgiy Mirsky, 'The Soviet perception of the US threat', in David W. Lesch and Mark L. Haas (eds), *The Middle East and the United States: History, politics, and ideologies*, 5th edition, Westview Press, Boulder, CO, 2012, pp. 148–56.
18. Treisman, 'Why Russia protects Syria's Assad'.
19. ibid.
20. Trenin, 'Why Russia supports Assad'.
21. Khaled Yacoub Oweis, 'Syria toll rises, Russia opens way to UN resolution', Reuters, 2 August 2011, available at: http://in.reuters.com/article/2011/08/02/idINIndia-58575020110802
22. Quoted in Robert O. Freedman, 'Russia and the Arab Spring: A preliminary appraisal', in Mark L. Haas and David W. Lesch (eds), *The Arab Spring: Change and resistance in the Middle East*, Westview Press, Boulder, CO, forthcoming (November 2012).
23. ibid.
24. 'News agency: Russia opposes calls for Syrian president to resign', CNN.com, 19 August 2011, available at: http://articles.cnn.com/2011-08-19/world/syria.world.reaction_1_syrian-president-bashar-al-assad-president-assad-syrian-people?_s=PM;WORLD
25. Randa Slim, 'Where's Syria's business community?', *Foreign Policy*, 8 August 2011, available at: http://mideast.foreignpolicy.com/posts/2011/08/05/wheres_syrias_business_community
26. For more on the development of Turkish-Iranian relations, see Gallia Lindenstrauss and Yoel Guzansky, 'The rise and (future) fall of the Turkish-Iranian axis', Foreign Policy Research Institute, 27 April 2011, available at: www.fpri.org/enotes/201104.lindenstrauss_guzansky.turkey_iran.html. Regarding the Gaza flotilla incident in 2010, in which Turkey criticized Israeli actions that led to the deaths of Turks and others on board ships heading to aid the Palestinians in the Gaza Strip, one Palestinian editor of the daily newspaper *al-Quds al-Arabi*, while bemoaning the tepid response of many Arab countries, stated that the Turkish prime minister was 'more Arab than the Arabs'. See ibid.
27. Anthony Shadid, 'Syrian unrest stirs new fear of deeper sectarian divide', *New York Times*, 13 June 2011, available at: www.nytimes.com/2011/06/14/world/middleeast/14syria.html?pagewanted=all
28. Quoted in Susanne Gusten, 'Mandate for a new Turkish era; Erdogan boldly changes tack with broad outreach to a region in turmoil', *International Herald Tribune*, 16 June 2011.
29. Mark L. Haas, 'Turkey and the Arab Spring: Ideological promotion in a revolutionary era', in Haas and Lesch, *The Arab Spring*.

30. Meir Javedanfar, 'Iran and Turkey circle Syria', *The Diplomat*, 9 July 2011, available at: http://the-diplomat.com/2011/07/09/iran-and-turkey-circle-syria/
31. Khaled Yacoub Oweis, 'Assad: Syria won't stop fight against "terrorists"', Reuters, 10 August 2011, available at: http://in.reuters.com/article/2011/08/09/idINIndia-58697320110809
32. ibid.
33. 'Ahmet Davutoglu live blog', Al-Jazeera Blogs, available at: http://blogs.aljazeera.com/liveblog/ahmet-davutoglu?page=1
34. 'Middle East allies call for Syrian government to reform', CNN.com, 29 August 2011, available at: http://articles.cnn.com/2011-08-29/world/turkey.syria_1_local-coordination-committees-syrian-revolution-government-of-syrian-president?_s=PM;WORLD
35. Haas, 'Turkey and the Arab Spring'.
36. 'Obama, Erdogan agree to "increase pressure" on Syrian regime', Radio Free Europe/Radio Liberty, 21 September 2011, available at: www.rferl.org/articleprintview/24335058.html
37. Abdo, 'How Iran keeps Assad in power in Syria'. As Ali Nader, an Iranian analyst, stated: 'Iranian conservatives . . . worry that Turkey is presenting an alternate model to the Islamic Republic in the region . . . The Iranian government claimed that the Arab Spring has been inspired by the Iranian Revolution of 1979 . . . Turkey [is] basically offering itself as [an alternative] model for the Arab population in the region. This contradicts with Iranian interests.' Quoted in Haas, 'Turkey and the Arab Spring'.
38. There were many scholars who said that a Turkish-Iranian breach was inevitable because of the multitude of differences and contradicting interests between the two countries, although few saw that the cause of the breach would be Syria. On the other hand, many said the same thing about Syria and Iran when that alliance began to take shape in the 1980s, and it lasted for a generation.
39. Oweis, 'Assad says Syria won't stop fight against terrorists'.
40. Anthony Shadid, 'Qatar wields an outsize influence in Arab politics', *New York Times*, 14 November 2011, www.nytimes.com/2011/11/15/world/middleeast/qatar-presses-decisive-shift-in-arab-politics.html?pagewanted=all
41. ibid. A number of prominent Sunni Islamists call Qatar 'home' or have a residence there, such as the influential Sunni religious leader Shaykh Yusuf Qaradawi, a leading Libyan Islamist, Ali Sallabi and Hamas' Khalid Meshaal; there was also speculation that the Taliban may open an office in Doha.
42. 'Syria unrest: Government pledges political reforms', BBC News, 25 March 2011, available at: www.bbc.co.uk/news/world-middle-east-12853634
43. Nicole Gaouette and Gopal Ratnam, 'Clinton says US won't intervene in Syria, sees progress in Libya fight', Bloomberg News, 28 March 2011, available at: www.bloomberg.com/news/print/2011-03-27/u-s-won-t-intervene-in-syria-unrest-clinton-says-on-cbs.html
44. ibid.
45. Bill Spindle, Nour Malas and Farnaz Fassihi, 'Protests explode across Syria', *Wall Street Journal*, 23 April 2011, available at: http://online.wsj.com/article/SB10001424052748703521304576278491441761116.html
46. Mark Hosenball and Matt Spetalnick, 'US slaps new sanctions on Syria over crackdown', Reuters, 29 April 2011, available at: www.reuters.com/article/2011/04/29/us-syria-usa-sanctions-idUSTRE73S4PP20110429
47. Anthony Shadid, 'Syria proclaims it now has upper hand over uprising', *New York Times*, 9 May 2011, available at: www.nytimes.com/2011/05/10/world/middleeast/10syria.html
48. Liz Sly, 'Blooms of Arab Spring fading', *Washington Post*, 13 May 2011, p. A1.

49. Arshad Mohammed and Andrew Quinn, 'US slaps sanctions on Syrian president, top aides', Reuters, 18 May 2011, available at: www.reuters.com/article/2011/05/18/us-syria-usa-idUSTRE74H4XX20110518
50. 'Syria's opposition dismisses amnesty gesture', Al-Jazeera, 1 June 2011, available at: www.aljazeera.com/news/middleeast/2011/06/20116153830904339.html
51. Robert Fisk, 'Who cares in the Middle East what Obama says?', *Independent*, 30 May 2011, available at: http://independent.co.uk/opinion/commentators/fisk/who-cares-in-the-middle-east-what-obama-says-2290761.html
52. 'Activists at Syrian "national dialogue" call for end to violence', CNN.com, 10 July 2011, available at: http://articles.cnn.com/2011-07-10/world/syria.unrest_1_syrian-people-syrian-activists-president-bashar?_s=PM:WORLD
53. 'Syria's Assad "is not indispensable", Clinton says', Reuters, 11 July 2011, available at: www.reuters.com/article/2011/07/11/syria-usa-clinton-idUSWEN523220110711
54. Mark Landler and David E. Sanger, 'White House, in shift, turns against Syria leader', *New York Times*, 12 July 2011, available at: www.nytimes.com/2011/07/13/world/middleeast/13policy.html
55. 'Syria condemns US "provocation" amid riot row', Al-Jazeera, 12 July 2011, available at: www.aljazeera.com/video/middleeast/2011/07/2011712134513429175.html
56. The administration was still hedging its bets somewhat, and it may have been influenced by the Turks. Shortly after these harsh comments against Assad, while meeting Turkish officials a week later, Clinton expressed the hope that the Syrian opposition 'can provide a pathway, hopefully in peaceful cooperation with the government to a better future'. Foreign ministers from the EU then sent Assad 'another implicit lifeline' by urging him to implement promised reforms. 'Syria's struggle', *New York Times*, 18 July 2011, available at: www.nytimes.com/2011/07/19/opinion/19tue2.html
57. Fareed Zakaria, 'The strategist', *Time*, 30 January 2012, available at: www.time.com/time/magazine/article/0,9171,2104842,00.html
58. ibid.
59. Blake Hounshell, 'Why Obama must be cautious on Syria', CNN.com, 3 August 2011, available at: http://articles.cnn.com/2011-08-03/opinion/hounshell.syria.obama_1_syrian-opposition-people-al-assad?_s=PM;OPINION
60. Laura Rozen, 'International outcry grows over Syria violence, but response so far constrained', Yahoo! News, 1 August 2011, available at: http://news.yahoo.com/blogs/envoy/international-outcry-grows-over-syria-violence-response-far-161544901.html
61. Laura Rozen, 'Clinton: Syria government responsible for 2,000 deaths', Yahoo! News, 4 August 2011, available at: http://news.yahoo.com/blogs/envoy/syria-endgame-u-mulls-world-opinion-hardens-against-205303810.html
62. 'US, Europe call for Syrian leader al-Assad to step down', CNN.com, 18 August 2011, available at: http://articles.cnn.com/2011-08-18/politics/us.syria_1_president-bashar-al-assad-president-assad-syrian-people?_s-PM;POLITICS
63. ibid.
64. On 30 August, the United States added Syrian Foreign Minister Walid al-Mouallem and Bouthaina Shaaban to the sanctions list. Both Mouallem and Shaaban had been known for years to be some of the strongest advocates for improving Syrian relations with the United States, for entering into peace negotiations with Israel, and for political reform at home.
65. 'Syria condemns Obama's call for Assad to step down', Yahoo! News, 20 August 2011, http://news.yahoo.com/syria-condemns-obamas-call-assad-step-down-081442392.html
66. 'New al Qaeda leader slams Syrian president, praises protestors', CNN.com, 28 July 2011, available at: http://articles.cnn.com/2011-07-28/world/al.qaeda.leader.message_1_al-qaeda-leader-al-zawahiri-leader-osama-bin?_s=PM:WORLD

8 All In

1. Rami G. Khouri, 'Assad, going down', *New York Times*, 31 August 2011, available at: www.nytimes.com/2011/09/01/opinion/assad-going-down.html. It is important to note – and this is something I know from personal experience – that the titles of opinion pieces and essays are rarely chosen by the authors themselves. More often an editor on the publication in question chooses the title/headline, which is usually something much more sexy and attractive to prospective readers than that offered by the author. Indeed, sometimes the article itself adopts a quite different line from that which is indicated in the title/headline. But the mere fact that editors are choosing these titles reflects the popular discourse at the time and therefore the point I am making.
2. Blake Hounshell and Josh Rogin, 'The last stand of Bashar al-Assad?', *Foreign Policy*, 1 August 2011, available at: www.foreignpolicy.com/articles/2011/08/01/the_last_stand_of_bashar_al_assad
3. David Ignatius, 'Plotting a post-Assad road map for Syria', *Washington Post*, 20 July 2011, available at: www.washingtonpost.com/opinions/plotting-a-post-assad-road-map-for-syria/2011/07/20/gIQANBQcQI_story.html
4. Barbara Slavin, 'Beginning of the end for Assad?', Inter Press Service, 16 November 2011, available at: http://ipsnews.net/print.asp?idnews=105852
5. Roula Khalaf and Abigail Fielding-Smith, 'Tyrant now a pariah', *Financial Times*, 11 August 2011, available at: www.ft.com/cms/s/0/19622120-c334-11e0-9109-00144feabdc0.html#axzz1wXYnzfbN
6. Elizabeth Kennedy, 'Syria hits point of no return amid broad isolation', Yahoo! News, 21 August 2011, available at: http://news.yahoo.com/syria-hits-point-no-return-amid-broad-isolation-093933874.html
7. 'The squeeze on Assad', *The Economist*, 30 June 2011, available at: www.economist.com/node/18895586
8. Tony Badran, 'How Assad stayed in power – and how he'll try to keep it', *Foreign Affairs*, 1 December 2011, available at: www.foreignaffairs.com/articles/136707/tony-badran/how-assad-stayed-in-power%E2%80%94and-how-hell-try-to-keep-it
9. 'Syria will not bow down', CNN.com, 20 November 2011, available at: www.cnn.com/2011/11/20/world/meast/syria-violence/index.html?hpt=hp_t3
10. Bruce Bueno de Mesquita and Alastair Smith, 'Assessing Assad', *Foreign Policy*, 20 December 2011, available at: www.foreignpolicy.com/articles/2011/12/20/is_assad_crazy_or_just_ruthless?page=full
11. Robert Fisk, 'Syria is used to the slings and arrows of friends and enemies', *Independent*, 1 February 2012, available at: www.independent.co.uk/opinion/commentators/fisk/robert-fisk-syria-is-used-to-the-slings-and-arrows-of-friends-and-enemies-6297648.html
12. On the Friday following the August establishment of the SNC, the protests were dubbed 'The Syrian National Council Represents Me', although it is difficult to assess how widespread this actually was or whether it was a media mechanism by opposition groups to drum up support for the SNC.
13. Syrian National Council, 'Announcement of the Founding Statement of the United Opposition National Council in Istanbul', 3 October 2011, available at: www.syrian-council.org/
14. Karen DeYoung, 'Clinton meets with Syria opposition', *Washington Post*, 6 December 2011, available at: www.washingtonpost.com/world/middle_east/clinton-meets-with-syria-opposition/2011/12/06/gIQApzQ9ZO_story.html
15. Nada Bakri, 'Syria demands that nations reject opposition council and protect its embassies', *New York Times*, 9 October 2011, available at: www.nytimes.com/2011/10/10/world/middleeast/syria-warns-countries-not-to-recognize-opposition.html

16. Bassem Mroue, 'Syrian lawmaker criticizes opposition council', Yahoo! News, 3 October 2011, available at: http://news.yahoo.com/syrian-lawmaker-criticizes-opposition-council-100447057.html
17. Muhammad Atef Fares, 'Anatomy of an opposition', *Syria Today*, 28 December 2011, available at: http://syria-today.com/index.php/politics/17464-anatomy-of-an-opposition
18. ibid.
19. Peter Harling, 'Beyond the fall of the Syrian regime', International Crisis Group Report, 27 February 2012, available at: www.crisisgroup.org/en/regions/middle-east-north-africa/egypt-syria-lebanon/syria/op-eds/harling-beyond-the-fall-of-the-syrian-regime.aspx
20. Muhammad Atef Fares, 'Anatomy of an opposition', *Syria Today*, December 2011, available at: http://syria-today.com/index.php/december-2011/916-politics/17464-anatomy-of-an-opposition
21. ibid.
22. Nir Rosen, 'Syria: The revolution will be weaponised', Al-Jazeera, 23 September 2011, available at: www.aljazeera.com/indepth/features/2011/09/2011923115735281764.html
23. ibid.
24. Nir Rosen, 'Q&A: Nir Rosen on Syria's armed opposition', Al-Jazeera, 13 February 2012, available at: http://aljazeera.com/indepth/features/2012/02/201221315020166516.html
25. ibid.
26. Hugh Macleod, 'Meet the Free Syrian Army', *Global Post*, 3 November 2011, available at: http://mobile.globalpost.com/dispatch/news/regions/middle-east/111102/syria-free-syrian-army-bashar-al-assad
27. Note the different spelling; he is no relation to Bashar al-Assad.
28. ibid.
29. Peter Keller, 'Ghosts of Syria: diehard militias who kill in the name of Assad', *Guardian*, 31 May 2012, available at: http://guardian.co.uk/world/2012/may/31/ghosts-syria-regime-shabiha-militias/print
30. ibid.
31. Dan Bilefshy, 'Factional splits hinder drive to topple Syrian leader', *New York Times*, 8 December 2011, available at: www.nytimes.com/2011/12/09/world/middleeast/factional-splits-hinder-drive-to-topple-syrias-assad.html?pagewanted=all
32. Fares, 'Anatomy of an opposition'.
33. Nicholas A. Heras, 'The Free Syrian Army: Syria's future army of liberation?', siyese.com, 13 December 2011, available at: www.en.siyese.com/opinion/the-free-syrian-army-syrias-future-army-of-liberation-by-nicholas-a-heras/
34. 'Report: Syrian abuses could be "crimes against humanity"', CNN.com, 1 June 2011, available at: http://cnn.com/2011/WORLD/meast/06/01/syria.unrest/index.html?hpt=hp_bn2
35. 'UN Security Council issues statement condemning violence in Syria', CNN.com, 3 August 2011, available at: http://cnn.com/2011/WORLD/meast/08/03/syria.unrest/index.html?hpt=hp_bn2
36. 'Al-Assad rejects calls for ouster as UN team visits Syria', CNN.com, 21 August 2011, available at: http://cnn.com/2011/WORLD/meast/08/21/syria.unrest/index.html?hpt=hp_t2
37. ibid.
38. International Atomic Energy Agency (IAEA) inspectors traveled to Syria in the wake of Israel's September 2007 attack on a suspected nuclear reactor site, in order to investigate whether or not Syria was indeed attempting to build one. Some of Assad's closest advisors, particularly Vice President Farouk al-Sharaa, urged him not to allow the inspectors into the country, on the grounds that it was an infringement of Syria's

sovereignty. Other advisors – chief among them Foreign Minister Walid al-Mouallem – urged the president to cooperate with the IAEA and allow the inspectors in. The result was a compromise: the IAEA inspectors would be allowed in, but their movements in Syria would be restricted. Since, in the end, there was not full cooperation, Syria did not receive the credit it wanted for allowing the team to enter the country in the first place; if anything, the restrictions gave the impression that the government was hiding something. On the other hand, once inside the country, the inspectors found enough suggestion of foul play to recommend further investigations, if not actually to condemn the government outright. Later on in the uprising something similar would happen with Arab League observers sent to Syria (see below).

39. 'Arab League to US: Stop interfering in Syria', Associated Press report in AzCentral.com, 13 July 2011, available at: www.azcentral.com/news/articles/2011/07/13/20110713syria-arab-league-backing-html
40. 'Syria's struggle', *New York Times*, 18 July 2011, available at: www.nytimes.com/2011/07/19/opinion/19tue2.html
41. For a good essay on this, see Sean Mann, 'How the Arab League turned against Syria', *Open Democracy*, 9 February 2012, available at: www.opendemocracy.net/print/64090
42. Reinforcing this monarchical alliance of sorts, the Gulf Cooperation Council (GCC) states suggested that Jordan and Morocco might become members of the GCC. This made absolutely no sense geographically, but it would further characterize the organization as one made up of pro-Western Sunni Arab monarchies (ibid.).
43. ibid.
44. For a good analysis of this AL initiative, see Sami Moubayed, 'An offer Syrian shouldn't have refused', *Mideast Views*, 22 September 2011, available at: www.mideastviews.com/articleview.php?art=547
45. ibid.
46. 'Arab League demands Syria end violence against citizens', CNN.com, 1 November 2011, available at: http://edition.cnn.com/2011/10/31/world/meast/syria-unrest/index.html?eref=rss_topstories&utm_source=feedburner&utm_medium=feed&utm_campaign=Feed%3A+rss%2Fcnn_topstories+%28RSS%3A+Top+Stories%29
47. 'Regime backers express anger at other nations after Arab League suspends Syria', CNN.com, 12 November 2011, available at: www.cnn.com/2011/11/12/world/meast/syria-unrest/index.html?hpt=hp_t1
48. 'Arab League votes to impose sanctions against Syria', CNN.com, 27 November 2011, available at: www.cnn.com/2011/11/27/world/meast/syria-unrest/index.html?hpt=hp_t2
49. 'Syria signs Arab League plan, minister says', CNN.com, 19 December 2011, available at: www.cnn.com/2011/12/19/world/meast/syria-unrest/index.html?hpt=hp_t3
50. ibid.
51. Sami Moubayed, 'Observers court controversy in Syria', gulfnews.com, 3 January 2012, available at: http://gulfnews.com/opinions/columnists/observers-court-controversy-in-syria-1.960231
52. Richard Gowan, 'Don't write off the Arab League in Syria . . . yet', *Foreign Policy*, 6 January 2012, available at: http://mideast.foreignpolicy.com/posts/2012/01/06/dont_write_off_the_arab_league_in_syriayet
53. ibid.
54. Mohamed Fadel Fahmy, 'Arab League calls for unity government in Syria', CNN.com, 22 January 2012, available at: www.cnn.com/2012/01/22/world/meast/syria-unrest/index.html?hpt=hp_t1
55. Rania Abouzeid, 'The Arab League to Syria's president: it's time for you to go', *Time*, 22 January 2012, available at: www.time.com/time/world/article/0,8599,2105066,00.html
56. ibid.

57. 'Syria rejects new Arab League plan to end crisis', CBC News, 23 January 2012, available at: www.cbc.ca/news/world/story/2012/01/23/syria.html
58. 'Arab League's Syria mission extended by a month', CNN.com, 25 January 2012, available at: www.cnn.com/2012/01/24/world/meast/syria-unrest/index.html?hpt=hp_t1
59. Mick Krever, 'Draft resolution calls for al-Assad to step down', CNN.com, 27 January 2012, available at: www.cnn.com/2012/01/27/world/meast/un-syria/index.html?hpt=hp_t1
60. ibid.
61. 'UN Security Council talks Syria peace as deaths mount', CNN.com, 1 February 2012, available at: www.cnn.com/2012/02/01/world/meast/syria-unrest/index.html?hpt=hp_t3
62. Roshanak Taghavi, 'Regional pressure against Iran raises specter of civil war in Syria', *Urban Times*, 16 February 2012, available at: www.theurbn.com/2012/02/civil-war-syria/
63. Julian Borger, 'Draft resolution to UN calls for Syria's Assad to step down', *Guardian*, 31 January 2012, available at: www.guardian.co.uk/world/2012/jan/31/un-resolution-syria-assad-step-down
64. ibid.
65. 'Syria: Russia opposes UN resolution against Assad', *Democracy Now!*, 31 January 2012, available at: www.democracynow.org/2012/1/31/headlines
66. Jeffrey Laurenti, 'Navigating Arabs' Syria roadmap through the UN', *Huffington Post*, 1 February 2012, available at: www.huffingtonpost.com/jeffrey-laurenti/syria-un-security-council_b_1247461.html
67. 'Russia, China veto UN action on Syria; opposition group calls for strike', CNN.com, 4 February 2012, available at: http://articles.cnn.com/2012-02-04/middleeast/world_meast_syria-unrest_1_syrian-people-syrian-national-council-syrian-observatory/3?_s=PM:MIDDLEEAST
68. 'Rockets, mortars rain down on Syrian city, opposition says', CNN.com, 6 February 2012, available at: http://edition.cnn.com/2012/02/05/world/meast/syria-unrest/index.html?iref=allsearch
69. 'Russia, China veto UN action on Syria; opposition group calls for strike', CNN.com.
70. CNN television report by Ivan Watson, 20 February 2012.
71. 'UN Security Council fails to pass resolution on Syria', CNN.com.
72. For example, see a *New York Times* editorial entitled 'In Syria, we need to bargain with the devil', by Nicholas Roe in the 6 February 2012 issue. In it, while noting its slim chances of being implemented, Roe calls for a grand bargain of sorts with Assad that would not remove him from power immediately. See also Julien Barnes-Dacey, 'Syrian rebels will have to deal with Assad', *Financial Times*, 15 March 2012, available at: www.ft.com/intl/cms/s/0/92c7187e-6d00-11e1-a7c7-00144feab49a.html#axzz1wXYnzfbN
73. Shadi Hamid and Marc Lynch, 'Who will save Syria?' *Time*, 179: 10 (12 March 2012), pp. 34–7.
74. 'Arab League proposes peacekeeping force, support for Syrian rebels', CNN.com, 12 February 2012, available at: www.cnn.com/2012/02/12/world/meast/syria-unrest/index.html?hpt=hp_t1
75. 'Journalists' bodies returned', *New York Times* report in *San Antonio Express-News*, 4 March 2012, p. A13.
76. 'Syria promises referendum results as EU imposes new sanctions', CNN.com, 27 February 2012 (original report no longer available online).
77. Lauren Williams, 'Syrian civil resistance activists try to steer revolution off its violent path', *Daily Star* (Lebanon), 15 March 2012, www.dailystar.com.lb/ArticlePrint.aspx?id=166579
78. 'Homs under fire as Syria awaits referendum result; rift develops in opposition group', Al-Arabiya, 27 February 2012, available at: http://english.alarabiya.net/articles/2012/02/27/197219.html

79. ibid. The Syrian Patriotic Group has also been translated as the Patriotic Action Front. Regardless, by May 2012 this group seemed to have faded, due to internal disputes.
80. Tim Lister, 'The elusive tipping point in Syria', CNN.com, 2 March 2012, available at: http://security.blogs.cnn.com/2012/03/02/the-elusive-tipping-point-in-syria/?hpt=hp_c1
81. ibid.
82. ibid.
83. 'Syria crisis: Opposition sets up military bureau', BBC News, 1 March 2012, available at: www.bbc.co.uk/news/world-middle-east-17217284
84. Williams, 'Syrian civil resistance activists try to steer revolution off its violent path'.
85. ibid.
86. ibid.
87. Quoted in Aron Lund, 'Divided they stand: an overview of Syria's political opposition factions', Olof Palme International Center, Foundation for European Progressive Studies, May 2012, Uppsala, Sweden, p. 2.
88. ibid.
89. 'Assad's wife to Jordanian queen: Our situation is excellent', Ynetnews.com, 28 February 2012, available at: www.ynetnews.com/articles/0,7340,L-4195876,00.html. Hamas Prime Minister Ismail Haniyeh told congregants at Egypt's famed Al-Azhar mosque that 'We commend the brave Syrian people that are moving toward democracy and reform', the first time a senior Hamas figure had publicly displayed support for the Syrian protestors. 'Crackdown continues; nations meet', Associated Press report in *San Antonio Express-News*, 25 February 2012, p. A11.
90. 'Homs under fire as Syria awaits referendum result; rift develops in opposition group', Al-Arabiya.
91. 'US officials mull possibility of arming Syrian rebels', CNN.com, 22 February 2012, available at http://security.blogs.cnn.com/2012/02/22/u-s-officials-mull-possibility-of-arming-syrian-rebels/?hpt=hp_bn2
92. ibid.
93. ibid.
94. Lister, 'The elusive tipping point in Syria'.
95. ibid.
96. 'Arab League proposes peacekeeping force, support for Syrian rebels', CNN.com.
97. At the time of writing, there have been two more meetings of the Friends of Syria: one in March and one in April.
98. Barbara Starr and Jamie Crawford, 'US sees no fracturing of Assad regime', CNN.com, 1 March 2012, available at: http://security.blogs.cnn.com/2012/03/01/u-s-sees-no-fracturing-of-assad-regime/?hpt=hp_t1
99. Quoted in Marc Lynch, 'Pressure not war: a pragmatic and principled policy towards Syria', Center for a New American Century, Policy Brief, February 2012, p. 2.
100. 'Homs under fire as Syria awaits referendum result; rift develops in opposition group', Al-Arabiya.
101. Associated Press, 'Crackdown continues; nations meet'. Of course, Syrian opponents in the country held up large banners saying, 'Iranian and Russian bullets are tearing apart our bodies' (ibid.).
102. 'Syria constitution vote called "window dressing"', CNN.com, 15 February 2012, available at: www.cnn.com/2012/02/15/world/meast/syria-unrest/index.html?hpt=hp_t1
103. Patrick J. McDonnell, 'Syria says constitution approved; scores of deaths are reported', *Los Angeles Times*, 28 February 2012.
104. Sami Moubayed, 'Syria's new constitution: too little, too late', *Mideast Views*, 14 February 2012, available at: www.mideastviews.com/print.php?art=560

105. Neil MacFarquhar, 'Syrians vote in election dismissed by foes as a farce', *New York Times*, 7 May 2012, available at: www.nytimes.com/2012/05/08/world/middleeast/syrians-vote-in-parliamentary-elections.html
106. Associated Press, 'Syria tallies ballots from parliamentary election shunned by opposition, dismissed by US', 8 May 2012, available at: www.mail.com/news/world/1265264-syria-tallies-ballots-parliament-elections.html
107. 'UN observers stayed with Syrian rebels after attack', BBC News, 16 May 2012, available at: www.bbc.co.uk/news/world-middle-east-18084824
108. Starr and Crawford, 'US sees no fracturing of Assad regime'.
109. ibid.
110. Quoted in Lund, 'Divided they stand', p. 34.
111. Ian Black and Julian Borger, 'Search for a Syria strategy focuses on stiffening fragmented opposition', *Guardian*, 7 February 2012, available at: www.guardian.co.uk/world/2012/feb/07/syria-strategy-opposition-arab-west
112. Patrick Seale, 'Assad family values', *Foreign Affairs*, 20 March 2012, available at: www.foreignaffairs.com/print/134595

9 Whither Syria?

1. The atrocities perpetrated by Syrian government forces have been repeatedly reported. But as the uprising intensified, there has been an increasing number of reports of human rights violations and criminal activity by opposition forces. For the latter, see Anne Barnard, 'Syrian insurgents accused of rights abuses', *New York Times*, 20 March 2012, available at: www.nytimes.com/2012/03/21/world/middleeast/syrian-insurgents-accused-of-rights-abuses.html?_r=1&pagewanted=all and Gert van Langendonck and Sarah Lynch, 'Syrian activists to rebels: Give us our revolution back', *Christian Science Monitor*, 16 April 2012, available at: www.csmonitor.com/World/Middle-East/2012/0416/Syrian-activists-to-rebels-Give-us-our-revolution-back
2. See an interview with reporter Nir Rosen for an on-the-ground perspective of daily life in Syria. Nir Rosen, 'Q&A: Nir Rosen on daily life in Syria', Al-Jazeera, 20 February 2012, available at: www.aljazeera.com/indepth/features/2012/02/2012220164924305314.html
3. Bruce Bueno de Mesquita and Alastair Smith, 'Assessing Assad', *Foreign Policy*, 20 December 2011, available at: www.foreignpolicy.com/articles/2011/12/20/is_assad_crazy_or_just_ruthless?page=full
4. ibid.
5. Arabic is his first language and, as is the case with many educated Syrians (a kind of cultural leftover from the days of the French mandate period), his second language is French.
6. And on two separate occasions, in 2005 and 2007, in chapters on Syria in the annual Freedom House volume that rates countries worldwide on such indices as corruption, transparency, political freedom, etc., I gave Syria some of the lowest scores in the volume. People used to ask me how I could give Syria such low ratings and still maintain access to its president (who, they naturally thought, would cut me off because of my criticisms). I told these people – and it is the truth – that I actually sent copies of the volumes to President Assad and to the Syrian ambassador to the United States, Imad Moustapha.
7. The assertion that Bashar al-Assad (and his wife Asma) were 'out to lunch' or in their own little world, detached from the violence of the uprising, was said to have been supported by the efforts of opposition elements, as well as the infamous computer hacking group known as 'Anonymous', which hacked into the emails of both Bashar and Asma al-Assad, as well as some other leading Syrian officials. Critics pointed out that, while Syrians were dying, Asma al-Assad was spending thousands of dollars buying luxury items online, while Bashar was making purchases of music and apps from

Apple's iTunes. Others, however, countered that the emails, some of them intimate exchanges of affection between the two, only served to humanize them at a time when they had been demonized. Such was the outcry over the shopping that the EU soon thereafter slapped sanctions specifically on Asma al-Assad (as well as Bashar's mother).

8. My thanks to Roger Owen for suggesting this verbiage to me at a conference at UCLA in May 2012. He and Sami Zubaida are currently examining the political sociology of how leaders imagine their people in ways that are often distorted.
9. Massoud A. Derhally, Flavia Jackson and Caroline Alexander, 'Assad detachment from Syria killings reveals life in cocoon', Bloomberg News, 14 December 2011, available at: www.bloomberg.com/news/2011-12-13/assad-s-detachment-reveals-life-in-cocoon.html
10. Ironically, the Islamist threat and subsequent massacre at Hama in 1982 occurred twelve years into Hafiz al-Assad's presidency, about the same amount of time that elapsed before the current uprising threatened his son's hold on power.
11. Anne Applebaum, 'The long, lame afterlife of Mikhail Gorbachev', *Foreign Policy*, July/August 2011, available at: www.foreignpolicy.com/articles/2011/06/20/the_long_lame_afterlife_of_mikhail_gorbachev?page=full
12. Barbara Starr, 'Sources: Syria's president holding firm', CNN.com, 9 March 2012, available at: http://security.blogs.cnn.com/2012/03/09/u-s-intel-sources-syrias-president-holding-firm/?hpt=hp_t1
13. ibid.
14. David S. Cloud, 'Obama rules out unilateral US military action on Syria', *Los Angeles Times*, 7 March 2012, available at: http://articles.latimes.com/2012/mar/07/world/la-fg-syria-obama-20120307. Former US Secretary of State Henry Kissinger wrote an interesting editorial arguing against outside military intervention in Syria on the grounds of upsetting the regional and international balance of power, especially if it is based on humanitarian rather than strategic motives. He stated that, 'In reacting to one human tragedy, we must be careful not to facilitate another'. 'Syrian intervention risks upsetting global order', *Washington Post,* 1 June 2012, available at: www.washingtonpost.com/opinions/syrian-intervention-risks-upsetting-global-order/2012/06/01/gQA9fGr7U_print.html
15. ibid.
16. Well into 2012 there have been increasing reports of deadly clashes between anti-Assad and pro-Assad groups in Lebanon. See, for instance, a *New York Times* report of gun battles between these two sets of groups in Beirut itself. On this occasion, both sides were Sunni Muslim: the pro-Assad faction was the Arab Movement Party, from a largely Sunni Muslim neighborhood in south Beirut (where pro-Assad Hizbullah is also prevalent), although most Sunnis in Lebanon are arrayed against Assad. There have also been reports of fighting along these lines in Tripoli, Lebanon's second-largest city, as well as reports of minority Alawites in Lebanon (the same sect as Assad) fighting against Syrian Sunni Muslims living in Lebanon (or having relocated there since the uprising). Reported as 'Syrian conflict spills into Lebanon', *San Antonio Express-News*, 21 May 2012, available at: www.mysanantonio.com/news/article/Syrian-Conflict-Spills-Into-Lebanon-3575121.php
17. Nir Rosen, 'Q&A: Nir Rosen on Syria's protest movement', Al-Jazeera, 16 February 2012, available at: www.aljazeera.com/indepth/features/2012/02/20122157654659323.html. See also Nicholas A. Heras and Christos Kyrou, 'Lessons from incipient civic movements in the broader Middle East', International Affairs Forum, 29 February 2012, available at: www.ia-forum.org/Files/VYKNGW.pdf
18. Moni Basu, 'Libyans face tough challenges in building a new nation', CNN.com, 26 January 2012, available at: www.cnn.com/2012/01/26/world/africa/libya-challenges/index.html?hpt=hp_bn2

19. See Neil MacFarquhar and Hwaida Saad, 'Dozens of children die in brutal attack on Syrian town', *New York Times*, 26 May 2012, available at: www.nytimes.com/2012/05/27/world/middleeast/syrian-activists-claim-death-toll-in-village-soars.html?ref=world. The Syrian government blamed 'terrorists' for the killings, although amateur video footage and reports, as well as the reports of remaining UN observer forces, tend to suggest that the massacre was committed by pro-government forces. Indeed, if this was carried out primarily by the *shabbiha*, it provides further evidence of the excesses of militias that the government may no longer be able to control. In response to the international outcry over Houla, on 3 June Assad gave his first public address since January. In it he denied government responsibility, blamed armed gangs and terrorists for the killings and promised to launch an investigation into the incident: 'Truthfully, even monsters do not do what we saw, especially in the Houla massacre. The criminal or criminals who committed this crime and others are not criminals for an hour or criminals for a day, they are constant criminals and are surely planning other crimes. At this time we are facing a war from abroad, dealing with it is different from dealing with people from the inside.' See 'Syrian president condemns Houla massacre, rejects accusations', CNN.com, 3 June 2012, available at: http://cnn.com/2012/06/03/world/meast/syria-unrest/index.html?hpt=hp_t2. In addition, an international incident involving Syria could also alter the equation against the Syrian regime. For instance, on 22 June 2012 a Turkish air force jet was shot down by Syrian ground artillery fire after the jet entered Syrian airspace just off the Syrian coast along the border with Turkey. Turkish officials admitted that the plane probably crossed into Syrian airspace, and both Syrian and Turkish rescue teams worked together to try to locate the downed pilots. It does not appear that this incident will lead directly to any Syrian-Turkish conflict, but an already tense relationship was injected with another dose of tension, as both countries took measures to beef up their border defense against the other. This is exactly the type of thing that could easily spiral out of control, galvanizing a more robust international reaction and placing more pressure on Russia to flip on Assad, something the Syrian regime no doubt wants to take care to avoid if at all possible.
20. 'Putin looking ahead to 2018', a *New York Times* report carried in *San Antonio Express-News*, 3 March 2012, p. A13.
21. Sami Moubayed, 'Will there be a Kremlin U-turn on Syria?', *Mideast Views*, 6 March 2012, available at: www.mideastviews.com/articleview.php?art=565
22. ibid.
23. ibid.
24. ibid.
25. Barbara Slavin, 'Pressure mounts on Russia to switch horses in Syria', *Al-Monitor*, 5 June 2012, available at: www.al-monitor.com/pulse/originals/2012/al-monitor/pressure-mounts-on-russia-to-swi.html. Speaking in Sweden on 3 June, Secretary of State Clinton commented: 'Assad's departure does not have to be a precondition, but it should be an outcome so that the people of Syria have a chance to express themselves. In my conversations with [Russian] Foreign Minister Lavrov he himself has referred to the Yemen example. And it took a lot of time and effort with a number of countries who were involved at the table, working to achieve a political transition. And we would like to see the same occur in Syria' (ibid.).
26. Henry Kissinger, 'Syrian intervention risks upsetting global order', *Washington Post*, 1 June 2012, available at: www.washingtonpost.com/opinions/syrian-intervention-risks-upsetting-global-order/2012/06/01/gJQA9fGr7U_story.html
27. For the best analysis of the United States and the 1979 Iranian revolution, see Gary Sick, *All Fall Down: America's tragic encounter with Iran*, iUniverse, New York, 2001.
28. Slavin, 'Pressure mounts on Russia to switch horses in Syria'.
29. Robert O. Freedman, 'Russia and the Arab Spring: A preliminary appraisal', in Mark L. Haas and David W. Lesch (eds), *The Arab Spring: Change and resistance in the Middle East*, Westview Press, Boulder, CO, forthcoming (November 2012).

30. ibid.
31. Helene Cooper and Mark Landler, 'US hopes Assad can be eased out with Russia's aid', *New York Times*, 26 May 2012, available at: www.nytimes.com/2012/05/27/world/middleeast/us-seeks-russias-help-in-removing-assad-in-syria.html?pagewanted=all. This article points out that one of the main problems of this model is that Putin, in his super-nationalist mode, might reject the Yemeni option simply because the United States supports it. The key, as pointed out in this book and by a number of commentators and officials, is to somehow allow Moscow (if it is willing) to take ownership of this option to resolve the crisis. Putin and Obama reportedly had a tense meeting in Mexico on the topic of Syria at the G20 summit on 18 June 2012, which appeared to confirm that the Russian president was going to maintain a hard line in terms of continuing to support Assad. Commenting on Russian sentiments, Fred Weir writes that 'the West, they claim, is out of legal bounds and pursuing its own geopolitical interests thinly disguised as a humanitarian "responsibility to protect" in a manner that is reckless, hypocritical and – perhaps the unkindest cut – incompetent'. Russian scholar Yevgeny Satanovsky, in a clear reference to US policies in Afghanistan and Iraq, states: 'The West talks in terms of noble goals, but their actions tend to wreck any stability, threaten the lives of millions, and leave people worse off than before ... the Russian aim is to try to minimize negative outcomes'. Fred Weir, 'Russia's rational and moral stance on Syria', CNN.com, 21 June 2012, available at: http://globalpublicsquare.blogs.cnn.com/2012/06/21/russias-rational-and-moral-stance-on-syria/?hpt=hp_bn2
32. The highest-level minister to date to reportedly defect was the deputy oil minister in early March. While this should not be dismissed, he is not a senior member of the military, security or the government – and certainly not the inner circle. On 21 June 2012, a Syrian air force colonel defected by flying himself (and possibly one other) in his MIG jet to Jordan. This is one of the higher-profile military defections, as it included the MIG as well as the fact that the air force, from which Hafiz al-Assad emerged to become president, has always been considered fiercely loyal to the regime. In addition, it has been reported that into June 2012 the United States, Syrian opposition groups and their allies have stepped up their efforts to encourage defections in the Syrian military, even offering monetary compensation. See Ruth Sherlock, Suha Maayeh and Peter Foster, 'Leading Syrians prepare to defect', *Daily Telegraph*, 21 June 2012, available at: http://www.telegraph.co.uk/news/worldnews/middleeast/syria/9347971/Leading-Syrians-prepare-to-defect.html
33. Jonathan Steele, 'Most Syrians back President Assad, but you'd never know from western media', *Guardian*, 17 January 2012, available at: www.guardian.co.uk/commentisfree/2012/jan/17/syrians-support-assad-western-propaganda
34. Charlotte McDonald, 'Do 55% of Syrians really want President Assad to stay?', BBC News, 24 February 2012, available at: www.bbc.co.uk/news/magazine-17155349
35. 'Syria: Bashar al Assad vows to crush terrorism in new campaign of fear', *Daily Telegraph*, 6 March 2012, available at: www.telegraph.co.uk/news/worldnews/middleeast/syria/9125504/Syria-Bashar-al-Assad-vows-to-crush-terrorism-in-new-campaign-of-fear.html
36. The Annan plan had six points, calling for: 1) an inclusive Syrian-led political process to address grievances; 2) a commitment to halt the fighting by government forces and opposition groups supervised by a UN mechanism, probably UN observers; 3) timely humanitarian aid; 4) speeding up the release of those people who had been 'arbitrarily detained', including those who had engaged in 'peaceful political activities'; 5) ensuring 'freedom of movement' for journalists; and 6) respecting peaceful demonstrations and freedom of association.
37. Since presidential statements are non-binding, Russia's support for it was more of a publicity stunt by Moscow in its attempt to shore up relations with the Sunni Arab states. The relationships had been frayed over Russia's continuing support for Assad.

38. 'Attacks pick up in Syrian cities after UN monitors leave, opposition says', CNN.com, 24 April 2012, available at: www.cnn.com/2012/04/24/world/meast/syria-unrest/index.html?hpt=hp_t3
39. Jim Muir, 'Syria crisis: Can UN mission succeed?', BBC News, 24 April 2012, available at: www.bbc.co.uk/news/world-middle-east-17829440
40. As Bashar al-Jaafari, the Syrian ambassador to the UN, stated when asked about the Friends of Syria conference, 'The so-called conference of the enemies of Syria is in itself a violation and contradiction of Kofi Annan's mission. This is a parallel track set up by enemies of Syria to compete with Kofi Annan's mission, maybe to undermine his mission'. Neil MacFarquhar and Rick Gladstone, 'Red Cross proposes daily cease-fires in Syria', *New York Times*, 3 April 2012, p. A7 (not available online). For more on Gulf Arab support for the opposition, see Karen DeYoung and Liz Sly, 'Syrian rebels get influx of arms with gulf neighbors' money, US coordination', *Washington Post*, 15 May 2012, available at: www.washingtonpost.com/world/national-security/syrian-rebels-get-influx-of-arms-with-gulf-neighbors-money-us-coordination/2012/05/15/gIQAds2TSU_story.html
41. Aron Lund, 'Divided they stand: An overview of Syria's political opposition factions', Olof Palme International Center, Foundation for European Progressive Studies, Uppsala, Sweden, May 2012, pp. 33–4. The *New York Times* reported on 21 June 2012 that the CIA has been operating secretly in southern Turkey (which hosts some 30,000 Syrian refugees by time of writing), helping allies vet and select which Syrian opposition groups should receive arms being funneled by a clandestine network into Syria across the Turkish border, these arms being primarily paid for by Turkey, Saudi Arabia and Qatar. The CIA wanted to make sure that the weapons, mostly automatic rifles, rocket-propelled grenades, anti-tank weapons and ammunition, did not wind up in the hands of Islamic extremist groups affiliated with al-Qaida or other undesirables. The CIA officials also hope to learn more about and establish stronger ties with various Syrian opposition groups. Eric Schmitt, 'C.I.A. said to aid in steering arms to Syrian rebels', *New York Times*, 21 June 2012, p. A1. On increasing Saudi financial aid to the Free Syrian Army to purchase more weapons and ammunition and encourage defections from the Syrian army, all with the support of the United States, see Martin Chulov and Ewen MacAskill, 'Saudi Arabia plans to fund Syria rebel army', *Guardian*, 22 June 2012, available at: http://www.guardian.co.uk/world/2012/jun/22/saudi-arabia-syria-rebel-amry/print
42. 'Activists threaten to desert Syrian National Council', *Now Lebanon*, 17 May 2012, available at: www.nowlebanon.com/NewsArchiveDetails.aspx?ID=397397
43. Robert Fisk, 'Syria is used to the slings and arrows of friends and enemies', *Independent*, 1 February 2012, available at: www.independent.co.uk/opinion/commentators/fisk/robert-fisk-syria-is-used-to-the-slings-and-arrows-of-friends-and-enemies-6297648.html. As Fisk wrote in the article, the Baath regime 'is a tough creature, its rulers among the most tenacious in the Middle East, used to the slings and arrows of their friends as well as their enemies'.
44. Richard Cincotta, 'Life begins after 25: Demography and the societal timing of the Arab Spring', Foreign Policy Research Institute, 23 January 2012, available at: www.fpri.org/enotes/2012/201201.cincotta.demography_arabspring.html
45. Ed Husain, 'Life after Assad could be worse', *New York Times*, 6 February 2012, available at: www.nytimes.com/roomfordebate/2012/02/06/is-assads-time-running-out/syria-after-assad-could-be-even-worse
46. Sharmine Narwani, 'Syria is not Tunisia or Libya', *New York Times*, 6 February 2012, available at: www.nytimes.com/roomfordebate/2012/02/06/is-assads-time-running-out/syria-is-not-tunisia-or-libya. Also, see Camille Otrakji, 'Ten reasons why many Syrians are not interested yet', The Syria Page, 14 January 2012, available at: http://creativesyria.com/syriapage/?p=79. In it, the author lists reasons why, in his view,

Syrians are largely not supporting the uprising, primarily because they know that what might emerge in the aftermath of the fall of Assad would be much worse. It is a middle-ground narrative that currently (at the time of writing) seems to be gaining traction.

47. 'EU agrees on new sanctions on Syria, targets Assads' luxury lifestyle', Al-Arabiya, 23 April 2012, http://english.alarabiya.net/save_print.php?print=1&cont_id=209638
48. Liz Sly, 'A year into uprising, Syrian protestors say they won't give up', *Washington Post*, 14 March 2012, available at: www.washingtonpost.com/world/as-violence-in-syria-escalates-a-year-into-uprising-protesters-say-they-wont-give-up/2012/03/14/gIQAGeA2BS_story.html
49. Lund, 'Divided they stand'.
50. Nir Rosen, 'Islamism and the Syrian Uprising', *Foreign Policy*, 8 March 2012, available at: http://mideast.foreignpolicy.com/posts/2012/03/08/islamism_and_the_syrian_uprising
51. At the time of writing, the latest have been two suicide blasts in Damascus on 10 May, killing fifty-five people and leaving many more injured. The previous blast occurred in the capital on 27 April, when a suicide bomber detonated an explosives belt near members of the security forces, killing nine. Two suicide bombers struck Damascus on 17 March: near-simultaneous attacks on two heavily guarded Syrian intelligence compounds killed at least twenty-seven people. There was a suspected suicide attack on 6 January at an intersection in Damascus (twenty-six killed) and there was an attack on 23 December 2011, again aimed at Syria's intelligence agency buildings (over forty-four killed). A shadowy group calling itself the Al-Nusra Front has claimed responsibility for some of these attacks (although it denied the 10 May bombings). Most Western intelligence analysts suspect this group is an al-Qaida-like organization composed of *salafi* Islamist extremists – or some such loose conglomeration.
52. ibid.
53. David W. Lesch, *The New Lion of Damascus: Bashar al-Asad and modern Syria*, Yale University Press, London, 2005, pp. 240–1.
54. Peter Harling, 'Beyond the fall of the Syrian regime', International Crisis Group Report, 24 February 2012, available at: www.crisisgroup.org/en/regions/middle-east-north-africa/egypt-syria-lebanon/syria/op-eds/harling-beyond-the-fall-of-the-syrian-regime.aspx
55. Ian Black, 'Syria's Bashar al-Assad vows to display captured foreign mercenaries', *Guardian*, 16 May 2012, available at: www.guardian.co.uk/world/2012/may/16/syria-bashar-assad-vows-display-mercenaries
56. David W. Lesch, 'Tear down this wall, President Assad', *Foreign Policy*, 23 May 2011, available at: http://mideast.foreignpolicy.com/posts/2011/05/23/tear_down_this_wall_president_assad

Epilogue

1. I developed and organized the Harvard–NUPI–Trinity Syria Research Project, 'Obstacles to a Resolution of the Syrian Conflict' in the late autumn of 2012. It is sponsored by Harvard University (specifically, the Harvard Negotiation Project in the Harvard Law School), NUPI (the Norwegian acronym for the Norwegian Institute for International Affairs), and my institution, Trinity University in San Antonio, Texas. Essentially, we are an independent team of researchers interviewing with similar sets of questions as many of the actors relevant to the conflict as possible, including the Syrian opposition in and outside of Syria, Syrian government officials, officials at the United Nations, and top government officials in the capitals of countries in and outside of the region who are involved in the conflict. The object is to compile a database of information on the origins and course of the conflict, the obstacles to a resolution of the conflict to date, and ideas about the future of Syria. This body of information may

then be useful in generating potential conflict resolution outcomes. As of this writing, the project is about halfway through, with the end of summer 2013 being the target date for completion. The end product will be a detailed report of our findings accompanied by recommendations regarding conflict resolution.

2. Officially known as the 'Action Group for Syria Final Communiqué' of 30 June 2012. The Action Group consisted of the secretaries-general of the United Nations and the Arab League, the foreign ministers of China, France, Russia, United Kingdom, United States, Turkey, Iraq (as chair of the Arab League Summit) and Qatar (as chair of the Arab Follow-up Committee on Syria for the Arab League) and the EU High Representative for Foreign and Security Policy. For a text of the document see: http://blog.unwatch.org/index-php/2012/07/01/full-text-action-group-for-syria-final-communique.
3. Frederic C. Hof, 'Syria: Will Geneva Happen? Should it Happen?', *Atlantic Council*, 20 May 2013, available at: http://www.acus.org/print/76364
4. On 6 March 2013, the Arab League, meeting in Doha, adopted a resolution authorizing the Syrian National Coalition to represent Syria at the Arab League.
5. In an interview with Syrian state television in April 2013, Assad said: 'There is no option but victory, otherwise it will be the end of Syria, and I don't think that any Syrian citizen will accept such an option. There is an attempt to invade Syria, the forces are coming from outside, from different nationalities, they are using different tactics from what the colonization powers have used.' Steve Almasy, 'Al-Assad to Western nations: Syrian rebels will turn on you', CNN.com, 17 April 2013, available at: www.cnn.com/2013/04/17/world/meast/syria-assad/index.html?hpt=hp_t3
6. As an indication of the rather complicated nature of the Syrian conflict, I firmly believe (as do a number of opposition leaders with whom I have spoken) that if there was a real democratic and legitimate election today in Syria where every Syrian could vote (even those who have left the country), Bashar al-Assad would win – and probably by some margin. Again, this is not so much because he is so popular – obviously he has mortgaged away much of the popularity he once enjoyed – but rather because the majority of Syrians who are still sitting on the fence would simply vote for the known quantity, and after such wanton destruction and chaos for more than two years, many simply want a return to some kind of normalcy, even if it means a return to the authoritarianism that preceded the uprising.
7. For more on this, see David W. Lesch, 'The Risks of Going into Syria', *Current History*, 111, No. 748 (November 2012), pp. 299–304.
8. Fareed Zakaria, 'With or Without Us', *Time*, 13 May 2013, available at: www.time.com/time/printout/0,8816,2142505,00.html
9. Frederik Pleitgen, Sara Sidner, and Hada Messia, '42 Syrian soldiers dead in reported Israeli strike, opposition group says', CNN.com, 6 May 2013, available at: www.cnn.com/2013/05/06/world/meast/syria-civil-war/index.html?hpt=hp_c3
10. On these doubts about Syria's use of chemical weapons, see Sharmine Narwani, 'Chemical Weapons Charade in Syria', *Al-Akhbar*, 27 April 2013, available at: http://english.al-akhbar.com/print/15644
11. Mark Landler and Rick Gladstone, 'Obama Considers Expanding Support for Syrian Rebels', *New York Times*, 30 April 2013, available at: http://nytimes.com/2013/05/01/world/middleeast/bomb-in-central-damascus.html?ref—iddleeast&_r=0&pagewanted=print
12. ibid.
13. Chelsea J. Carter, 'Obama: Do not foresee scenario of American boots on ground in Syria,' CNN.com, 4 May 2012, available at: www.cnn.com/2013/05/03/world/meast/us-syria-obama/index.html?hpt=hp_t1
14. ibid.
15. As one opposition military commander told me, 'Jabhat al-Nusra has snipers, and I'll take one of them over fifteen men with Kalashnikovs'. There have been reports of

battles between jihadist elements and other Syrian opposition groups; indeed, one of the leading *salafist* military commanders with whom we met was injured in March 2013 in a pitched battle against Jabhat al-Nusra. I do not know if it was ideologically motivated or simply some sort of territorial or power dispute.

16. Quoted in Steve Almasy, 'Al-Assad to Western nations: Syrian rebels will turn on you,' CNN.com, 17 April 2013, available at: www.cnn.com/2013/04/17/world/meast/syria-assad/index.html?hpt=hp_t3. See also Anne Barnard, 'Syria playing on fears of jihad,' *International Herald Tribune*, 25 April 2013, p. 1.
17. A small but representative poll was taken by Christopher Phillips in 2009 regarding the question of identity in Syria. A third of those asked identified themselves as Syrian first, a third Arab first, and a third Muslim first. See Christopher Phillips, *Everyday Arab Identity: the Daily Reproduction of the Arab World*, Routledge, London, 2013.
18. Quoted in Peter Bergen, 'Syria rebel group's dangerous ties to al Qaeda,' CNN.com, 10 April 2013, available at: www.cnn.com/2013/04/10/opinion/berger-al-qaeda-syria/index.html
19. ibid.
20. There have continued to be disturbances and exchanges of fire along the UN-patrolled demilitarized zone (DMZ) in the Golan between Israeli forces and forces inside Syria. Into 2013, the main reason is because the Syrian government has lost control of territory near and adjacent to the Golan, which has since been occupied by an array of opposition forces. In one instance a number of UN forces with UNDOF (United Nations Disengagement Observer Force), which patrols the DMZ, were taken captive by a Syrian opposition group, although they were later released. It is certainly a situation that the Israelis are monitoring closely. In addition, there were reportedly Israeli strikes in Syria in January and twice in early May 2013 (the second reportedly killed dozens of Syrian soldiers at a research facility outside of Damascus), apparently targeting Syrian depots storing arms or convoys carrying arms headed to Hizbullah in Lebanon. Israel has made it very clear that it will do what is necessary to prevent arms from Syria (and most likely originating in Iran) from reaching Hizbullah when it has identified a target of opportunity, as Hizbullah could use these arms, particularly longer-range missiles, to hit deep inside Israel. The Israelis frame their attacks as being to protect Israel rather than involving themselves in the Syrian conflict, but they have nevertheless placed the Syrian opposition in something of a quandary. On the one hand they don't mind seeing Syrian government forces and installations degraded; on the other, they don't want to appear to be on the same side as the Israelis, realizing Syria's constituency is still vehemently anti-Israeli. The opposition's awkwardness could be seen in the official media statement from the Syrian Coalition Media Office on 5 May 2013 following the second of the purported attacks in May: 'The Syrian Coalition condemns the Israeli attacks on the Syrian Center for Scientific Research in Jamaraya near Damascus. The Coalition holds the Assad regime fully responsible for weakening the Syrian Army by exhausting its forces in a losing battle against the Syrian people; who are the reason for its existence. It is clear that the regime … is instead weakening Syria in the face of the enemy.' 'Statement Regarding the Israeli Attack on Syria,' Media Statement, Syrian Coalition Media Office, Istanbul, Turkey, 5 May 2013.
21. For a more updated version of these three scenarios, see David W. Lesch, 'The Unknown Future of Syria,' *Mediterranean Politics*, 15 March 2015, available at: http://dx.doi.org/10.1080/13629395.2013.764656
22. Tom Watkins, 'Sectarian violence reported in Syrian city of Baniyas,' CNN.com, 4 May 2013, available at: www.cnn.com/2013/05/04/world/meast/syria-violence/index.html?hpt=hp_t1
23. On Nasrallah's remarks and Turkey's dilemma, see Semih Idiz, 'Turkey Faces Lose-Lose Situation Over Syria,' *Al-Monitor*, 2 May 2013, available at: www.al-monitor.com/

pulse/originals/2015/05/turkey-syria-policy-hezbollah-risk.html?utm_source=&utm_medium=email&utm_campaign=7125

24. Gideon Rachman, 'Syria and the undoing of Obama's grand strategy,' *Financial Times*, 3 May 2013, available at: www.ft.com/intl/cms/s/0/57c06b02-b0b8-11e2-80f9-00144feabdc0.html#axzz25XYDhUml
25. For instance, see David Rothkopf, 'The Ugly Choice in the Middle East,' *Foreign Policy*, 23 April 2013, available at: http://carnegieendowment.org/2013/04/23/ugly-choice-in-middle-east/g192; and, ironically, the noted anti-Assad commentator Daniel Pipes, 'The argument for Assad,' *Washington Times*, 11 April 2013, available at: www.washingtontimes.com/news/2013/apr/11/pipes-argument-assad/print/
26. On this, see Aron Lund, 'The Free Syrian Army Doesn't Exist,' *Syria Comment*, 16 March 2013, available at: www.joshualandis.com/blog/?p=18104&print=true
27. 'Kerry-Lavrov statements called first hopeful news on Syria in a while,' CNN.com, 8 May 2013, available at: www.cnn.com/2013/05/08/world/meast/syria-civil-war/index.html?hpt=hp_t2
28. ibid.

Index